DUCK HAWKING
AND THE ART OF FALCONRY

By Joe Roy III

ISBN-13: 978-0-88839-033-2 *[2017 Trade Softcover]*
ISBN-13: 978-0-88839-553-5 *[2004 Trade Hardcover]*
Copyright © 2004 Joe Roy III
2017 B&W Reprint

Cataloging in Publication Data

Roy, Joe, 1962-

    Duck hawking and the art of falconry / Joe Roy.

Includes bibliographical references and index.
ISBN 0-88839-553-1

    1. Falconry. 2. Fowling. I. Title.

SK321.R68 2004   799.2'32   C2004-903870-2

All rights reserved. No part of this publication may be reproduced, stored in a retrieval system or transmitted, in any form or by any means, electronic, mechanical, photocopying, recording, or otherwise, without the prior written permission of Hancock House Publishers.

                      Printed in the USA

Production: Theodora Kobald
Editor: Nancy Miller
Cover Design: Rick Groenheyde

Published simultaneously in Canada and the United States by

HANCOCK HOUSE PUBLISHERS LTD.
19313 Zero Avenue, Surrey, B.C. V3Z 9R9
(604) 538-1114 Fax (604) 538-2262

HANCOCK HOUSE PUBLISHERS
#104- 4550 Birch Bay-Lynden Rd, Blaine, WA 98230-9436
(800) 938-1114 Fax (604) 538-2262
www.hancockhouse.com   sales@hancockhouse.com

Contents

Contents 3
Preface 5
Foreword 6
Introduction 9
1   The Falconer's Greatest Assets 13
2   Falcons 20
3   Shortwings 29
4   Ducks 40
5   Dogs 74
6   Weight Management 84
7   Pitch 99
8   Pigeons 108
9   Thermals 122
10 Orchestration 162
11 Field Craft 171
12 Speculation Flights 196
13 Weather 202
14 Scouting 214
15 Entering 233
16 Slip Selection 249
17 Pond Burnout 255
18 The Psychology of Catch and Release 257
19 Coup de Grace and Field Dressing 277
20 Lost Hawks 280
21 The Future of Falconry 305
Glossary 310
Bibliography 313
Index 315

Dedicated to Sydney for rocking my world,
and to my children, Cassie, Aussie,
Tyger and Storm for letting me be their Dad.

In memory of Latham and Shaman–
two liked-minded souls who lived for the hunt

...

Preface

Because water plays such a pivotal role in most duck flights, it warrants special consideration and tactics. As a struggling upstart duck hawker, I had access to reams of falconry-related literature. However, there was relatively little written dealing specifically with duck hawking, and what little there was tended to be superficial at best. Within the pages of this manuscript, I have outlined the tactics, techniques and concepts I have found to be particularly effective for hawking ducks. I've also included sections that deal with the training and management of game-hawks in a broader sense. I've chosen to use anecdotal stories throughout the text in order to illustrate actual field application and make for a more interesting read. My greatest aspiration with this book is to illuminate duck hawking in the positive light for which it is most deserved.

Foreword

Duck hunting may well be the most popular from of our sport, at least with longwings. So why is it so hard to find out the details of how to do it? For years, this challenging and often spectacular form of the sport has been described "off to the side" in short articles and digressions. There are now whole monographs on accipiters! While I love them, I question whether the number of goshawkers comes anywhere close to those who hawk ducks with falcons. But, at long last, we have a manual on "the science" of duck hawking by a master falconer (and good storyteller) who has spent a lifetime honing his skills.

To say that this book is detailed is an understatement. Joe presents precise descriptions of everything from weight management to choice of dogs. He tells you how to analyze weather, how to select your slips, how to fly on spec, and how to scout your terrain—things you would otherwise have to learn by trial and error, with emphasis on the error.

I might emphasize the importance of two chapters in particular. The first is on the use of pigeons. Most of us who have been hawking for years know at least something about homing pigeons, and even have developed a strong interest in pigeons themselves. But because of a certain squeamishness about "bagged" quarry, hardly anything detailed has been written about the use (not abuse!) of the strong homer. Joe Roy will tell you tricks like using hilltops to produce an even more difficult flight for your falcon, and an ever better and more accomplished pigeon as well as falcon. He tells you how to "read" and condition your hawk by selecting easy or difficult pigeons, reminding you: "Remember, we are not training with pigeons to educate falcons on how to catch pigeons, but rather to instill specific behavioral qualities as well as develop fundamental skills...."

The other absolutely indispensable chapter is the one on entering. Speaking strictly for myself, I have always found this the trickiest, most important, and potentially the most dangerous (at least to future performance!) part of flying game. As Roy says "...I would speculate that this is the particular phase of falconry that generates the most frustration for novice and master alike." And for ducks the problems can be multiplied because of how the duck will use the water, not to mention that many longwings do not find ducks as appealing as they do gallinaceous birds. With Roy's advice, you may still make mistakes, but he has anticipated most of them and will guide you through the inherent uncertainties. He also gives an ethical and, again, detailed account of how to (and how not to) use bagged game to teach your hawk.

You will learn a lot from Joe Roy, even if you are an experienced duck hawker. For that matter, you will learn more than you think, even if you pursue other quarry, about how to think like and, as he says, "be the hawk." He gives thought to such oft-neglected details on how to kill cleanly; he offers a detailed critique of leg vs. tail mounts for transmitters; he even has a chapter on catch and release. If there is an issue he hasn't considered, I can't find it.

But above all, he brings our ancient practice a mixture of reverence for the hawks, quarry, and the whole subtly changing and elusive world we perform in, with the hard-earned knowledge of someone who isn't afraid to go out and do—to make mistakes, to risk it all in order to achieve what he actually calls art. ("As an artist, I'm constantly trying to perfect my art form.")

And he remembers what is most important. "With such an emotional investment riding on wings and a prayer, sometimes we lose sight of falconry's primary function. Above all else, falconry is a discipline to be enjoyed. In the most fundamental of ways, the most successful falconers are those who find the most pleasure in whatever falconry the choose to experience."

Read Joe Roy, and learn from him. Then take your hawk out, and go and do likewise.

—STEPHEN BODIO

Introduction

Falconry is a hunting art dating back thousands of years. That some twenty-first century people would rather hunt with hawks, falcons and eagles, when more easily mastered and higher yielding techniques are readily available is indicative of profound motivational forces. From an evolutionary viewpoint, we have only recently begun to rely upon the domestication and industrialization of food sources rather than the subsistence hunting and gathering of our ancestral heritage. Hunting cooperatively with raptors is a conduit, jamming us into direct contact with our primordial past. There are those who refer to falconry as a blood sport, a term that I am uncomfortable with. It is not the word "blood" I dislike but rather the word "sport." For me, the act of taking quarry with trained game-hawks is a sacred event, and I cannot equate it with badminton, baseball or cricket. Death plays a vital role in the scheme of falconry, but blood is not the element of fascination nor the essence of the art. The interaction of predator and prey is what provides the adrenaline surge that feeds the falconry addiction. Through falconry, we vicariously live the life of the predator we once were, filling a perceptible void.

Raptors have permeated my life literally since childhood. My very first falconry experiences were with a tiercel prairie falcon named Kopi. Back in the early seventies, I was a young boy living in a housing tract in Southern California, and a gentleman named Joe Naud moved into the house next to mine. Joe was a falconer with a magnetic personality and a great sense of humor. Aside from his prairie, Joe had a Harris hawk, and from the first day I saw these birds fly I was captivated. Joe wanted to teach Kopi to wait-on and, much to my pleasure, enlisted my help to achieve this behavior. I can still remember bubbling with anticipation as I rode the bus home from grammar school. I'd run home from the bus stop and Joe would be waiting for me in his garage with Kopi on his fist. We would hop in his little Triumph TR7 and head for the fields. I was always impressed by the way Joe could handle that sports car, running through the gears with the hooded falcon on his left hand. Once we were into the field, Joe would pass the falcon to me. In an effort to clue Kopi into the benefits of height, Joe would have me hike to the top of a cliff. When released, the tiercel would sail out over the valley where Joe would be hiding in the bushes far below, ready to toss the pigeon as the falcon flew overhead. On one occasion, Kopi unexpectedly blasted off my fist in hot pursuit of some small bird that had gotten up a short distance ahead. At that moment something happened to me internally—I had just caught a glimpse of the spectacle that would literally alter my life forever. The tiercel didn't catch the bird, but for an instant I grasped the essence of falconry and an indelible impression was imprinted on my soul.

All too soon my time with Joe came to an end when he took a job training raptors for Marine World (then known as Africa USA) in San Francisco. Before Joe finalized his relocation, he drove the company van back down to Southern California with a harpy eagle in the back. I have a vivid memory of sitting in that van just staring at the massive eagle perched in the rear. Talk about lasting impressions—sitting face to face with a predator of that magnitude inspired an awe in me that exists to this day.

Since those early attempts, I have flown a wide assortment of game-hawks at a variety of quarry with special emphasis on hawking ducks with falcons. My first encounter with duck hawking occurred when I was sixteen years old and attending a California Hawking Club field meet with my latest passage redtail. The year was 1978, a time when peregrines were few and far between, gyrfalcons were more myth than reality and the term "hybridization" wasn't even in my vocabulary yet. During the meet, I tagged along with a convoy of cars and trucks following notorious duck hawker Mike Connoly. Mike was scouting slips for his infamous Peales falcon, Witch. Any opportunity to watch a peregrine fly, let alone a bona fide slayer of ducks, was genuine cause for excitement. For me, the most poignant aspect of the ensuing flight was its aerial nature and the speed with which both falcon and duck contested the sky. The visual splendor of well-matched predator and prey flying in heated, high stakes competition was nothing short of exhilarating to witness. My enthusiasm for duck hawking has spanned the years, indeed my passion for duck hawking defies all logic excepting perhaps to like-minded individuals who similarly crave high-octane falconry.

By the very nature of waterfowl habitat, duck hawking is a unique branch of the art. Over the past decade or so, I have sensed an almost cavalier attitude toward duck hawking in some circles. Some have alluded to ducks as inferior quarry, particularly in relation to sage grouse. I'm quite certain I could guide such skeptics to duck slips that would prove infinitely more difficult than anything they encounter on the open sage. There is a world of difference between taking ducks on the rise as they exit small ponds and killing ducks well up in the sky far beyond the perimeter of their big water sanctuary. Ducks are intelligent, swift and evasive; they have virtually infinite stamina. In terms of sheer dramatic appeal, stoops at ducks can rival that of any other. In his book *Observations on Modern Falconry*, Ronald Stevens notes "falcons that are large and powerful enough to fly mallard with success provide what is probably the finest sport to be obtained in Britain.... She is an exceptionally good hawk that is not out flown by them." If one is so fortunate as to live in good duck country, his or her falcon may pursue well over a dozen species of waterfowl flown under incredibly diverse conditions. Learning to recognize and predict the minor nuances, as well as blatant differences between various species of ducks, the habitats they frequent and the escape tactics they employ is critical in orchestrating well-conceived slips. More importantly, insightfulness elevates the level of intimacy we feel for the quarry we pursue. This, in turn, enriches the falconry experience in ways beyond kill ratios and other such academics.

Falconry is about experiencing life as we once did, for the urge to hunt dwells in the deepest pools of our genetic history. I've spent half my life hawking ducks and am only now savvy enough to realize how very much I still don't know and haven't yet seen. Duck hawking boring? Repetitive? Only to the fool who thinks he's seen it all.

CHAPTER 1

The Falconer's Greatest Assets

As children, we are taught that there are two categories of literature: fiction and nonfiction. Like most kids, I thought everything belonging to the latter category was to be considered gospel. As I got older I began to realize that there was a good deal of misinformation out there, in print and otherwise. Many falconers have benefited from the written words of those falconers who graciously enlightened us by sharing their experiences in letters, books and magazines. By the same token however, I believe that if we are not careful, we can rely too heavily on others and their interpretation of events to dictate our reality. This situation has the potential to stifle our creativity and stunt our growth. Even as I write this book, I am sure there are those who have had differing experiences and drawn conclusions that, in some ways, contrast those of mine. Nonconformity of thought is a fascinating aspect of falconry and part of the attraction for me. There isn't one rigid path to which one must adhere. Falconry is an art that lives and breathes and is practiced by many diverse cultures and individuals. As our personal knowledge in the art grows in relation to our experiences, we begin to comprehend the relevance of that which we've read. Likewise, in some instances we detect contradictions and discrepancies. Through experimentation, trial and error, we begin perfecting that which works for us and eliminating those practices that do not. Our own philosophies develop and opinions emerge.

Falconry is a cerebral affair requiring a degree of intellect and an eye for detail. The falconer's ability to comprehend the workings of the raptor mentality is what makes training possible. Thus, the greater our understanding of raptorial thought processes and instinctive inclinations, the more effectively we may construct training protocol.

Falconry is also an ancient art that is steeped in tradition. However, I believe that at times a traditionalist approach becomes an impediment. I was recently surprised to find that there are still some purists who shun the use of telemetry. While this seems absurd to me, presumably the inclusion of such modern technology is an unwelcome intrusion of something sacred to traditionalists. So long as they fly indigenous species only, who could condemn them? Nonetheless, anything, whether it be traditions, assumptions or preconceived notions, that prevents us from exploring alternatives or broadening our perspectives has the potential to limit our progression on all levels. An open mind cultivates innovation, helping us to envision creative solutions to behavioral hurdles and explore untapped potential. I believe training hawks requires a certain amount of creativity and flexibility. As trainers we are not building model airplanes, we are molding minds and developing skills. Raptors are hatched with the necessary physical and psychological characteristics required to be successful predators. Falconers merely shape the bird's rudimentary thoughts and behaviors to make falconry possible. I have come to realize that the biggest obstacle the game-hawk is likely to encounter on the path to perfection is the falconer himself. It is up to us as falconers to develop techniques that don't prevent our game-hawks from reaching their full potentials, and our greatest assets in regard to this endeavor are our experience, knowledge and intuition, working in combination.

The longer we practice falconry, the more experiences we acquire and the deeper the depth of our knowledge. Experiences become more meaningful if we diligently engage in observation. Observation is not just spending time in proximity with something, but actively analyzing that which is being observed. Observation is a skill; the more we practice, the better at it we become. One of the finest falconry books ever written is not coincidentally titled *Observations on Modern Falconry*. The author, Ronald Stevens, obviously recognized the importance of observation. The more time spent monitoring and examining raptors, the clearer the information flows from hawk to man, like second nature. The more intimately we know individual hawks, the easier it becomes to understand just what they are doing and exactly why they are doing it. The same can be said of child rearing. I never cease to be amazed by the things that parents will do in regards to their children, such as the types of behaviors they will reinforce and unwittingly reward. The child wants something, initially the parent says "No." The child acts out in defiance (negative behavior), the likes of which include breath holding, stomping, yelling, tantrums, etc., all designed to soften, embarrass, guilt or frustrate the parent into giving in. These events are not random—they are devised and are the culmination of previous episodes during which the parent helped teach these skills to the child. The child would not behave in this manner if the end result was a negative experience. The child behaves in this fashion because it works! In the end the parent acquiesces and the child gets what it wants. These early lessons occurring during the most formative years of an individual's life are not shucked off with the onset of adulthood. Rather, these lessons act as a roadmap, guiding the individual through the course of his or her life. In this case the message is simply, "be an ass, you get what you want." This analogy is very relevant to falconry—if you really want to mess up your training then positively reinforce a negative behavior. If a falconer is not carefully observing situations and monitoring his own behaviors, he may unwittingly reward negative behaviors or fail to reinforce positive behaviors.

    Virtually all the chronic behavioral problems seen among falconry birds can be traced to falconer error. Problems with biting, footing, hooding, screaming, raking, etc., become chronic only if they serve a purpose. Sometimes the cause of a problem is blatantly obvious. Take for example, biting and footing maliciously directed at the falconer's hands. Some raptors bite handlers any chance they get. This aggression is typically an exhibition of fear and can be traced to inadequate manning, along with a healthy dose of positive reinforcement. The first time the falcon bites your hand and you pull away, the bird has achieved its desire—to rid itself of your hand. Now the precedence has been established and you can count on the falcon biting your hands as a means of ridding itself of them again. If a hawk foots the handler while feeding on the glove it is an act of aggression usually stemming from possessiveness. Of course, being footed by a large hawk is quite painful and an excellent example of the type of behavior that is preferably preempted, especially since raptors do not respond well to negative reinforcement. Starting with the very first meals eaten in the presence of the falconer, the hawk should be familiarized with having the trainer's hands in close proximity to its food. If the hawk looks "iffy," a feather or stick can substitute for the hand initially. In very short order the hawk accepts that the hand is of no threat to itself or its meal and that there is nothing that it can do to make it go away anyway, so it learns to see the hand as nothing more than a mild distraction at worst. Thus, the hawk is properly habituated right from the start.

Raptors are very habitual organisms. This works well for the falconer provided the hawk is forming good habits only. Continual observation allows falconers to recognize events, behaviors, mannerisms and trends as they happen and predict them before they begin. Interpreting and evaluating that which we have observed illuminates strengths as well as flaws in our training/hawking regimen. Mentally recording the day's events (and journaling) provides necessary decision-making data. This data becomes more useful through active contemplation. Information is a tool and, like any tool, is only productive when in use. Often at night, I lie awake in bed reflecting on the day's flights, assessing how things went for each hawk and correlating recent performance trends. I can then construct a plan for the following day, suited to meet the needs of each individual raptor. By anticipating tomorrows slips based on today's performance, I can help ensure that the hawk is being managed as efficiently as possible. This pre- and post-flight analytical process is extremely useful to a falconer with an agenda, some sort of criteria or aspiration.

Without a critique of the previous flight it is difficult to make directional changes in flight style. If a falcon has had bad luck or poor slips for a day or two I'll make a point of providing a superior slip the next time out. If a falcon has been pounding easy duck slips and is high on confidence, I may plan for a more difficult slip the next day to broaden her horizons. If a falcon became bored and strayed today, I'll be sure to serve with expedience tomorrow. Conversely, if the falcon's pitch plateaued at a sub-standard altitude today, I'll make a point of keeping her on the wing tomorrow until she ascends to a pitch I'm satisfied with. Determining the night before what type of slips I'm looking for allows me to plan which areas I should be traveling through during my search the next day.

Sometimes the hawk behaves in a manner that appears unexplainable on the surface and we become perplexed. Fortunately, for every question there is an answer somewhere. One way or another, the information is there; the raptor is telling us what we need to know in order to solve the riddle. Projection is the tool of choice to solve the puzzle, and it is the falconer's ability to project (more than anything else) that reflects his abilities as a trainer. Projection is a process of moving beyond ourselves through mental imagery. We take on the persona of an object that we want to better understand. Through projection we think like a bird because in essence we are the bird. Projection is extremely beneficial because not only does it make it possible for us to ascribe meaning to the behaviors we have witnessed, but also projection helps us conjure ideas and tactics to shape or reshape desired behaviors. The more sentient we are toward our hawks, the easier it becomes to project ourselves into them.

A natural byproduct of projection is intuition, which is a sort of instinctive knowledge. During these quiet moments of introspection we are primed to receive information, a thought, an epiphany, a breakthrough. There is a fuzzy area between focus and a blank mind, a sort of relaxed concentration or meditative state. I seem to hit this state most often at night, during the transitional stage between wakefulness and sleep. If I have successfully swept the clutter from my mind, I sometimes access an all too infrequently used portion of my brain and occasionally receive insight or perhaps clarity on a previously convoluted issue.

My work often takes me on the road, lecturing in metropolitan areas for several days at a time. Afterwards, I anxiously head home, watching the city dissipate in the rearview mirror, my soul yearning for the solitude of the forest. Peaceful time spent among the trees restores a sense of balance and can be very inspirational, providing an excellent opportunity for me to seek answers to questions and hopefully receive pristine images in return. Sometimes intuition arrives at less serene times and locations, such as while in the shower or watching television. It is likely that each of us receives intuitive guidance in our own unique ways. The important thing is to realize that we are all capable of channeling this positive energy and benefiting from it. Utilizing an intuitive approach to raptor management and life in general allows us to envision productive methods and solutions that may have otherwise eluded us.

Establishing criteria and setting goals are other tactics that falconers can benefit from. There is a natural evolution that takes place among falconers. Initially we are happy just to have a hawk and ecstatic if it doesn't fly away. Through small increments we progressively perfect our methodology and our art, setting ever-higher standards. In so doing, we continually achieve an elevated falconry experience and sense of satisfaction. It is equally important that we recognize goals as they are fulfilled and not minimize each milestone achieved. Wanting more is a part of the human psyche and can be the driving force behind perfection. This mentality is a double-edged sword, in that it can indeed encourage us to practice outstanding falconry, but if we are not careful we may find ourselves eternally unfulfilled due to some perceived or imagined flaw in the hawk's performance. Falconry is the epitome of an emotional rollercoaster capable of eliciting extreme highs and lows in short order. When falconry is good, it's damned good; when falconry is bad, it's just damned. With such an emotional investment riding on wings and a prayer, sometimes we lose sight of falconry's primary function. Above all else, falconry is a discipline to be enjoyed. In the most fundamental of ways, the most successful falconers are those who find the most pleasure in whatever falconry they choose to experience. It would be foolhardy to go to such great lengths, exerting such effort in the pursuit of falconry and not enjoy the scenery along the way, even when things aren't great. It would be absurd not to savor the good times. Nonetheless, I find that I must periodically remind myself to live in the moment and revel in the spectacle unfolding before my eyes. Some of the happiest moments of my life are those in which I sit alongside the falcon and dog after an awesome flight, engulfed in the here and now.

Occasionally I remind myself to completely appreciate each game-hawk I fly. Even the greatest of game-hawks are temporary—we would be wise to delight in them while we can. Relatively few genuine game-hawks live to a ripe old age and die from natural causes, though many live longer than their wild counterparts. Game-hawks are exposed to so many potentially deadly elements in the field. The loss of a well-loved game-hawk is always difficult; to lose such a bird through falconer error is even tougher as we compound the grief with a healthy dose of guilt. Life presents ample opportunity for us all to make mistakes. The hard truth of falconry is that due to its very nature, it is unforgiving of all but the smallest mistakes, and sometimes even those will spoil the entire day, if not the season. Avoiding mistakes is crucial, nonetheless making some mistakes is inevitable. Learning from mistakes is essential. No mistake should be a total loss because they all offer the gift of enlightenment if we choose to learn from them. To not learn from a mistake is a tragedy in and of itself and leaves us destined to stumble on the same barriers over and over.

CHAPTER 2

Falcons

Waterfowl vary so significantly in both size and habit that it would be presumptuous to state which type of falcon makes the best duck hawk. Even so, we falconers that seriously hunt ducks with falcons are curious as to which types of falcons would be most effective for the kind of duck hawking we do. This question pertains not only to species and subspecies but also to gender. I would speculate that for most species of large falcons there is a facet of duck hawking at which they could excel. Once a specific falcon type and gender have been selected, there are still some decisions yet to be made, i.e., eyas, imprint, chamber, hacked, passage, etc. Often these choices are made out of convenience, necessity or psychological considerations. In some cases there are extenuating circumstances or legalities involved, which take precedence over preference.

When I compare the myriad of falcons available to the average falconer today, as opposed to when I was a boy, I can't help but feel as though we've all been blessed. As a child, I had resigned myself to the possibility that I may never have the opportunity to fly any falcon whatsoever. Between the crash of the anatum peregrine, tightening restrictions and the antifalconry propaganda being spewed by the likes of the Audubon Society and the Sierra Club, things appeared dismal to say the least. I wonder if American falconers who have joined our ranks after captive breeding exploded on scene can fathom falconry in an era during which available falcons were scarce and falconry's very existence was tenuous. We are fortunate indeed in this new millennium to be faced with the enviable dilemma of selecting from a plethora of desirable falcons. With an ever-increasing number of breeding projects springing up every year, more and more falcons (including exotics) will find their way into the hands of skilled duck hawkers, presenting unique opportunities all but unimaginable in the not so distant past.

In spite of this rosy outlook, there are still some disappointing restrictions. Even though the anatum peregrine has been de-listed, there is still no "take" of peregrines throughout most of the U.S. Some states, however, are beginning to open up. Thus, the legacy of American falconers flying wild-taken peregrines is currently experiencing a renaissance. The captive-bred hen anatums that I have flown were fine duck hawks, and I think it safe to say that peregrines in general make excellent duck hawk candidates. Hopefully someday soon, there will be a take of passage tundra falcons. These legendary migrants from the north formed the backbone of American duck hawking with the generation of falconers preceding mine and up until about the 1970s. The reputation of these "beach birds," as they came to be called due to being namely trapped on beaches, still lingers, having been deemed to be in a class unto themselves. These pale falcons manned down very rapidly and were often free flown within days of their capture, regaling falconers with their polished passage style. Due to their migrational urges, tundra falcons were routinely lost, well before the molt, a factor which probably only added to their mystique. I can't help but wonder about the passage tundra's potential in the hands of a skilled, telemetry-equipped falconer. Someday, I hope to have the opportunity to find out! In the mean time, there are certainly enough outstanding falcons out there to satisfy everyone's taste. A few of the northern states comprise the lower fringe of the occasional gyrfalcon's wintering grounds, some of which allow for a limited gyr take. At one time, even California allowed a passage gyr harvest, but those days ended simultaneously with the closure of the Harris take after a few Californians were busted for illegally trapping Harris hawks in Arizona.

When peregrines became all but impossible to legally

acquire, many falconers in the western U.S. switched to the prairie falcon, whose diet generally consisted of fewer birds (less volume) than that of the peregrine and was therefore less affected by the ravages of DDT. It didn't take long for duck hawkers to realize that these desert predators, which were relatively prevalent throughout portions of the western U.S., were not the docile beach birds they so relished. Prairie falcons gained a reputation for being less inclined to "go up" (mount to lofty pitches) and being prone to throwing tantrums. They were, however, equally regarded for being extremely aggressive, hard-hitting game-hawks. Eventually, some falconers developed methods that allowed them to realize the potential of the prairie. Until I saw Gerald Richards fly his prairies, I had bought into the prairies won't go up high rhetoric. After watching Gerald's birds fly, I became aware that the prairie was both willing and able to mount to a tremendous pitch. Getting them to do so boils down to using the right kinds of motivational tactics.

The prairie has proven itself to be a more than competent slayer of ducks. At times, the energy with which they strike their victims supercedes gravitational laws. One day while visiting a prairie eyrie, I unintentionally spooked a barn owl into flight at the base of the cliff. The irate hen prairie vented on the hapless owl, striking it twice. The second hit was lethal, killing the owl instantly. What was most impressive about that unfortunate incident was that the prairie had little height or speed advantage over the owl prior to impact. Obviously the prairie packs a hell of a wallop, and a wild haggard must know a thing or two about where to deliver the blow.

The hardest-hitting falcon I've flown was a hen peregrine x prairie hybrid. These hybrids were popular in the 1980s as they quickly made their mark within the falconry community. The hen I flew for several seasons was a hard-core body slammer. I often flew her in thermals and saw some tremendous stoops and some hellacious impacts. This was not a falcon of finesse; she was all about delivering devastating blows to her quarry. When she struck mallards, the sound carried for a considerable distance and is perhaps best described as that of a baseball bat fully connecting with a melon. Instances of individuals killing themselves on impact are not unheard of and broken legs have also been reported. Nonetheless, peregrine x prairie hybrids are hearty, weather resistant and relatively easy to maintain in good health. As imprints, some individuals may be a bit cantankerous at times, but nothing beyond the realm of acceptability. I have always found it strange how these proficient duck/game-hawks became obscure in a relatively short period of time. As pure strains of peregrines became more available and affordable, these hybrids took a back seat. I wouldn't be shocked if some day peregrine x prairie hybrids were revived at least on a small scale.

There are, of course, many other hybrids. Gyrs have been crossed with prairies and the progeny have been met with mixed reactions. They gyr x prairie has commonly been accused of having a difficult disposition, in fact one prominent breeder told me years ago that he would only produce this cross upon special request because of the inherent difficulties in their personalities. Even so, the gyr x prairie maintains a steadfast group of followers who regard this hybrid with the utmost respect. This discrepancy probably reflects not only variations in individual falcon's personalities, but is probably indicative of some falconers having mastered dealing with these falcons' mentalities.

Out of all the various hybrids that have been produced, by far it is the gyr x peregrine that has created the biggest stir. In recent years, the gyr x peregrine hybrid phenomenon has taken the falconry community by storm. While I readily admit to bias, I beg your indulgence whilst I sing the praises of this hybrid with which I have had the privilege of spending countless days in the field over the past twelve years. From a falconry perspective, the gyr x peregrine hybrid embodies all of the most desirable characteristics one could ask for in a falcon. Ideally, a hybrid should represent the most desirable characteristics from both gene pools, and in this case they do. They are very fast, extremely maneuverable and extraordinarily agile! They are capable of ascending at an enviable rate and are inclined to do so. Historically, the gyr has been a challenging falcon to keep healthy. Foot problems (bumble foot) were a common complaint among Old World falconers. Frounce (trichomoniasis) and aspergalosis routinely terminated fresh-trapped gyrs. Improvements in gyr husbandry, advancements in avian medicine and nutrition have undoubtedly saved the lives of many modern-day gyrfalcons. Nonetheless, hard luck stories of dead gyrs abound, the majority of which involve captive-bred eyases. These days avian malaria seems to be one of the bigger health concerns for captive gyrs, but West Nile virus seems to be vying for center stage.

The average falconer residing in a temperate climate will likely enjoy a lower mortality rate flying gyr hybrids as opposed to pure gyr strains. Gyr x peregrine hybrids benefit from the enhanced immune system of the purebred peregrine, which evolved in a more temperate climate. As generations of captive gyrs perpetuate the domestic stock, survivors will gradually reflect the more resistant members of the captive gene pool. In the mean time, gyrs will most likely continue to experience comparatively high mortality rates, particularly in warmer and damp climates.

The gyr x peregrine hybrid has provided a win/win situation for both breeders and falconers alike. Many of the hens produced in the U.S. are exported to foreign markets where they fetch a fine price. Meanwhile, the tiercels are sucked up by a grateful domestic market, fortunate indeed to be able to fly such gifted falcons. These teircels have unquestionably raised the bar of waiting-on falconry.

The first time I laid eyes on a gyr hybrid was sometime around 1985 when a friend and I visited Steve Baptiste in Nevada. I had a chance to watch Steve work a couple of the gorgeous falcons I had seen blocked out and was duly impressed by their obvious strength and the way they cut through the air. During the mid-1970s, Gerald Richards conceived the "sky trials" concept, originally known as pigeon derbies. The goal was to provide a forum for long-wingers to gather and display the talent and ability of their proteges in a structured, competitive environment. The sky trials venue provides an excellent and otherwise largely impossible opportunity for falconers to mingle and visually compare the results of their training regimen with that of other falconers throughout rather large regions. It is also unique in that one can compare the flight characteristics of a variety of falcons flying under similar conditions and at similar targets, i.e., pigeons. Furthermore, these events encourage an exchange of information among falconers, since nobody is rushing to get to the next field or pond. Having a chance to see many fine falcons flying and stooping, one after the other, taking their best shot at highly conditioned and very illusive homing pigeons is both enjoyable and insightful. Only a small percentage of the falcons served will touch, let alone kill, a homer. Even so, some falconers still complain about the image these events project to the public. Ironically, I've never heard anything negative said about the sky trials from any of the hundreds of public spectators I've mingled with over the years. Thus, the only complaints of which I'm aware are those from nonparticipating falconers.

While a good sky trials falcon isn't necessarily a good game-hawk, probably the vast majority of well-performing contestants have likewise excelled as game-hawks. Sky trials are by no means scientific, but an analysis of the statistics is nonetheless enlightening, at least in terms of falcons versus smallish, illusive targets. For about the last fifteen years, gyr x peregrine hybrids have been a dominating force in this competitive arena. In California, ten out of the last fifteen sky trials held by the California Hawking Club have been won by gyr x peregrine hybrids, nine of which were tiercels. In 2000, gyr x peregrine tiercels took the first three slots. Clearly, something is going on here. In categories such as mounting (feet per minute), pitch, agility (footing) and pursuit, the gyr hybrid really shines. Watching falcons pitted against such challenging targets gives one a good perspective of tiercel hybrids' unique ability. In the world of duck hawking, the targets (ducks) are much easier to hit. Nonetheless, there's ample opportunity for a physically endowed falcon to make good use of such talents.

In 1992 I was in line for a female Peales falcon from Dave Jamieson's "Sky Out Falcons" project but his Peales production was limited that year. Dave offered me a tiercel gyr hybrid instead. At the time I was hawking mostly mallards; I hadn't heard anything about the hybrid tiercels and big ducks so I was hesitant. I definitely didn't want to show up at my mallard slips undergunned. Dave assured me that the tiercels were fully up to the task, and he seemed confident I'd be happy with the switch. In fact, his exact words were, "You'd be a fool not to." At that, I signed on and things haven't been the same since.

The average tiercel gyr x peregrine is certainly capable of taking the biggest, baddest, fastest ducks out there. To say that these feathered athletes can catch large ducks is akin to saying that cheetahs can catch Thompson's gazelles. There's just so much more. A lot of falcons can catch ducks, but I don't believe that any of them can do it quite the way the tiercel gyr x peregrine can (yes, I'm definitely biased).

The gyr x peregrine is a midrange size and in some ways their size works in favor of the duck hawker. The tiercel gyr hybrid strikes a slightly less formidable pose than that of a larger falcon in the eyes of waterfowl. Large ducks are more apt to underestimate the strength, will and tenacity of the tiercel and are thereby more likely to put themselves in harms way, i.e., flush. Also, the lighter weight of the tiercel requires that he climb higher in order to generate enough momentum to knock big birds out of the air—a task that a larger, heavier falcon could accomplish from a lesser pitch. During a recent phone conversation I had with Steve Chindgren of Utah, Steve stated that this was one of the reasons he preferred to fly tiercel gyr x peregrines on sage grouse. Steve's infamous tiercel, Jomo (thirteen years old at time of writing), has probably killed more sage grouse than any other game-hawk, dead or alive. Quite an accomplishment for any falcon let alone a tiercel considering the boomers (male sage) can weigh six and a half pounds. Tiercel gyr hybrids can take duck hawking to another level, therein showcasing ultralong stoops and generating scorching velocity, enviable agility and precision impacts. In the field, these falcons are the epitome of an aggressive game-hawk, yet they remain level headed and docile at home. As a game/duck-hawk, it's difficult to assign a flaw to this hybrid.

In spite of such accolades, gyr hybrids have recently been

embroiled in controversy. Interestingly, it would appear as though the biggest detractors are individuals who have never flown them. I've heard two separate arguments against hybridization. One such argument revolves around the potential threat hybrids may pose if permanently lost to the wild. The fear being that these falcons could then conceivably reproduce with wild falcons and contaminate the gene pool. The mandatory imprinting of hybrids in the U.S. directly addresses this issue, thus reducing the potential for an imprinted hybrid to naturally pair bond and copulate with a wild falcon. The fact that female gyr x peregrine hybrids are most often infertile further reduces the threat of contamination. It could be argued that any hybrid competing to occupy a breeding territory is a waste in itself whether progeny are produced or not. Perhaps, but in the grand scheme of things, even this scenario poses an insignificant threat to wild populations. If, against all odds, an imprint hybrid did manage to procreate with a wild native falcon, the net result of the intermingling would have a negligible impact on the wild gene pool. Within a couple of generations, the wild "pure" genes would begin to saturate the ensuing progeny; mathematically the out-crossed genes would be overwhelmed or swamped.

And as far as contaminating the pure genes of the anatum peregrine, that is a misnomer in itself. The original peregrines released in the U.S. post-DDT era consisted of genes from at least seven subspecies, many of which were entirely exotic races to begin with—not that many people are complaining! Just to be sure that I wasn't missing some important aspect of the hybrid issue and how they may threaten indigenous populations, I spoke with various knowledgeable people, most notably Dr. Tom Cade. Nobody with whom I spoke, including Dr. Cade, felt that gyr hybrids posed a significant threat to wild gene pools in North America. Tom, in fact, is rather a fan of gyr hybrids himself, which tends to be the case for any falconer who has flown one! I do feel it is important to minimize the risk of loss whenever flying any nonindigenous raptor. It is highly recommended that all hybrids be flown with high-quality radio telemetry equipment. It would be a shame to lose access to such a fine and readily available falconry resource due to misconceptions or excessive losses.

There is a second argument I've seen lodged at gyr hybrids, revolving around fair play issues. Apparently, some people consider such hybrids as "designer falcons" with an unfair advantage in the field. The contention is that such hybridization unduly tips the scales in favor of the predator and unfairly disadvantages the quarry. In fact, one letter to the editor published in a falconry periodical described such hybridization as "loading the dice," insinuating that those individuals flying hybrids were merely interested in ensuring maximum kill ratios with a disregard for ethics. Admittedly, I don't personally know the individual who wrote the letter, but I would speculate that the person has never flown a gyr hybrid because he or she appears to be coming from a place of limited experience and understanding. While I can't speak for all others, I'm compelled to set the record straight, as I would hate to see the sentiment of the falconry community and its governing bodies tainted by some ill-informed misrepresentation. The way I see it, from my limited perspective, falconry is an art. As an artist, I'm constantly trying to perfect my art form. This correlates directly to field performance. After one has mastered the act of taking game with falcons, the seemingly natural progression is to then take game in as spectacular fashion as possible—stretching the envelope of preconceived flight parameters. When flying longwings in wide-open spaces, this often equates to extreme pitches, though other facets of the falcon's performance are equally important. Flying a 780-gram falcon that regularly mounts in excess of 1,000 feet and head shoots large ducks well up in the sky after they have come off big water isn't exactly tantamount to an unfair advantage. It is more about doing something you love as well as you can possibly do it. A falconer who is truly committed to artistry doesn't go to such great lengths to develop game-hawks of this caliber solely in order to fill more freezer space with the corpses of his egotistical excess. To say as much is naive at best! Whatever hawk, falcon or eagle one chooses to fly and how one flies it is truly the purest expression of one's self.

CHAPTER 3

Shortwings

Most falconers who have flown several great game-hawks would probably be hard pressed to pick a favorite if asked. However, if they were asked to name the one hawk that taught them the most, I suspect that the majority of falconers could put their finger on that one particular bird that most enabled them to pierce the inner circle. For me the choice is easy, that special hawk would be an eyas goshawk named Girl.

Girl came to me when my life was in turmoil. I was twenty-one years old and had been living with friends for a couple of years. Previously, within a span of two months, a drunk driver killed my mother, and my fiancée went off to college and on to marry someone else. I was enrolled in the local junior college and was working part-time as a security guard and then a pizza maker. I decided that it was time to fly a goshawk, and it was probably the best decision I made all year.

Usually, the things that are most precious to us don't come easily, and this hawk was no exception. I racked up 1,500 miles driving to remote forests, camped and hiked for many days. Eventually, all the effort paid off and I was able to pull a gorgeous hen. Together we had a phenomenal season, terrorizing game everywhere we went. Initially we focused on hunting the abundant cottontails inhabiting both chaparral and tumbleweed/grassy habitats. Multiple kills quickly became the rule and it was then that I first began to practice catch and release techniques. Looking for greater challenges, we began making trips to the desert, embarking on a successful campaign hawking blacktail jackrabbits. Next, we set our sights on waterfowl and I became instantly addicted to duck hawking.

Our first attempts at taking ducks were literally trial and error incarnate. I'd never seen anyone hunting ducks with an accipiter; indeed, I'd only seen one or two ducks taken in my entire life and those were with falcons. There didn't seem to be a whole lot of recent literature on the subject either. Though I knew virtually nothing about ducks, and even less about how to catch them with hawks, I was eager to learn, and I had an awesome goshawk. What we lacked in know-how, we made up for in enthusiasm and drive. We began prowling streams, ditches and ponds, quickly learning where the coots, pintail, teal, mallards and others were hanging out. I began to see flights the likes of which I'd never heard described before. If we had a couple of days of hard luck, we'd revert to flying bunnies for a day—in essence we flew them as if they were bagged game because they were so easy for the gos to catch and they restored both of our confidences. Afterwards, we'd go back to the trenches, matching our wits with those of the waterfowl. We put a ton of coots in the bag before we developed a strategy and the level of skill necessary to take ducks. Ultimately, I learned that if I could provide good slips, the gos could score.

At the time I was hawking my gos strictly off the fist, so ducks needed to be flushed in close proximity. This required a degree of stealth that had not been necessary for the rabbit and sparrow hunting I'd done with previous hawks and falcons. I found that I was playing a larger role in the hunting process and my competency, or lack thereof, had a greater impact on the success or failure of our hawking endeavors. This I found to be both challenging and rewarding. The art of falconry is first and foremost a hunting art. As a duck hawker, I really began to consider myself a hunter. And the quality of the hawking experience was a direct reflection of not only my ability to train and handle raptors efficiently, but also my ability to manipulate circumstances and the quarry I pursued.

Throughout this period I felt a bond develop between this hawk and me at a level that I'd never felt before—a kind of codependent partnership, or so I thought. One day, I ran into some trouble while flying ditches near the coast. The gos had killed a coot and I had fed her a little but we pressed on, hoping for a duck slip. Eventually I spotted three mallards in a ditch, running along the base of a small hill. I mentally marked their location before dropping down below the embankment in order to approach unseen by the ducks. Unfortunately I'd either miscalculated or the ducks had moved because I somehow managed to come up over the top ten yards too far down. Startled, the ducks made for the sky, the gos pursued the mallards, pumping hard for seventy yards, but was unable to make up the distance. Aborting the chase she flew up the hillside and landed on some brush. I pulled out the lure to call her in, but as she headed down the hill, a pair of crows and a haggard redtail distracted her. She set her wings, caught the updraft and began to rise. She slowly drifted around the corner of the hill and out of view. At the time I didn't own any telemetry equipment, so instead of a quick retrieval I spent the next four hours looking in vain until darkness suspended the search. I went home permeated with an awful feeling of emptiness. From that moment on I put my life on hold, including my job at the pizza place, and concentrated all of my efforts on recovering the hawk. The following morning, I was out searching before light, using a coot carcass and a live pigeon for lures. There was a golf course around the backside of the hill and I spoke with the groundsmen but no one had seen my hawk. After nine hours, there was still no sign of her; I went home empty-handed again. On the third day I was back at it, beginning at first light. After another six hours of calling, whistling and swinging lures all over the surrounding area, I was physically and emotionally depleted and had serious doubts as to whether I would see her again. I decided to check by the golf course again and was summoned over by one of the groundsmen who said he had seen my hawk and that she had killed a coot. I found it hard to believe, since I'd spent so much time in the vicinity and seen nothing to indicate that she was still in the area. Nonetheless, I checked it out and, sure enough, a coot had been killed. It was obviously a raptor kill and the coot had been virtually entirely consumed right there on the green. I figured that with a crop like that, if it was my gos, she wouldn't be far. I walked to some nearby trees, swinging a lure and down she came. I was simultaneously relieved, exhausted and ecstatic.

When I returned to work, the restaurant manager pulled me aside for one of those serious lectures they like to give when an employee has missed work and needs to "refocus." He looked me in the eye and said, "Joe, you've got to decide what's more important—your job or your bird." I looked him in the eye and said, "That's easy, I can replace this job way more easily than I can replace my hawk!" The conversation came to an abrupt halt and the subject was never discussed after that.

Girl and I resumed our outings. By the end of the season we had a basic understanding of the fundamentals of duck hawking and we were catching ducks with some regularity. The molt arrived and I spent the summer dreaming of the ducks we would catch next season. September rolled around; I was enrolled in the final courses I needed to graduate from the junior college and to be eligible to apply for work as a game warden for the state of California. Just when you think you have some sort of game plan, life has a way of throwing curve balls. Out of the blue, I was offered an opportunity to spend a couple of months training birds of prey at a theme park in Florida. I declined at first because all I wanted to do was finish school and fly my hawk. Eventually I was persuaded, and my new boss and I set off for an adventure. We traveled cross-country in a Toyota pick-up with most of our earthly belongings—his dog, two falcons, an eagle and my goshawk. Surprisingly, we arrived in Florida without incident. The bird of prey department was staffed by an all-female ensemble and the park's main attraction was a mermaid show; this situation made my decision seem all the more sensible.

One day, my boss and I drove out to a remote location to work the new eagle and, by chance, we spotted a group of black ducks on a pond butted against the side of a small hill. It was a terrific set up and I thought it would be perfect for the gos' first setup since leaving California. I drove back to the park to pick her up and returned to the pond within an hour. Much to my relief, the ducks were still there. I marked their exact location, then took the gos out of the truck and made a textbook approach. We used the hill to conceal our advance, and when we emerged at the top of the hill we took the blacks completely by surprise. The ducks were still some distance from us, but the hill gave us sixty feet of vertical advantage. These ducks were in trouble! They flushed clean and the gos blazed off the fist, her descent ignited by a gravity assist. She was smoking when she slammed into a hen thirty yards out. Not bad for the first slip of the season! I returned to the park one happy austringer with a cropped gos and a great deal of optimism.

As the weeks wore on, however, hawkable setups were difficult to find. The bunnies that we had always fallen back on in Southern California were equally difficult to find in this new land. Our work at the park was extended and it became evident that we would be in Florida for the duration of the season. Soon winter was in full swing (such as it is in Florida), yet we didn't experience a heavy influx of the northern migrants we'd hoped for. There were some hooded mergansers showing up at various ponds, but the setups were more conducive to longwings, so my boss flew his falcon on the mergs and I shifted my attention to hawking tree squirrels with my gos. It was during this period that I really began to appreciate the versatility of the gos as she began to add another species of game to her repertoire. By the same token, I began to comprehend the falcon's ability to take waterfowl under a broader range of circumstances than the accipiter.

Goshawks are truly marvelous creatures, deserving of falconry's highest honors. I don't believe anyone can claim to have had the full-spectrum falconry experience without having shared the field with a goshawk. The energy, enthusiasm and physical capabilities endowed in this species are formidable. They are predators second to none. Goshawks and falcons are dissimilar in so many ways, it almost seems absurd to make comparisons, yet a brief analysis in terms of duck hawking potential is in order. Aside from the obvious physical differences, there is a profound separation of psyche. I have never known another creature with such intense predatory propensities as the goshawk. Their urge to kill transcends their physical need to consume. It is this mentality coupled with explosive acceleration, perseverance and incredible dexterity (footing) that has earned the goshawk a special niche in the hearts of austringers around the world. The gos' ability to accelerate and hit top speed so quickly are precisely what makes this species such a dynamic duck killer. Though the gos boasts appreciable top end speed, she (like the peregrine) will be regularly outflown by most species of waterfowl in a protracted horizontal tail chase. Goshawks are not prone to waiting-on, like falcons; rather their flight is more a point A to point B affair. This is a limiting factor in the goshawk's ability to fly ducks on most large bodies of deep water. Goshawks excel when they can be slipped closely as ducks are flushed out over land. The goshawk's range can be extended with elevation, as in flying from trees, poles, etc. Nonetheless, the gos generally needs to connect before ducks can reach top speed. Goshawks can be effective from long range when flying dryland ducks or ducks in shallow water fields, and they reportedly take ducks consistently when flown under these conditions. Unlike accipiters, falcons are easily taught to fly above the falconer and wait-on at height, giving her a tremendous speed advantage. Generally speaking, the higher the falcon's pitch, the larger the area she can effectively cover below her; this area is referred to as the killing cone. Thus, high-flying falcons are limited less by pond size than they are pond location. Powerlines, fences, tree cover, etc., all of which can easily impede or kill a falcon, can usually be successfully navigated by the gos. The choice as to whether to fly a shortwing or a longwing in pursuit of waterfowl is not so much a question of which is better than the other, it is more an assessment of the kind of waterfowling one has access to and personal flight/lifestyle preference. If the setups are predominantly conducive to one or the other type predator, the falconer may have little choice in the matter. In most of the areas I've flown, falcons would have an edge over shortwings due to their ability to take ducks under a wider range of circumstances. But, with the exception of one tiny area of Florida, my hawking has virtually always been in the western part of the U.S., much of which is wide-open country. In other parts of the country, it is probably vice versa. From a broader perspective however, goshawks cannot be beaten in terms of overall versatility. Whereas most North American falconers limit their large longwings hunting to upland game birds or waterfowl, austringers flying goshawks can fly feather today, bunnies tomorrow, jacks the next, or just about anything else they choose...decisions, decisions.

Throughout this chapter, I have intentionally focused on the northern goshawk (*Accipiter gentilis*) because its combination of size, speed and strength makes it an ideal candidate for waterfowling. This by no means is meant to imply that other shortwings are not capable of consistently taking ducks. The average Cooper's hawk (*Accipiter cooperii*) may be a bit undersized for the larger ducks, though some do take them. Nonetheless I have often imagined what a Cooper's on teal flight might look like, and if the reality is anything like what I've imagined, it must surely be some flight. The Harris (*Parabuteo unicinctus*) is of course capable of handling ducks of all sizes. I take an occasional duck with my tiercel and could no doubt take them regularly if I chose to do so. However, since I have chosen to fly waterfowl and upland game birds with two falcons all season long, the Harris offers a nice change of pace. I thoroughly enjoy the opportunity to switch gears and hawk primarily ground game with my Harris, mixed with an occasional slip at waterfowl or game birds. I am unaware of anyone seriously flying redtails (*Buteo jamaicensis*) on waterfowl, but a friend of mine experimented with waiting on redtails and ducks, he feels the potential may be there. Certainly wild bald eagles (*Haliaeetus leucocephalus*) and golden eagles (*Aquila chrysaetos*) take waterfowl both from the surface of the water and in the air. And I even met a guy in Florida that had taken a mallard with his red-shouldered hawk (*Buteo lineatus*).

Undoubtedly, there are many ways for a creative austringer to take ducks with a variety of raptors other than longwings. Nonetheless, I'd like to proceed with a description of the tactics I'm most familiar with involving taking ducks on the rise with gos or Harris hawks. Under this premise, we expect to place the hawk reasonably close to the ducks as they flush in order to take advantage of the hawk's explosive acceleration. As with longwings, it is often preferable to spot and mark ducks before removing the hawk from the truck. Most of the information contained in the chapter on scouting is applicable with some modifications. When flushing ducks for falcons, it's important to know where the ducks are before going over the top of the ditch, dyke, etc. However, there is usually some room for error. As long as the ducks clear land, the falcon's pitch and positioning can usually compensate for imperfect flushes. When flying shortwings, there is little tolerance for such errors. Even if the ducks do clear land, coming over the top anywhere but in the right spot is likely to result in the ducks making the most of their exaggerated lead and leaving the hawk in the dust. If the hawk has an appreciable vertical advantage, such as when she's released from higher ground, it will really enhance her speed and stretch out her effective range. When flying areas with suitable elevated perches (or bringing one's own T-perch), the hawk can be cast up to a tree or pole, positioning her well above the ducks before the flush for additional speed. When flying ditches or streams lined with trees, the hawk can be encouraged to leap frog her way along the watercourse, staying just ahead of the austringer who follows along behind the hawk. When ducks are casually encountered, they will usually flush and fly along the top of the water only to splash in as the hawk approaches; therefore, it is important to try to surprise them, intercepting them at hard angles in order to push them directly away from water, giving the hawk an honest shot. When ducks have been located, always note their position using a visual reference, anything that will serve as a landmark to guide you to the exact spot when you are approaching, and the ducks are no longer in view. A bush, fencepost, rock or any other identifiable object will suffice, so long as the ducks are accurately marked. Otherwise, the odds of properly slipping the hawk will be seriously undermined. Of course there's always the possibility that the ducks will move after you mark them and before you flush them, so no matter how well you've got them marked you could still be off. Getting to the ducks and flushing them quickly after having marked them, will help limit the distance they may travel. Sometimes the austringer can sneak a peak just before coming over the top to flush and confirm the ducks exact position, but it's a risky move and can backfire. Sometimes the austringer will have virtually no choice but to try to get one last visual conformation before the flush because the ducks are floating downstream or otherwise actively paddling around. When doing some of this tedious marking, hawks that are hooded are likely to be more manageable than hawks that are not. A hawk that isn't hooded is probably going to be very hyper; the stealthier you behave, the more keyed up she becomes. Having a hawk bating off the fist, even with bells taped, is counterproductive when you are trying to keep a low profile.

When hawking ditches, an accomplice can come in handy. When my friends in Southern California hawk ditches together, they'll have one man act as a spotter, maintaining visual contact with the ducks from a distance, as the austringer approaches from an obscured angle. Using simple, predetermined hand signals, the austringer is guided by the spotter to precisely the right point for the flush. Regardless of how the approach is made, once the ducks are lined up, the hood is popped and the hawk is given a couple seconds to orient and then taken directly in for the flush. If the sudden appearance of man doesn't terrify the ducks, screaming at them should. When ducks are panicked, they're far more likely to flush clean. If they're flushed gingerly, they may act more rationally and then they're much more likely to use water in order to evade capture. A good clean assist off the fist will catapult the hawk into the air and have her up to full speed quickly. When all goes to plan, the hawk slams into a duck for a precision bind making it look all too easy.

Sometimes ducks will be situated in areas that make a completely concealed approach impossible; often it's just those critical last few yards that create the impasse. In such cases, the austringer can try covering the ground at a fast gate or even a run, launching the hawk as the ducks begin to rise. In some instances it may be necessary to shield the hawk's view of the ducks in order to prevent a premature bate, or fly her directly out of the hood as the ducks get up. Sometimes, however, a preemptive strike is the best possible option. At such times, the hawk is cast off toward ducks, which may not even be visible to her at this point; this is all right as long as she's headed in the right direction. Ducks in vulnerable locations may flush automatically when they see the hawk coming and realize they're under attack, hopefully by then the hawk has covered enough ground to make up the deficit in the approach. However, often they will attempt to stay on the water and casually submerge as the hawk flies overhead. This can usually be prevented if the austringer is prepared to make the typical flushing commotion (running, yelling, throwing things, etc.) at just the right moment. This method should not only get the hawk within range, but she'll also have a full head of steam when she gets there.

There's another variation of this method that is particularly handy with the Harris and it, too, involves a preemptive maneuver. When ducks have been spotted, the austringer makes his usual approach, but stops well before reaching the ducks. The hawk is then cast into a tree, on a pole or set on the ground. The austringer then covers most of the remaining distance between himself and the ducks and then calls the hawk his direction. Food is not used as a prompt; the objective is not to call the hawk to the austringer (in which case she'll be slowing down, in anticipation of landing and being fed), but rather to encourage the hawk to fly past the austringer. Hawks that have been conditioned to respond to hand signals may be moved forward in the usual manner. Its probably best not to use vocal cues to move the hawk during this phase, lest we give the ducks more insight than we'd like them to have just yet—silence is golden. As the hawk begins its "fly by," the austringer prepares to execute the flush, which is done in similar fashion as the previous example. As the hawk approaches, hopefully full steam, the austringer estimates how close to let her get before making the flush. The ducks need to have time to get up and clear land. Otherwise, they'll just splash back in or the hawk will be binding to a duck over water.

Some setups are difficult to scout without prematurely flushing any ducks that may be there. These sets are better flown speculatively. They are approached with the hawk on the fist or flying from trees. If on the fist, I prefer unhooded for this tactic. These flights possess a unique flavor drenched in anticipation. The hawk (especially a gos) feels like a bundle of nerves, head snapping this way and that, muscles contracting with the sound of each snapping twig. At such times, I sense her energy flowing into my hand, up my arm and into my core. Engulfed in the moment, I am no longer a vicarious onlooker, I become a predator—the hawk and I hunting as one. When at last a duck suddenly erupts from cover, my body responds with a burst of adrenaline as the hawk explodes off my fist. In that instant, my heart leaps and my spirit flies with the hawk as she fulfills her predatory role…awesome!

CHAPTER 4

Ducks

Ducks are a fascinating collage of feathered diversity. Just as falcons have evolved to be efficient aerial predators, so too have ducks evolved to excel in aquatic environments. They have also developed sophisticated attributes geared toward avoiding predation. The evolutionary competition between predator and prey forms the backbone of the falconry premise. Thus, an understanding of this intricate relationship is as fundamental to falconry as the falcons themselves. By recognizing some of our own survival instincts, we are better able to relate to other species and interpret their behaviors.

Ducks, like people, are social and exhibit a flock mentality. Armed with this basic bit of information, we are much better equipped to orchestrate coherent duck slips. Ducks are smart, and when it comes to self-preservation they are most resourceful. Serious duck hawkers would do well to scrutinize duck behavior before, during and after the flush. In so doing, behavioral patterns will begin to emerge, after which comes predictability. When you know what a duck is going to do before he does, it is a lot easier to manipulate the slip to your advantage. If you can get inside the duck's head, the battle is half won. Once we realize that a duck will react differently when it is alone as opposed to a part of a group, we can appreciate what naturally follows. While there are many variables that can alter the progression and outcome of a duck slip, the concept of observation is what is vital at this point.

Our very human nature suggests that mistakes are inevitable. Ironically, mistakes often offer the best opportunities from which to learn...if we're paying attention. Ducks, too, make mistakes, and often the mistakes they make are forced errors in which the falconer has played a pivital role. Sometimes, however, they err in judgment.

A hen mallard that I had flushed under an anatum peregrine made one such error. The duck got off the pond well, then bailed into a small creek, thus thwarting the falcon. Instead of remounting, the anatum landed on the ground beside the duck. The width and depth of the water were just enough to keep the falcon at bay, but not so big that the mallard could make a graceful exit. I sat some distance away and waited to see what would happen next. After a couple of minutes of what could best be described as a Mexican standoff, the duck made her move. In spite of the outcome, one has to give credit to the duck for having guts. She marched herself right out of that creek and stomped directly at the peregrine, chattering as she went. In one fell swoop, the falcon leapt off her feet and pounced squarely on the mallard's back. And that was that. I have no doubt that the mallard misinterpreted the falcon's reluctance to enter the creek, believing it was she the falcon was intimidated by, not the water. So much for intimidation.

Yes, ducks do make the occasional unforced error, but, rest assured, ducks are of sound mind and body. While numerous intelligent organisms have adapted to life in a liquid environment, few are as at home in both the water and sky alike. Interestingly, the nonhunting public at large seems to be of the impression that ducks are stupid (thanks in part to Hollywood's notorious Daffy and Donald Ducks) and that they are slow or ungainly in the air. Nothing could be further from the truth. The magnificent peregrine in all her aerodynamic glory simply can't match some of the flight performance capabilities of an average mallard. Once a mallard slip flattens out into a tail chase, the mallard can fly faster, steeper and longer than the peregrine. If we were to accuse the mallard of being slow, what then does that say for the peregrine? The very idea of a heavily wingloaded mallard leaping vertically into instant flight from the surface of the water is in itself a testament to engineering genius. That ducks are cosmopolitan and abundant organisms is evidence of a very successful evolutionary tactic.

Ducks namely seek water for food and shelter, relying on flight for safe and rapid transportation. Flight has enabled ducks to exploit the finest habitats the earth has to offer year round, regardless of distance. Some species utilize two or even three continents over the course of a single year, flowing with the cyclical patterns of the ever-changing seasons. The fluid movement of ducks across the landscape is perhaps the ultimate use of migratory potential. Duck migration is fascinating and steeped in mystique. There can be huge fluctuations in local duck populations over the course of a relatively short period of time, in some cases overnight. Duck hunters who rely upon an influx of migrants hope and pray for the right combination of meteorological conditions to bring ducks in plentiful hordes and keep them there. Even though we can get a pretty good idea of the nesting conditions and hatch rate up north, those of us living to the south never quite know what to expect. Of course we always wish for a good hatch, but even a great hatch by no means guarantees a great duck-hunting season. I do the bulk of my duck hawking in California's Sacramento Basin, where even in below-average years, the overwinter duck population is quite large. Yet the conditions for duck hawking can at times be far from ideal. Due to a combination of wetland habitats and flooded rice fields, there's usually more than enough water around to keep the ducks happy, but it isn't until rains have filled ephemeral ponds and formed puddles in fields, that the region's full duck hawking potential can be realized. The sooner the precipitation comes to the south and cold settles into the north, the longer ducks will be in the valley. Last year we had the making of a great duck season with the exception of one crucial element—timing. Winter arrived a bit late, as did many of the ducks. Just before duck hawking became optimal, the hunting season came to an end.

The timing of weather systems is crucial in the world of waterfowl hunting. Correlating the dynamics of habitat conditions, hatch rates, populations, hunting seasons, bag limits, etc., is a major concern for hunters and governing agencies alike. The fact that many species of ducks heedlessly traverse across international borders hasn't exactly simplified matters. Identifying migration corridors as well as destinations has certainly been a perplexing proposition. About 100 years ago, Americans began marking wild ducks with numerical leg bands. As hunters bagged and reported marked ducks, a database was established, offering a rare glimpse into the previously enigmatic lifecycles of waterfowl. Banding is still very much part of the on-going quest to better understand and manage duck populations. Recently, radio telemetry has become increasingly useful, as transmitter-equipped ducks are tracked and monitored via satellite. This technology goes where no band has gone before, divulging a much broader picture of not only where ducks are going, but also by which routes they get there and how long they are staying. In January of 2000, fifty hen pintails wintering in California's Sacramento Valley were radio tagged and tracked throughout the spring and summer. Most of them left California in March or April, heading north via two primary migration corridors. They flew through Oregon, Washington and Montana in order to reach their breeding grounds on the Canadian prairies of Saskatchewan and Alberta. Most of the hens didn't settle due to drier than normal conditions and continued flying until they reached better conditions in the Canadian Arctic. Meanwhile, a small contingency of the study hens had lingered in staging areas in Northern California and southern Oregon well into April and early May. When they finally departed, they flew directly across the Pacific Ocean to western Alaska. Surprisingly, one of these hens then proceeded to cross the Bering Strait and spent the summer in Siberia. Thus, we clearly see the multinational implication of our waterfowl.

Ducks are among the most highly managed resources on our planet. Accurate and detailed information help make effective management a reality, as does millions and millions of dollars, much of which is paid directly by hunters. Most North American duck populations are currently in good shape; unfortunately, this hasn't always been the case. Throughout much of the last two centuries, ducks and their habitats have suffered mightily. Until most recently, man has little understood and appreciated wetlands. Drainage of North American wetlands has resulted in large-scale loss of habitat. Elimination of wetlands has had an adverse impact on the environment and the organisms dependant upon them including waterfowl.

American duck populations were also threatened, rather assaulted, by market hunters. Beginning around 1890, Americans developed an insatiable taste for fowl. Duck flesh became a commodity like gold or timber and it was readily available for the taking. Over the next two and a half decades, Americans consumed untold numbers of ducks. Alas, the seemingly endless supply of succulent duck meat collapsed as duck populations crashed, no longer able to support the overwhelming demand. Before the smoke had cleared, many species were imperiled, and the wood duck had nearly been shot to extinction. Finally, in 1918, the federal government stepped in and enacted the Migratory Bird Treaty Act, which gave them control over all migratory birds. Stressed out duck populations got a reprieve with the abolition of market hunting. The feds were then obliged to construct the framework for a sustainable set of hunting regulations. By 1951, the International Association of Game, Fish Conservation created the "Flyway Councils" in order to assist the government in managing waterfowl populations. The council divided North America into four quadrants: Pacific, Central, Mississippi and the Atlantic. These flyway designations are commonly confused with migration corridors, which they are not. In fact, some species may traverse two or three of these flyways during the course of their migration. The four flyways were divided on a purely geographical basis. The segregation of the flyways is instrumental in allowing waterfowl to be managed on a regional basis.

Waterfowl management has certainly come a long way. No doubt some of the grievous mistakes we've made in the past, whether by greed, necessity or ignorance, have helped launch a more conservative agenda. Recently, gun hunters were mandated to use only nontoxic shot while hunting waterfowl. Lead shot, which has always been preferred due to its low cost and ballistic performance, is now banned. Previously, ducks would routinely ingest toxic lead pellets (shot) while bottom feeding, thus shotguns killed many a duck long after they had been fired. Carnivorous birds (including trained falcons) have benefited from the ban because any ducks that have either ingested or been shot with lead posed a threat to any birds eating them. Once in a while, my falcons catch a duck that has been "peppered" by a gun hunter. There are always ducks flying around out there laden with shotgun pellets. As time goes by, more and more of them will be carrying something other than lead and I'm all for that!

Waterfowl identification is a crucial component of duck hawking. An accurate assessment of a potential slip can only be made when the falconer knows what he's looking at. Identification, like most everything else, gets easier with practice. Viewing high-resolution photographs, such as those found in field guides and duck magazines, can be a great way to learn. Direct field observation regarding physical characteristics, i.e., size, shape, colors, wing-beat, vocalizations, etc., as well as habitat preferences and behavioral patterns is essential. Most of the pertinent ducks can be put into one of two major categories: puddle ducks or diving ducks.

Puddle Ducks

There are eleven species of puddle ducks, or dabblers, in North America. Puddle ducks are reasonably adept at walking on land, and some species are known to forage in this fashion, gleaning leftovers in harvested fields, etc. However, the majority of feeding occurs in water at a depth of one foot or less, where ducks "tip" on end and forage partially submerged. Puddlers are crepuscular but may feed at any hour, sometimes even switching to a nocturnal schedule under heavy hunting pressure. Diet consists of mostly vegetable matter, though invertebrates are also consumed. As the breeding season approaches, invertebrates make up a larger portion of their diet and become vitally important to hens, providing the nutrients required to produce a clutch of approximately a dozen eggs.

Eggs are laid in a nest lined with down from the hen's breast.

Nests are primarily on the ground, hidden in thick upland grass or under brush, and may be as far as a mile or more from the nearest water. Once the final egg has been laid, the hen alone then incubates the clutch for twenty-one to thirty-five days, depending on the species in question. Hatching is synchronized, the entire brood emerging from their shells within five to six hours of one another. Puddle ducklings, like all the rest, are precocial and are capable of walking, swimming, and eating shortly after hatching. Ducklings follow the hen to water on what must be a harrowing journey for all but the shortest of jaunts. During this procession, the brood may be exposed to various obstacles and predators along the way. It seems that every year, news cameras capture some hapless mother duck attempting to lead her brood across some busy road, right through traffic. Upon reaching the relative safety of water, the lucky survivors become highly predatory, feeding almost exclusively on insects during this critical growth phase.

By the eight or ninth week, mallards are able to fly. Subarctic pintails are able to take advantage of the extended photoperiod, eating profusely, and are flying by about their sixth week. Green-wing teal, by virtue of their miniscule size, mature at lightning speed and are flighted by day thirty-four. Puddle ducks sexually mature in their first year with pair bonding taking place on the wintering grounds. Hens have their pick of drakes as they are outnumbered and older drakes have a leg up, so to speak, on younger inexperienced drakes, and are more likely to pair up. Once selected, the drake will stick like glue to his hen, defending her from any and all would-be suitors.

By late winter (in some cases, much earlier) mallard flocks splinter off, as pairs seek seclusion. This is a welcome occurrence for falconers, as pairs begin showing up at isolated set-ups that had until now been vacant. Also, the odds of happening into a duck slip are increased with this expanded distribution of many pairs as opposed to a single flock.

A hen is philopatric and as spring approaches, she will return to the place of her hatching, or where she had previously reproduced. For most species, this will mean a lengthy northern migration. Wherever she may go, her drake will follow.

Through thick and thin, he'll be right there—at least until the hen stops copulating. That's right, once the sex is over and the clutch is complete, he's outta' there, which may not be as cold as it appears. Incubating hens suffer quite high mortality rates, more so today than in the past. In a man-altered prairie habitat, raccoons have managed to expand their range and are voracious killers of nesting hens, clutches of eggs, and hatched ducklings. Raccoons are fond of water, so even species of diving ducks, which nest over water, are not immune to raccoon predation. Furthermore, man has altered the composition of prairie predators by eliminating the wolf and curtailing coyote populations, which in turn has allowed the red fox, a notorious duck killer, to flourish. Against predators such as these, a drake could offer no protection; indeed his mere presence would tend to attract more predators. Better that he should go his own way. Besides, there may yet be hens in need of his "services." If for any reason a clutch fails, the hen will likely recycle, in fact, puddle duck hens have been known to make as many as six attempts. Time, of course, is of the essence if she is to have any hope of rearing a brood, and she'll not dally long between failed clutches; she'll select an alternate mate right quick. Happy day for the drake that happens to be in the right place at the right time. Male waterfowl are, interestingly enough, members of an elite, if small, number of birds in possession of a penis. Presumably because copulation takes place in water, actual penetration, as opposed to mere cloacal contact, is a more surefire means of fertilization. Ultimately, the drake having made his most important contribution to the reproduction cycle by way of genetic excellence will seek out a quiet, secluded body of water where he can begin to moult. He'll have nothing more to do with hen(s) he has fertilized nor the offspring they bear.

Ducks go through two moults annually, one of which involves a rapid loss of flight feathers. Moulting in this manner will leave a mallard flightless for a period of about three weeks. This, of course, would prove fatal to most species of birds, but ducks, provided they have chosen their moulting location wisely, find relative safety on water. During this summer moult, both hens and drakes will take on a drab appearance that will be much more profound in the otherwise colorful drakes. Not to worry, come fall the drake will undergo his second moult, wherein he'll not lose his flight feathers or ability to fly, but he will replace his camouflaged plumage with the regal, spectacular colors of a stud looking to party. The puddler hen's subsequent moult will flash up her look some, but she'll always pale in comparison to her drake, excepting in the case of American black ducks and mottled ducks, which exhibit no such plumage dimorphism between the sexes. In all cases, save gadwalls, puddle ducks of both sexes sport a very ornate patch of iridescent secondaries known as the speculum.

As a group, puddlers are vocal, and the voice of most hens sounds like the quack of a hen mallard. Drake pintail and widgeon make whistling sounds especially while flying. There can be no finer sound on a cold January morning than that of flocks of pintail whistling overhead as they carve their way across the sky.

All puddle ducks are aerodynamic wonders capable of vertical lift off and rapid acceleration and they possess surprising agility. Thankfully, these ducks frequent the kinds of shallow water habitats that make them vulnerable to falconry tactics.

MALLARD

Mallards are perhaps the most versatile duck on the planet. As a species, they are icons of adaptability. No doubt, their ability to adapt and even thrive in a man-altered environment has played a vital role in their proliferation. In light of the fact that my falcons take more mallards than any other duck, I'm pleased to say that they rate very high in terms of hawkability. When I muse over mallards, I conjure images of large, beautiful, swift, intelligent and, thankfully, abundant quarry. Mallards are great ducks to fly on just about any set. Their hefty size helps ease their anxiety of flying under falcons, making them cooperative in the flush. When mallards are in a mixed flock, they help out by pulling less cooperative species along with them when they go. Smaller ducks that fly out with mallards are more likely to withstand the falcon's first stoop before trying to turn and regain the pond. Due to the mallards' size and strength, it takes a decent hit to knock them down. They can down right intimidate some falcons, especially those that don't fly them regularly. Even duck hawks with extensive mallard experience can succumb to intimidation tactics, particularly when not driven by hunger.

Last season I watched a drake mallard pull of just such a maneuver. Having been knocked down in a plowed field by an experienced, intermewed falcon, it appeared as though the drake had no recourse. Apparently, he didn't see things that way. When the falcon circled in for the kill, the mallard stood, fully erect, head back, beak open, quacking in unabashed defiance. The falcon kept circling, reluctant, looking for a chance to attack from behind. Nothing doing. The drake stood his ground and faced off the falcon each time it passed by. Showing impressive intelligence and poise, the duck waited until the falcon's back was turned and looking away, then he made his break. By the time the falcon caught on, it was too late; in the face of long odds, the mallard escaped, averting what had once seemed an inevitable fate. This was a prime example of the kind of quarry mallards can be—tough! Any falcon that will consistently slam mallards should be up for just about anything else within reason.

AMERICAN WIGEON

Wigeons are flat out one of my all-time favorite ducks. Their midrange size makes them a very enticing target for falcons, which attack them with reckless abandon. There is no other duck that uses the air space surrounding a pond quite like a wigeon. They are extremely maneuverable and highly evasive. Their sharp turning radius permits them to maintain good airspeed while twisting, turning and circling around the perimeter of a pond in an effort to avoid the stooping falcon.

I can still remember the first time I flew a wigeon set; it was bizarre. I had a peregrine waiting on at a meager pitch when I flushed. The falcon stooped and managed to put a hen back in, which was subsequently reflushed, with identical results. The wigeon got up a third time and the falcon was in hot pursuit, but this time the duck didn't splash back in or make a clean break.

Instead she began a series of high-speed revolutions around the perimeter of the small pond, gaining height as she went, the peregrine following in suit. Up they climbed in tight spirals, both birds flying for all they were worth. At 350 feet, the wigeon, convinced she could indeed contest the sky with the peregrine, made her move. She streaked across the sky full tilt, peregrine in tow. The wigeon had played it right. She was never to be seen again. The befuddled peregrine was picked up a half an hour later on her training grounds some fifteen miles away.

Whenever wigeon are involved, well-conceived tactics are called upon if the falcon is to prevail. The flush in critical. When scouting wigeon ponds, be especially attentive to outlying grassy edges where they may be foraging. Occasionally, European wigeon make their way to North America where they mingle with American wigeon. Aside from slight variations in plumage, falconers are unlikely to detect any differences between the two. I always love to fly wigeon and derive an extra measure of satisfaction when one is cleanly put to bag.

Pintail

Pintails are generally considered to be the most regal of ducks, and rightfully so. The elongated contour of pintails carving graceful lines in the sky above causes one to pause and take note. Their stately appearance and swift flight is nicely complimented by an uncanny intelligence. A clean pintail slip is cause for celebration. When found in mixed flocks, pintails are among the least likely to be taken by falcons. While many ducks will balk at the flush, pintails are probably the only ones that intentionally hesitate, knowing full well the others will draw the falcon's stoop. Once the falcon has killed, the pintail are then free to go as they please. This tactic is highly effective, but it can backfire. If for any reason, the falcon fails to kill from the first wave of ducks off the pond, it is the remaining pintails that then captivate the falcon's full attention, as was the case last year on the final day of duck season.

The rains had finally come and puddles had formed in the fields. One such puddle held approximately 150 wigeon and a smattering of pintail. A strong wind was kicking up making the unfortunately necessary downwind approach less than ideal. A deep irrigation canal ran past the puddle, separating it from a flooded rice field to the east. I cut Shaman, a gyr hybrid, loose. The dog and I dropped into the ditch out of sight, walking into the wind as the falcon mounted. By the time the pointer and I were parallel to the ducks, Shaman was at pitch, so over the top we went. The puddle erupted as ducks scattered downwind. I glanced up; to my surprise, Shaman was stooping a separate group of ducks flying over the rice field behind me. I yelled for the dog to stop and we ducked back into the ditch, hoping for a few ducks to stay put. The falcon failed to connect over the flooded check. In the meantime, every duck had cleared off the puddle save three—one wigeon and a pair of pintail. Shaman, now entirely focused on the hapless ducks in the puddle, positioned himself upwind of the set and some 300 feet up. Once again, the dog and I went over the top and Shaman had his choice of the remaining three as they fled downwind. Ultimately, it was the hen pintail upon which the ax fell.

Pintails are birds of open spaces. In Northern California, they are typically found on big water such as flooded rice fields making them additionally challenging quarry for the falcon accustomed to flying over smaller sets. California's central valley boasts one of the largest concentrations of wintering pintails anywhere. While viewing enormous flocks of pintail among the rice stubble, you get the impression that pintail numbers must be high. Yet, this is not the case. The overall pintail population remains well below historic levels. Whereas most duck populations have steadily increased over recent decades, pintail numbers continue to sag. As research has shown, they are extremely sensitive to what transpires on their critical breeding grounds in the prairie pothole region. Drought and agriculture are insidious threats to the pintail breeding cycle. The mixed and short grass prairies of the western Dakotas, Montana, Alberta and Saskatchewan form the nucleus of the pintail breeding range. Over the course of their evolutionary history, pintails have adapted to maximize their breeding potential in this semi-arid region. Breeding pairs of pintails are the first ducks to return to the prairie, timing their arrival to coincide with spring thaws in late March and early April. Aside from being the first to nest on the prairies, they also incubate for a shorter period and get through their brood rearing faster. All of which capitalizes on the use of spring runoff. During wet years, pintails utilize shallow, grassy basins covered in sheet water. These ephemeral wetlands support massive numbers of invertebrates, providing hens the necessary nutrients to produce a healthy clutch. Wet years also retard the farmers' spring plowing long enough for the pintail broods to have hatched and reached the relative safety of water before being tilled under. You really begin to appreciate what this means to pintail populations when you realize that more than half of the original prairie wetlands (much of which is ephemeral) have been drained or filled for agriculture. Furthermore, more than 75 percent of the prairie grasslands (nesting habitat) has been lost. Without a doubt, were it not for duck hunters and the monies they contribute to conservation and restoration, our beloved sprig would be in far worse shape than they are now.

WOOD DUCKS

If pintails are birds of open spaces, wood ducks are very much their counterpart, preferring sheltered ponds, wooded streams and other secluded haunts. Woodies also inhabit a special niche in my heart, offering challenging and unique hawking opportunities. They have adapted to a forested environment, hence the elongated tail for better maneuverability while flying through trees. They are cavity nesters, and readily utilize manmade nesting boxes. Unlike most other species of ducks, woodies occasionally perch in trees, something to keep in mind when scouting slips.

Wood ducks don't have the top end speed of other ducks of similar size and are relatively easily caught by falcons out in the open. The difficulty in catching them is a direct result of their preferred habitat. Even so, some of the locations where wood ducks hang out are totally flyable with a longwing. One such pond happens to be a favorite of mine in the Sierra foothills.

Nestled between hills to the north and south, the pond is open to the east with a shallow ravine running to the west.

When I scouted this pond one morning last December, I was delighted to find a squadron of Canadian geese and seven woodies. I fly this set exclusively in the early morning when the air is dense. On this day, even though the temperature was more than 40°F, my tiercel hybrid mounted well, climbing in steep concentric circles. Omen usually takes a fine pitch and this day was no exception. I covertly worked into a flushing position at the west end of the pond in order to flush the ducks out the open end to the east. When Omen was at about 1,000 feet, I moved in to flush and everybody, honkers and woodies alike, cleared the pond. Down came Omen in a vertical stoop, just as pretty as they come. The wood ducks arced to the south and disappeared behind some trees, trying to avoid the open ground and total exposure to the falcon. My view of the last section of Omen's stoop was likewise obstructed, as he vaulted below tree line, but I heard the impact, then the sounds of a lone woody tumbling through branches. I saw Omen pitch up, simultaneously the remaining six woodies came flying directly back to the pond and splashed in. The geese were long gone and as far as Omen was concerned so was the duck he'd hit—such was the cover it had fallen into.

I lowered out of sight and waited for Omen to remount before a second attempt was made. The ducks, who were so cooperative the first time around, were understandably far less willing to get up and go the second time, and who could blame them after what they'd just seen? As a result, on the reflush Omen was unable to connect as the ducks ratted around the pond and piled back in. By then, I knew things could really deteriorate, but I also felt the slip could still be pulled off with style. The intimidation of the woodies was total and this then was the crux to be surmounted. The solution lay in the positioning of the falcon.

Sometimes falcons give indications of comprehending these sorts of intricacies, as did Omen in this case. Instead of ringing the pond, he flew wide, remounting some eighty yards away over the field to the east. Distance served as a kind of disconnect and relieved a lot of the pressure that the woodies had been under. Omen was 800 feet up, still climbing and still wide when

I assaulted the pond a third time. This time the woodies made a break for it, flying up the ravine for all they were worth. If there had been a disconnect with the falcon, it had only been in the minds of the woodies. As soon as the ducks had lifted off, the falcon peeled into a long, slanted stoop. He blazed across the sky, covering tremendous ground at high speed, gaining on the woodies that had already disappeared through the trees. Omen passed overhead; then he, too, was swallowed from view. Even in my blindness, the sounds emanating from the woods painted a detailed picture of what happened next.

The tear of the falcon's stoop abruptly ceased with the clap of a high-speed bind. The unmistakable shriek of the woody reverberated through the canyon as the two entwined bodies fell to earth. Then all was silent, save the tinkle of Omen's bell, which led me to the site of the kill. So it goes when hawking woodies...

GADWAL

It is tempting to judge animal intelligence based on our own human perception. Thus, it is quite natural to call a pintail smart. In the same vein, it's sometimes tempting to label the gadwal as being clueless. I won't, however, go that far, as I suspect to do so would be an act of stupidity on my part. Nonetheless there is a certain naivety about the gadwal that doesn't exist in, say, the pintail or mallard. I'll cite an example. I located a pair of gadwals on a midsize pond, and put Omen into the air. He took a hellacious 2,000-foot pitch, at which point I went over the top of the dam to flush. The gaddies were reluctant to make a break, so they swirled around the pond for a bit. I kept the pressure on; the hen finally snapped, cleared the dam and roared off down the canyon. She didn't get ninety yards before the falcon connected. Meanwhile, the drake piled back in, which was good news for me because I still hadn't flown Shaman. I collected Omen and hiked back to my truck, feeding him along the way. I swapped falcons then returned to the pond. The drake was still there. I figured the drake would be more cooperative if I flushed him the same direction his hen had gone. I took up my position while Shaman mounted. He decided that 250 feet would be sufficient and as it turned out he was right. The drake was exceedingly cooperative, flying directly over the dam, where the falcon summarily took him.

This example isn't meant to imply that gadwals always make things easy on falcons. Sometimes they absolutely refuse to fly, demonstrating remarkable poise. Because I spend so much time flying mallards, I tend to use them as the benchmark by which all other ducks are judged. Don't get me wrong, gadwals are a great duck, but they don't have the size, strength or speed of the mallard, all of which means that when the gaddy does make a mistake, they are far more likely to pay the price.

During the 1990s, gadwal populations rose dramatically, which is great news for falconers. They are among the last ducks to lay eggs on the prairies, typically in early to mid-June. The advantage is related to the thick cover available this time of year surrounding the deeper marshes and ponds they prefer. Deeper water habitats are less impacted by both drought and plow. Gadwal ducklings switch to a largely vegetarian diet much sooner than most other ducklings, thus reducing the time frame when they are most at risk, foraging for insects in shallow water. Gaddies were the third most commonly bagged duck in the year 2000 by North American hunters and are certainly an important species to duck hawkers. Go gadwals!

SHOVELERS

On appearances alone, shovelers are unusual ducks. Aptly named for their absurd-looking bill, they feed upon more invertebrates than any other puddle duck. Though I fly them occasionally off small ponds, I mostly hawk them on the biggest water around—flooded rice fields. Shovelers aren't super fast and they appear to grasp this concept when falcons are involved. Even when flying them on only small or moderately sized ponds, they may be reluctant to flush, as the following story illustrates.

Looking through the dirty windshield of the mud-encrusted four-wheel drive, I centered my binoculars on a small patch of water, the only visible hint of a much larger pond, otherwise obstructed by mounds of earth. A drake shoveler came into focus. He was floating on what happened to be one of my deadliest sets. The pond itself is fairly big, but due to the irregular L shape, the bottom section can almost always be easily flushed. Aside from the fact that the drake was in a killer location, Shaman was next on deck and he had this pond wired; so, even before the flight had begun, I pretty much considered the duck to be in the bag. With the dog at heel, I released Shaman, noting his deep thrusting wingbeat which only confirmed what I already knew—this duck was as good as mine. If it's true that all good things come with a price, then this great slip is no exception. In order to access the pond, one must cross a substantial irrigation canal. While I had tons of confidence in Shaman, I double-checked his progress to make damn sure he was totally into the slip before stepping into the frigid water. He was.

I eased down into the murky water and began wading across, the water level creeping up on me with each step forward. Instinctively, I rose on my tiptoes trying to spare the more sensitive areas of my anatomy from the imminent, cold shockwave, but the effort was in vain. I sloshed my way out the other side, half the man I used to be, yet grateful it hadn't been any deeper. After all, I had breaststroked across that ditch on more than one occasion. Latham and I climbed the steep embankment stopping just below the top of the hill overlooking the pond. I verified Shaman's position, 400 feet straight up, and then peeked over the top to check the shoveler's whereabouts. The little dude was below me and just a little to my left—perfect! Without delay, the pointer and I vaulted over the top, doing our best to panic the drake into making the biggest mistake of its life. Our angle of approach was intended to separate the duck from the rest of the pond, pinching him out the nearest exit. The shoveler took off all right and it definitely looked as though he would just keep going. Thankfully, Shaman hesitated his stoop (a rarity for him) and the duck kept flying, looking even more like he planned on making a clean break for it. Shaman must have been thinking the same thing I was—"this duck's gonna clear," because he rolled into a mighty stoop.

The shoveler reacted instantly and was able to splash in at

the very last moment before clearing land. Shaman pulled up very sharply, converting speed back into height, thus maintaining a decent pitch. Latham, flusher dog from hell, was all over the duck. I quickly waded into the pond knowing full well the dog would have our duck friend back on the wing pronto. I wanted to be in a position to turn the duck should it seek refuge in the larger section of the pond behind me and around the bend. Sure enough, here came the shoveler, determined to reach sanctuary, but alas I was directly in his way.

Most ducks would have flared and swung wide. When they do so they are almost frozen for a fleeting moment, slowed by a nanosecond of indecision and air friction as they clear land. They are then tremendously vulnerable to a skilled duck hawk and when it comes to these sorts of tactics, Shaman is about as skilled as they come. This shoveler, however, kept his composure and buzzed right past me as if I didn't exist. Evidently, and rightfully so, he was convinced that the falcon was his biggest concern. I turned as he went by and watched him quickly disappear around the corner, Shaman hot on his heels. As I trudged my way back out of the pond, Latham zipped by, rounded the corner, then he, too, was out of view.

By the time I made it around the bend, the flight had taken on a new twist. Latham and Shaman had engaged a flock of five or six mallards, which had apparently been rafting on the larger section of the pond. I watched as the two of them masterfully worked the flock from above and below in a graceful and well-coordinated attack. I noted the shoveler floating off to one side as if some uninvolved spectator. The mallards split in half, three exited headed north, while the remainder of them settled back in. The three trailblazers cleared the dike and took refuge in the ditch just ahead of Shaman. Latham kept pressing the other mallards and succeeded in getting them back into the air. They naturally followed the same flight path as that of their predecessors—big mistake. Shaman was half way back to the pond when the panicked mallards flew under him. Finally able to seize the moment, Shaman inverted and rotated into a reverse stoop striking a hen with devastating ferocity. As I stepped Shaman off his kill and turned to leave, the shoveler caught my attention. I watched admiringly as the beautiful little drake took his cue to leave, no doubt headed for somewhere with fewer falcons.

Intelligence, cunning and impressive grace under pressure spared the crafty shoveler where so many others have fallen. I thought about that and about how fortunate I am to hawk quarry that still surprises and humbles me.

Teal

North America sports three species of teal: blue winged, green winged and cinnamon. Though tiny (1/2–1 1/3 lbs), all three are gorgeous in appearance. When I think of teal, I dredge up all these conflicting sentiments which, if you know teal, probably isn't surprising. Teal are a lot of fun to hawk, but they also have the potential to grind you up into fine dust and leave you feeling as inept as a pile of dog excrement. You can love them, you can hate them and I suppose you could even love to hate them. I think at least part of the reason teal can be so exasperating has to do with the size of the water they're often found on, i.e., small. It is very hard to call it quits and walk away from a teal flight after the first few stoops when the pond is so tiny. You keep telling yourself, "One more time, she's gotta connect on the next stoop!" Sometimes teal are taken on the next pass as predicted, often they are not. If you're the sort of person that likes to watch this cat and mouse stuff, by all means enjoy. If, however, the falcon in question is being managed and reserved for classic towering, clean kill stoops then certain boundaries may be in order when teal are the primary targets.

Teal flights demand a solid flight setup, precision orchestration and a sense of knowing when to say when. And when, hawking teal, you've got to expect the unexpected. They're so quick and agile that they can turn what was once a promising flight absolutely upside-down in a blink of an eye. They will use cover like none other and they can seemingly vanish, even when struck down in the middle of the desert. Of course, plenty of other strange things can happen out in the desert.

A couple of years ago I was headed for northeastern Nevada where I was scheduled to lecture. I stopped along the way long enough to hawk a mallard in a beautiful stream 5,000 feet up in the mountains of the Sierra Nevada range, then proceeded across Nevada almost to the Utah boarder. Exhausted, I pulled off the highway and drove out a ways into the desert where I could get some much-needed sleep. I unrolled my sleeping bag in the backseat of the truck and crawled inside. I woke at first light, but procrastinated getting up and into the frigid morning air. Outside the truck a passing shadow caught my eye. A flock of some sort, but I couldn't distinguish just what sort it was because the windows had totally frosted over on the inside. I half scrambled out of my bag and pushed the door open in time to identify them as sage grouse before they flew completely out of sight. I didn't want to fool around and miss my lectures, so I decided I would return afterwards and then look for a grouse slip. On my return I ran the pointer for an hour or two but he couldn't pick up any scent. I needed to be back in California that evening, so I reluctantly loaded Latham and headed west, figuring I'd fly a teal pond on the way back home.

    It was late afternoon by the time I found what I was looking for—a small stock pond with green-winged teal, not many, only two, but two would suffice. There was a farmhouse across the road so I pulled into the drive, knocked at the door and made my pitch. The lady on the other side of the threshold was attractive and she listened intently as I explained that I was just passing through and wanted to fly the pond just this once. Having a hooded falcon on my fist probably aided my cause, but I got the distinct impression that she would have said yes either way. I spoke briefly with the inquisitive woman, answering all her questions, which I hoped in some feeble way returned the generosity she'd shown me.

    I grabbed my binoculars and approached the pond. It was very small and provided no cover in which the teal could hide. I was reasonably sure I'd be able to flush the green-wings without too much difficulty, which was good because I'd left Latham in the truck. Even though the old highway was devoid of traffic, I didn't want to have to worry about Latham getting in the road. When I tried to flush the teal, I was met with a lot of resistance. Apparently, they resented the hell out of the falcon overhead. It quickly became obvious that the standard yelling and rock throwing routine wasn't going to cut it. There was no way those little buggers were going to leave the pond unless somebody was willing to get wet. As I said, I'd left Latham in the truck so I deduced that somebody was me. I wasn't excited about jumping in another pond in the dead of winter, but since this was the first slip I'd had all day, and by the looks of things probably the last, I thought I better get on with it. I didn't screw around; I just jumped in and tore after the ducks like some fool-headed Labrador retriever. I splashed and thrashed around and every time it looked like the teal were going to go, Shaman would rip past, changing their little minds right quick. Now, I'd flown enough teal to know they can be stubborn, but this whole thing was ridiculous! It took me another minute to figure out what was going on. One of the teal couldn't fly, something wasn't right with one wing. I directed my attention to the other one, but so long as his buddy wasn't going anywhere, neither was he.

There I was, waist deep in ice-cold water in the middle of the rat hunt from hell. Damn those teal! I stopped splashing long enough to take stock of the situation and check Shaman to see if he had any ideas (which he sometimes does), only when I looked up he wasn't there. Turns out, a flock of sage grouse had been lurking there in the sage surrounding the pond. I guess my antics weren't enough to unnerve the teal, but they were more than enough to send the grouse packing. Chalk one up for psycho pond man! I spotted Shaman just as be bottomed out of his stoop. Leveling out just above the sage, he quickly overhauled a grouse and plucked it from the air. Leave it to a sage grouse to spoil a teal flight. Okay, I'm kidding; nonetheless, the truth of the matter is that at least on that day a sage grouse made for much easier quarry than the diminutive teal. I make this observation not to minimize the grouse, a quarry of mythical proportion (and rightfully so) but rather to give credit where credit is due.

When it comes to self-preservation and falcons, teal like to keep a low profile and are not prone to premature flushes. I can't help but wonder if falcon avoidance isn't at least part of the reason why green-wings (among others) prefer to migrate at night under the cloak of darkness. Hell, when you're the smallest puddle duck around, you probably look for any advantage you can. During daylight hours, teal fly low in tight formation constantly twisting and turning as if being chased by some unseen phantom menace. I've seen them pull these same stunts to save their skins when the phantoms had been quite genuine. You get a whole new perspective on teal when you see them outmaneuver goshawks.

The teals' agility is mind blowing. They move so quickly while evading accipiters that the flight is a blur, challenging one's ability to comprehend what the eyes are beholding. If these ducks weren't so resourceful, it would almost be a shame to knock them down with falcons. Teal are a fine little duck and well deserving of the falconer's respect.

DIVERS

Diving ducks are an equally diverse bunch. They differ from puddle ducks in some fundamental ways. Divers lack the iridescent speculum we've come to associate with puddle ducks, though some may display white or gray wing patches. Divers are far less vocal and most vocalization is confined to elaborate courtship rituals. Diving ducks have a sex ratio with a numerical advantage favoring drakes far above that of puddler's. In keeping with a rather non terrestrial format, divers nests are built primarily in emergent vegetation over water. Rather than dabbling for food on or near the water's surface, divers are marvelously adapted to forage well beneath the surface where most of them feed primarily on invertebrates and in some cases fish. Oversized webbed feet placed further back on the body serve divers well under water, but make them awkward on land. With a smaller wing surface to body ratio, divers are more heavily wingloaded than puddle ducks. Wingload, of course, has a profound effect on aerodynamics, which is why we observe significant differences in flight performance between the two groups. With less available lift, divers can't spring into the air they way puddlers can. Divers require a running start to generate the speed necessary for take off. Once airborne, divers can be differentiated from puddlers by their shallower, faster wingbeat. They also have a much wider turning radius, which is especially apparent when they try to turn under a stooping falcon. Without the ability to turn sharply, divers are particularly vulnerable when trying to beat the falcon back to the pond. More often than not, they are struck down midturn. While none of the divers take off as quickly or turn as sharply, some of them do exceed the top end speed of the fastest puddle ducks. It is widely accepted that the canvasback is the fastest duck on the planet. At 100 miles per hour, a red-breasted merganser (subcategory diver) is the fastest duck ever clocked. Unfortunately, the blurb I read failed to state whether or not this was wind aided.

Most of the diving ducks make excellent quarry for falcons. Divers are often associated with big, deep water, with heavy concentrations wintering in coastal bays and lagoons, nonetheless they can commonly be found on easily hawkable water. Not all divers flush alike, as with puddlers, the difficulty level varies widely from species to species. The length of time a duck has spent on a particular body of water will greatly influence its willingness to flush under the falcon. Smaller divers, in particular, that have become very familiar with a certain pond may truly be impossible to flush. Hawking divers off big water can be a tough yet rewarding proposition. High-flying falcons are called for in order to effectively cover big water. A stupendous pitch will also give divers plenty of time to clear out and reach top speed. Hawking divers in this fashion is not to be confused with knocking down slow-moving targets at edges of ponds for such is not the case.

CANVASBACKS
Surely one of the great duck flights to be had includes high-flying falcons, big water and canvasbacks. In many hunting circles, it is the "can" which reigns supreme. They are also (not coincidentally) considered to be one of the best tasting of ducks. Throughout the market-hunting era, cans commanded premium prices, such was the demand for their flesh. It has been estimated that as many as 15,000 cans were shot daily on the Chesapeake Bay to fill the market and restaurant demand.

The cans' specialized diet accounts for their fine taste and contributes to their relatively small populations. Far more than any other duck, canvasbacks are adapted to feed upon the tubers and rootstocks of aquatic plants. Their unique profile, i.e., sloped foreheads and thick, muscular necks, are adapted to facilitate plant root excavation and extraction; sago pondweed, banana water lily and duck potato feature on the cans' menu. However, they've shown such a strong preference for wild celery that their Latin name, *Valisineria*, is derived from the word for celery. Unfortunately, rivers and estuaries, once pristine, became sewers and dumping grounds. Soil erosion, sedimentation, eutrophication, industrial waste, along with water control and diversion all wreaked havoc on the canvasbacks' habitat and the aquatic plants they depend upon. When drought struck the prairies in the 1980s, the canvasback population became seriously imperiled, thus prompting a temporary prohibition on all canvasback harvest. Studies have shown that in years of drought canvasback nests, which are usually constructed on floating mats of vegetation, become more accessible to mammalian predation and nest success ratios plummet dramatically, as was the case in the eighties. When the drought broke, canvasbacks rebounded, and by 1997, their numbers were 24 percent above long-term (1955–97) averages.

As a duck hawker, I hold the mighty canvasback in the highest of regards. They are a powerful and formidable duck, weighing 2–3½ pounds. They are extremely fast and they're also very cooperative about flying under falcons. This may be due to a heightened intolerance of man or it may be an elevated confidence in their supreme speed, perhaps both. In any case, canvasbacks are flushable from surprisingly big water. When flown off big water, cans have an opportunity to get up to full steam before the falcon is into them. Under these circumstances, the canvasback will prove to be a very worthy quarry indeed. Meek or timid falcons are unlikely to be willing to hit one of these airborne trucks flying at full speed and even less likely to be capable of delivering a knockdown blow. When it comes to this elite quarry, my best advice is to never pass up any reasonable opportunity to have a go at them. Put up your highest-flying falcon, let her take her best pitch and let the pieces fall where they may.

REDHEADS

Redheads are a close relative of the canvasback, hence the similarities in appearance. Like the can, redheads subsist on a primarily vegetarian diet. In recent years, redhead populations have soared. While this is good news, there is potential trouble looming on the horizon, not the least of which is the redheads' working relationship with canvasbacks. Studies conducted in the 1960s and 1970s revealed that though redheads outnumbered cans on the breeding grounds in the larger midcontinent marshes, cans still held a numerical advantage and bred more successfully in parts of the prairie pothole region. In southern Manitoba, cans outnumbered redheads by approximately two to one. Currently, redhead numbers are at least equivalent to that of cans in the pothole region and this could spell disaster for the canvasback. The peculiar "dual-nesting" strategy of the redheads is precisely the cause of alarm.

Redheads are parasitic nesters, which is to say they routinely lay eggs in the nests of other ducks, namely those of the canvasback. On breeding grounds with dense concentrations of redheads, virtually all canvasback nests in the area will contain some redhead eggs. A female canvasback will cease to lay eggs once her clutch of about eight eggs is complete. When redheads contribute to the number of eggs in the clutch, the result is fewer canvasback eggs laid and, therefore, chicks hatched. As the population balance continues to shift in favor of the redheads, nest parasitism will likely become increasingly detrimental to canvasback populations.

Also, due to the redheads' specialized winter habitat requirements, there is concern that they will deplete available food sources in critical locations. Most continental redheads prefer coastal bays and estuaries rich in submersed vegetation, especially shoalgrass. In the past few decades, shoalgrass has been in sharp decline, particularly on the Atlantic coast. As a result, today more than 80 percent of the redheads' continental population winters in the estuaries of the Laguna Madre of Texas and

Mexico. The Laguna Madres' shoalgrass is estimated to have been reduced by 40 percent since 1965 due to a salinity problem. When the estuary was permanently connected to the gulf by the construction of shipping lanes, the saline content was diluted. This resulted in the encroachment of other less saline tolerant vegetation, displacing the native shoalgrass. Since several thousand redheads rely upon the Laguna Madres' shoalgrass, there is cause for concern. In the mean time, those of us fortunate enough to hawk redheads will take great pleasure in these good times.

Though not as fast as their cousin the canvasback, I've seen redheads pull away from the tiercel gyr hybrid fair and square. Redheads are a stout duck weighing between 1 ½–3 pounds. They have a lack of tolerance for man and they aren't too shy about flying under falcons, though sometimes I'm sure they wish they hadn't.

One day I watched a falcon stoop right past the nose of a drake redhead. There was no contact but the falcon definitely left an impression. I suspect the drake thought he'd just seen the shadow of death as he flew through the falcon's jet wash. I've seen plenty of ducks lose heart and bail after being intimidated, but ordinarily they seek refuge in water or some other form of cover. Watching the redhead winnow down in a controlled landing on the barren earth forty yards from the pond was something I hadn't seen before (or since). Clearly the drake felt that he couldn't contest the sky with the falcon and decided he'd stand a better chance on the ground. I guess he hadn't counted on the dog.

RINGNECKS

I'm not quite sure what was the thinking when these ducks were named ringnecks. Yes, there's a slight chestnut ring around the drake's neck, but it's only visible at very close range. On the other hand, the white band around the bill of both sexes is very conspicuous. No surprise this duck is often as not referred to as ringbill. By either name, this midsize diver (1–2 pounds) is a welcome addition to any pond. They are not super fast but they are usually extremely cooperative in the flushing department.

Flocks that have been hawked a few times may get resistant, but fresh ringnecks are almost a sure thing. The flights tend to be a straightforward sort of affair that nicely compliments a towering stoop.

In *Gamehawking at Its Very Best*, Mike Connoly sums up the ringneck as such, "On a small pond, to find them is to catch them." This pretty much hits the nail on the head. Ringnecks are perhaps the ultimate duck with which to enter a duck hawk, especially if the falcon is small or timid. Unless you've got something more challenging in mind, you won't want to pass on an opportunity to fly these guys.

SCAUP—LESSER AND GREATER

Despite a twenty-year decline in their population, scaup or blue bills, as hunters commonly refer them to, are still the most numerous diver in North America. There are two types of scaup: lesser and greater. Lessers are by far the more abundant of the two comprising 85 percent of the total scaup population. Lesser scaup weigh between 1– 21/2 pounds, greaters weigh between 1 1/2–3 pounds. The greaters' wintering grounds are mostly restricted to the Pacific, Atlantic and Gulf coasts, plus the lower Great Lakes. The lessers' wintering range is extended notably inland. The breeding population of both species was estimated at 4,000,000 in the year 2000. This is well below the goal of 6,000,000 plus, set forth in the North American Waterfowl Management Plan (NAWMP). Over the past twenty years, scaup numbers have plummeted at a rate of 100,000 birds per year. About 60 percent of all scaup breed in the boreal forests and taiga plains of northwestern Canada, and it is in this segment of the breeding population where the decline is taking place. Nobody knows the exact cause of the decline but possible explanations have included environmental/habitat degradation and global climate change.

Wintering scaup are typically associated with big, deep water, yet they do frequent small ponds. Duck hunters consider blue bills to be one of the least wary of diving ducks, this being based on the ease with which they are lured into decoys. Falconers have also regarded them as easy quarry. Connoly dubs them "among the easiest of all ducks to take with a long-wing" due to their "paddling take-off and straight line flight." No surprise, he also rates them as excellent candidates with which to enter a duck hawk. Let us hope the current decline in the scaup population reverses itself soon.

Goldeneye

No secret where this duck got its name, both sexes sport conspicuous gold-colored eyes. Nevertheless, they are sometimes called whistlers because of the sound their feathers make while flying. There are two races of golden eye: barrows and common. Males of both types feature prominent white facial patches. The goldeneye is a relatively heavy duck, commons ranging between 1 1/2–3 1/3 pounds with barrows a bit lighter at 1–2 1/2 pounds. Goldeneyes are closely associated with big water and they have an enhanced tolerance for cold. Commons tend to migrate late, moving south only after forced to do so by freezing water. Some barrows in mountainous regions, don't migrate at all. While the barrows' range is rather restricted (primarily along the northwestern Pacific coast and sparingly in the Rocky Mountain states), commons winter throughout much of the U.S. They have a predilection for large freshwater lakes, bays and estuaries but also show up occasionally on the types of ponds typically flown by falconers.

Last year I took a hen from a mixed flock off a fairly small pond along California's southern coast. It was the canvasback that I was most interested in, but the tiercel I was flying had ideas of his own. The goldeneye went out with the bulk of the flock, presenting an irresistible and all-too-easy target as she flew directly under the waiting falcon. Meanwhile, the cans slipped out the back door without regard for the rest of the flock. I hefted the goldeneye; she was solid and felt considerable heavier than I would have guessed. On bigger water, goldeneyes may prove difficult to flush.

Ruddy

Ruddies are an unusual duck. When you look at one on a pond, you get the distinct impression you're looking at something quite unlike any other duck. Ruddies (named for the chestnut red nuptial plumage of the male) are segregated from the other divers into a subcategory known as "stiff tails." Their stiff tails, which are often held in an upright position, present a unique and clearly distinctive profile. Their bodies are not elongated as one might expect, but are almost round instead. These odd little ducks have been described as pugnacious, which comes as a bit of a surprise when you consider their size—a scant ½–1½ pounds.

If ever there was a duck at home on or under the water it is the ruddy. With huge feet (even for a diver) they are most ungainly on land. Ruddies namely winter on freshwater marshes in the south and bays along both the Atlantic and Pacific coasts, preferring shallow water. While I do take an occasional ruddy with my falcons, they are never my primary targets. The reason being, ruddies can be extremely difficult, even impossible, to flush.

One day last winter, I encountered a lone ruddy on a small coastal pond. I hadn't had much luck finding a slip that morning so I was tempted to break tradition and fly it. I considered the prospects, playing out various scenarios in my mind. Since I hadn't checked this pond all winter and therefore had no way of knowing how long the ruddy had been in residence, I knew it would most likely be a recipe for disappointment. My better judgment prevailed and I decided to pass. Just for curiosity sake, I lobbed a couple of dirt clods at the duck before I left, to see if in fact it could possibly have been flushed. No way! Even without the added pressure of a falcon overhead, the ruddy couldn't be budged. Apparently, he'd been on that pond for some time. When ruddies are new arrivals to a pond, they are much more likely to flush. Even so, I would consider the ruddy a duck of last resort, and if I were going to fly a pond with ruddies only, I'd be sure to have some sort of contingency plan in case they refused to fly.

BUFFELHEAD

The buffelhead is another micro member of the diving family, tipping the scales at ¾–1 ½ pounds. Adult males are strikingly handsome and easily distinguished on any pond. Buffelheads are cavity nesters (aspens with holes created by flickers are favored) and their long tails undoubtedly assist them in flying among trees. From a falconry perspective, much of what is said of the ruddy can be said of the "buffy." They can be brutally stubborn about leaving a pond. Unless you know for certain they are new arrivals, expect them to be completely uncooperative.

MERGANSER—HOODED, RED-BREASTED AND COMMON
Hooded, red-breasted and common mergansers comprise another subcategory of the diver family. They are collectively called fish ducks as they all have pointed, serrated bills designed to catch fish. My introduction to mergansers occurred in 1984 during the winter I spent along the Gulf Coast of Florida. My boss flew a peregrine x prairie hybrid and the vast majority of slips we had were at hooded mergansers. We hawked them through the winter, and they were certainly one of the highlights of our Floridian falconry.

"Hoodies" are the smallest of the merganser family weighing a slight 1¼–2 pounds. They are predatory, feeding upon fish, frogs, aquatic insects and crustaceans. Their flesh is probably best described as fishy tasting, which is why they are seldom gun hunted. Indeed, some falcons will vomit after consuming merganser, most however handle it fine.

Drake hoodies are stunningly beautiful and are among the most ornate birds in North America. Hooded mergansers are cavity nesters and prefer wooded places. Their winter range is somewhat restricted, namely residing within portions of the Pacific and Atlantic seaboards, sheltering in bays, marshes and estuaries. Further inland they are typically found within similar habitat to that of the wood duck. I've hawked them here in Northern California on wooded ponds and streams. Hoodies generally flush quite well, the first time around. They aren't super fast and may be overhauled by some of the faster falcons in an extended tail chase. The challenge and joy of hawking them is largely due to the terrain in which they're often found. When hooded mergs are situated in areas open enough to permit flying a longwing, the flights can be dramatic and are highly recommended.

Common and red-breasted mergansers are a whole lot bigger than their smaller cousin the hoody. Red-breasteds weigh between 1 1/2–3 pounds and the common mergansers are a whopping 2–4 1/2 pounds, making them second only to the common eider as North America's largest duck. The largest duck I've ever taken was indeed a drake common merganser. I released him unharmed before he could be weighed, but I can tell you he was a massive individual.

Common mergs are widely distributed throughout the U.S. during the winter, while the red-breasted mainly sticks to coastal regions and the Great Lakes. Common mergs tend to flush quite nicely. I suspect their size and strength emboldens them in the presence of falcons. Connoly likened mergs to "alligators with wings," suggesting they are dangerous and best left alone. Most experienced duck hawks are very quick to seize a combative duck's head, thus nullifying the merg's jagged bill. My falcons have had things well in hand whenever they've confronted these big dudes. Nonetheless, heeding Connoly's advice, excepting with very experienced falcons, would be a wise precaution.

Coot

American coots (*Fulica americana*) and Common Moorhens (*Gallinula chloropus*) are not members of the duck family. They do however superficially resemble ducks in some ways. Coots in particular are commonly found in the shallow pond habitats frequented by duck hawkers. Furthermore, all duck hawks find these ungainly waterbirds irresistible targets.

Unless you've seen a coot in the air, you really can't appreciate just how slow they fly. I've seen them run down by dogs and snapped out of the air! The very fact that coots are so excruciatingly slow is what makes them a less than desirable quarry with which to challenge any longwing. Coots are a bit of a wild card. Sometimes they'll sit tight, other times they'll flush right along with the ducks. Falcons have no qualms about coots and will quite often single out the only coot flying in the midst of all manner of duck. For this reason, most falconers don't relish the sight of a fresh coot on their favorite duck pond. Sometimes it seems as though the only way to catch a duck in coot-infested waters is to eliminate all the coots first. I've stepped falcons off several consecutive coot kills in the hopes of knocking a duck down on the next try. This sometimes works, but more often than not the coots prevail by sheer volume. There are times when duck slips are completely unavailable but a coot slip is possible. The longer it has been between duck slips, the more tempting coots become. Under these circumstances, a well-orchestrated coot flight may be preferable to no flight at all. Confident, hardcore duck hawks are generally no worse for the experience of killing a coot once in a while. But, extreme caution is advised in order to prevent a potential problem. At all costs, avoid allowing a duck hawk to become wed to (fixated with) coots, lest they become spoiled and refuse to stoop anything faster or tougher than those little black bastards.

Geese

There are a host of geese that may provide waterfowl hawking opportunities. Many species of geese have been thriving in our man-altered environment, and some are expanding their ranges dramatically. As a matter of fact, some species of geese have been deemed overpopulated! Lesser snows and Ross' geese numbers have more than tripled in the last three decades. This increase has had a negative impact on their fragile breeding habitat in the Arctic tundra. In desperation, biologists have initiated a spring "conservation hunt," aimed at reducing midcontinent snow goose populations. Large concentrations of various species of geese have caused extensive crop damage and some Canadian geese are now overstaying their welcome in urban areas. There are some nineteen recognized populations of Canadian geese ranging in size from 3–20+ pounds. Many of them are experiencing record high populations. Rarely have any of my falcons shown a lethal intention toward the large honkers I've flushed under them. Rather, they've learned to stoop between them, targeting any ducks trying to use the geese as a shield. This year, however, Omen did knock down a white-fronted goose with a vicious headshot. Some falconry birds do take a liking to geese, and wild gyrs have been observed successfully hunting them.

Geese are quite different from ducks in many respects, size being only the most obvious. Whereas most species of ducks form temporary ties, geese tend to be very family structured. For example, a drake mallard abandons his hen shortly after she begins incubation. He is then free to look for additional breeding hens—not so for the gander. Once a pair is established, the bond is very strong and usually permanent. He will stay with and defend his female throughout all stages of brood rearing. His protective nature is bestowed upon his progeny as well. The family migrates intact and stays together throughout the first year of the goslings' lives.

The close-knit goose society acts as an effective deterrent against some forms of predation. There is a one for all and all for one mentality that reportedly is directed at falcons engaged in ground combat with one of the flock. Such encounters have the potential to go awry very quickly and I've heard of at least one instance in which a falcon was actually killed in the melee. A good dog could conceivably move in much quicker than the falconer and provide the additional ground support the falcon needs in order to even out the odds. In any case, extreme caution is warranted whenever flying geese.

BRANT

Occasionally, I bump into Pacific brant. They aren't tremendously big; males weigh just more than 3 pounds and females weigh around 2 ¾ pounds. One day while hawking an estuary, Shaman peeled out of the sky and bound to a brant standing in the grass. I intervened immediately, stepping Shaman off what turned out to be one very emaciated brant. I left the brant there, no worse for the ordeal than he had been before it started. However, I suspect his fate had long since been sealed. Predators (like Shaman) are extraordinarily opportunistic and will capitalize on any weakness detected in the animals they encounter. This mindset lies at the very core of the predator mentality. To be weak is to be at risk.

Since this incident, I've learned about brant die-offs related to starvation. During the mid 1970s, a large number of Atlantic brant starved to death after unusually cold temperatures iced over the coast preventing them from reaching seagrass beds along the coast of New Jersey and New York. Considering that some Pacific brant migrate 3,200 miles in fifty to eighty hours, metabolizing one-third of their body weight in the process, you get a sense of how critical reliable food sources must be for this species.

While I've touched upon most species relevant to North American duck hawkers, this list remains incomplete in the sense that there are several excluded species that are certainly relevant in isolated areas or circumstances. I trust the reader will forgive me if I have omitted a personal favorite. Any omission is not intended to reflect negativity on my part. There are some ducks out there that I've never even seen, but I surely look forward to hawking them someday. I hope I have shed some light on these amazing birds, and, more importantly, I hope I've sparked a curiosity and interest to learn more. I have certainly learned some fascinating things about waterfowl since I began researching for this chapter. In order to fully appreciate any animal we pursue as quarry, we need first understand what that animal is and as much as possible about its life history. In so doing, we demonstrate respect, bring dignity to the hunt and take our falconry to a higher plane.

CHAPTER 5

Dogs

Several years ago, I was out flying a favorite falcon at a favorite ditch just as the sun began to set. The ditch was loaded with mixed ducks, so when the dog and I moved in with the falcon waiting above, I knew we had all the right ingredients for a sweet flight. Within moments, ducks were flushing wildly and the falcon began a barrage of hammering stoops. Ducks kept getting up off the water, and the falcon kept pounding them back down into the water and the thick patches of blackberries bordering the ditch. For a while, it rained ducks. Finally, a mallard was struck down away from the ditch and into the adjacent rice field where it was immediately seized by the falcon. At this point, the dog switched job titles from flusher to retriever. Probing through the underbrush with his sensitive nose, the dog successfully retrieved an additional two wood ducks that the falcon had knocked down.

Contrary to popular belief, falcons do occasionally cripple or kill prey items they can't recover. In fact, it was one such incident that first inspired me to incorporate a dog into my duck hawking. My peregrine x prairie hybrid (notoriously hard hitters) once pounded a duck to the ground but was unable to wing over before the duck got up and flew back into the pond. I watched the duck paddle to the middle of the pond, where it abruptly rolled over dead. Dogless, it was up to me to do the honors, so I swam to the middle of the pond and made the retrieve myself. Man, that water was cold! It wasn't long after that I began to bring a dog along.

My first hunting dogs, Ranger and Shunka were both German shorthair hand-me-downs. Ranger was a happy-go-lucky dog and made for good company, Shunka had been bred from extensive field trial lines and was aloof; they were both none too fond of water. One day my peregrine had splashed a mallard into a small pond and was waiting for the reflush. Both dogs refused to go in, so I did. There I was again, swimming and freezing my nether regions. While I was paddling around this pond, doing my darnedest to serve the falcon, I glanced toward the bank and there was good old Ranger and Shunka sitting side by side on their haunches watching the show with puzzled expressions on their faces. I remember thinking, "This just isn't right!" I knew then that it was high time I got serious about dog work.

Ordinarily, I'm a solitary hawker, so I rarely have the luxury of others helping flush ducks. Alone, I can't flush big water as effectively as I could with a troop, but this I accept as a small price to pay for the solitude I have come to enjoy. Not surprisingly, I have learned to rely heavily upon the canine factor for assistance in duck hawking and for companionship as well. My dogs are as passionate about hunting as I am. Under most circumstances, the dog has proven to be an invaluable asset, and I would honestly prefer the aid of a good dog over another human being based on merit. With a dog on hand, I stand a much better chance of orchestrating a successful flight *and* staying dry. A good dog is, as they say, "worth its weight in gold." A disobedient dog, on the other hand, is usually considerably worse than no dog at all.

When I was a boy, I spent many a summer on my grandparent's farm in Illinois. My grandmother had a succession of poodles, all named Pierre. Aside from being very similar in appearance, all of her poodles had something else in common—they were all mannerless, ill-tempered little heathens. Pierre(s) was one of those dogs that always made getting in or getting out of the house difficult. Not so much because of his ankle-biting tendencies as his propensity to bolt. Crack the door just a hair too wide and the little brown torpedo was off and running, and no form of persuasion would stop him. My grandmother loved those little dogs so they did have redeeming value, but as far as I was concerned, Pierre was nothing but a pain in the derriere. I'd be willing to bet that more than a few of you have come across a pooch displaying symptoms of "Pierre syndrome." Ironically, if just a little effort were geared toward behavioral modification, Pierre wouldn't have to be such a nuisance after all. Indeed, it's less trouble to train a dog than it is to live with an untrained dog.

Dogs are direct descendants of wolves and as such are very pack oriented. This quality lends itself nicely to a positive working relationship within a domestic environment, provided the human establishes himself as the indisputable leader—alpha. Dogs have a deep desire to please the alpha, which is a bit of a switch from the independent nature of the hawks we fly. Dog training and hawk training is conceptually similar, yet the ultrasocial nature of the dog will stimulate some divergences in training procedure. Nonetheless, the food association techniques we falconers have become so familiar with, along with a healthy dose of praise, is probably the fastest and easiest way to inspire the pup to perform rudimentary tasks: sit, stay, come, etc. I like to use hotdogs, the cheapest I can find, for reward. Periodically, throughout the day, the pup can be commanded, praised and rewarded with a small piece of hotdog for his efforts. With this sort of positive reinforcement, pups learn to recognize and respond to commands and signals in short order. Repetition is key. The pup doesn't need to be told to sit several times a day for months on end in order to learn or remember the command, but the redundancy of having to bend to the will of the trainer (alpha), regardless of what may be going around him, sets an important precedence. Keeping the lessons fairly brief and fun help the pup painlessly learn to do as he is told, when he is told.

This obliging mindset is what separates a workable/useful dog from the Pierres of the planet. A cooperative dog may not always see the logic or wisdom in your decisions, but he will not question your authority. He will make mistakes, may even feign deafness and ignore your commands on occasion, but that's to be expected. He's not a machine, he's a work in progress. Rome wasn't built in a day and likewise the pup will blossom over a period of time. If the dog is worked consistently, he'll more than earn his keep. And he will save the day often enough to compensate for his occasional blunder.

Long before I began working dogs with hawks, I viewed them as an unnecessary distraction from the main character—the hawk. My, how attitudes can change! I now view dogs as an integral part of the hawking program. Their companionship and contribution are priceless additions to the falconry experience. A dog will not only add to the productivity of the time spent afield, but it can also add greatly to the ambience. I can't imagine that anyone having enjoyed the participation of a good working dog would prefer not to work with a dog in the future. When I'm in the field with a falcon and without a dog, I feel naked and handicapped.

Some duck sets can be flown with or without a dog and there are some specific instances when the dog is better left in the truck. Wherever coots are mixed with ducks, there is a potential that they may be unintentionally flushed along with the ducks. With a dog in the water, the odds of flushing coots in unfortunately enhanced. Also, if the falconer hopes to fly multiple falcons in succession on the same set, he'll have much better odds of having ducks still on the water after the falcon stoops if the dog is not used. Far and away however, the majority of duck sets can be more efficiently exploited with the aid of a well-trained dog. There are a wide variety of dogs from which to choose and it's important to research the inherent characteristics of prospective breeds in order to select a dog that will most likely meet your expectations. Virtually any kind of dog could be used for duck hawking, but certain breeds offer more of the characteristics duck hawkers find useful. It is equally imperative to select a breed that resonates well with you on a personal level. After all, the time spent in the field will only constitute a small fraction the dog's life. Best pick a dog you can enjoy.

Duck hawking dogs are primarily used for flushing, so two major traits we're looking for in a dog are a strong desire to chase birds and a love of water. Dogs from one of the hunting lines, such as pointers, retrievers, setters, spaniels, etc., will all have a strong natural inclination to give chase, enhancing the dog's desire to flush. There are differences between the sexes but these differences are manifested more so in terms of personality and husbandry than field performance. Both male and female are fully capable at excelling in their work. Though having a dog with a good nose isn't as critical for duck hawking as it is for hawking game birds, it is still desirable. Not only is a good nose useful when retrieving ducks that can't fly, a good nose is invaluable when searching for ducks that have been knocked down in cover and won't fly. When my dogs relocate such a duck, they'll go up on point, which sets the stage for me to reinforce a remounting behavior in my falcons if I so choose. Ordinarily, I'll scoop up the duck and toss it high into the air, presenting the falcon with a clean target. This is usually preferable to an attempted reflush, which is as likely as not to go bad because ducks are prone to getting hung up the underbrush on take off. Sometimes, when the dog has located a duck which has been knocked down close to the water, I'll surreptitiously pick it up and tuck it under my coat until I've distanced myself from the water's edge in order to assure the falcon at least one clean shot at the duck before it can reach water and bail out. A pointed duck presents another alternative as a sort of back up. If you think there may still be flushable ducks in the vicinity, the pointed duck can be mentally marked and the hunt can continue with an assurance of the falcon eventually getting another chance at a duck, one way or another. If the resumed hunt proves fruitful, the previously marked duck can be left undisturbed. If however, the falcon fails to connect with another duck through no fault of her own, she may then be served the original duck, thus rewarding her loyal effort. It's always anticlimactic when having to call the falcon down to the lure after a protracted vain search for ducks, and never more so than when she has already knocked one down. No doubt about it, a pointed duck is a fantastic contingency plan, one that you'll be ever so grateful to have when your falcon is towering above at her finest pitch and there's nothing more to flush!

By now the reader has probably surmised that I use pointing dogs, specifically English pointers for my duck hawking. It is not that I believe pointers to be the superior flushing breed, on the contrary, I'm sure there are several other breeds better qualified for the task. I use the pointers because I have an affinity for the breed and because I spend a great deal of time hawking upland game birds. For me, there's nothing finer than watching a stylish pointer work a field and point birds with an aristocratic air, and I admire their enthusiasm in flushing ducks. I am happy to report that pointers can be used simultaneously for duck flushing and upland pointing with no negative side effects. Fine as they are, pointers aren't for everyone, not even most. The biggest complaint seems to revolve around the pointers' energetic personality and their propensity to run big. Ironically, these very traits have been genetically engineered over a period of centuries to create a dog that covers vast tracts of mostly open terrain very quickly, pointing any game birds they locate with their superb sense of smell. Thus, while not flawed, English pointers are higher maintenance than most breeds. Since they enjoy contact and flat out love to run, any pointer relegated to a life of confinement in a kennel without exercise and attention can't be expected to reach its full potential.

Dogs that are willing to swim after reluctant ducks are far more effective flushers than those that don't. Thus, from a hawking perspective, if the pointer has a shortcoming it is the dog's inability to withstand frigid water temperatures in the dead of winter. Duck hawkers living in colder climates would probably be better served by a dog from one of the retrieving breeds, since these heavier and well-insulated dogs can better tolerate frigid waters. Some lab strains have been bred to include an enhanced pointing gene, which would be of great interest to those duck hawkers who also fly upland game birds. This kind of dual-purpose genetics is found among several breeds, any of which may or may not meet your specific criteria. I recently read an interesting article about the less-renowned Chesapeake Bay retrievers. According to the article, a well-bred "Chessy" is dual purposed and is no longer the hard-headed, surly dogs they once were. Because Chessies are a relatively obscure breed, the ones that are being bred are more likely to originate from authentic hunting stock. Here in Northern California, I seem to be on the cusp of what is and is not tolerable swimming temperature for the pointers. This year I noticed that my pup Jessy, was more gung-ho about jumping in than was my old male, Latham. To my surprise, the pup, still green in her first year, actually did a better job of flushing some of my sets than Latham because she was willing to swim when he sometimes was not. However, even the reckless abandon of youth has its limitation.

A while back, we flew a small marsh and Jessy outdid herself by first flushing, then relocating the knocked-down duck. The funny thing was, when it was time to leave, she refused to swim back across the marsh as she'd done earlier and had to be coaxed to an area where the water narrowed and she could jump across. I've often thought that doggie wetsuits for the pointers might be just the ticket.

Though the intricate mechanics of dog training are beyond the intended scope of this book, I would like to pinpoint some behaviors, commands and cues that I have found useful. Basic obedience training, i.e., come, sit, stay, etc., is mandatory and a prerequisite to more advanced training. During duck hunting, it is sometimes necessary to direct the dog without the spoken word in order to avoid prematurely flushing sensitive ducks. Teaching the dog to respond to visual signals is very beneficial and is relatively easily accomplished. But in order for visual signals to work, the dog must be looking in your direction. More often than not, when working in toward a duck set, the dog is out front and therefore difficult or impossible to direct without an audible cue. Whistling is certainly less offensive to nervous ducks than is the human voice, but I've found that in close proximity finger snapping delivers a more authoritative message with less volume. My dogs are conditioned to turn and direct their attention toward me when they hear the snap, which is then followed up with visual signals.

Any dog with an enthusiasm for hunting will need little instruction on the actual flushing of ducks. Bird dogs bred from authentic hunting stock should be more than willing to participate. If getting dogs to flush ducks is easy, stopping them from flushing ducks is another story. Once flushing commences, dogs cross over, temporarily reverting to a wolflike mentality. Throughout the frenzied chase, dogs have only one thing on their mind, "GET THE DUCKS!" Sometimes this single-mindedness works to the advantage of the falconer and sometimes not. It does no good to flush ducks while the falcon is still hooded in the back of the truck. Likewise, there are a host of other inopportune moments to flush ducks and most of those moments occur after the initial flush. To the practitioners of classical waiting-on falconry, orchestration and timing is everything; too bad the dog doesn't see it that way. Rest assured, there will be times when the dog will be flushing like crazy and the falcon may just as well be in the truck with her hood on because she's not where you want or need her to be. The dog doesn't care about your sense of choreography. If you don't stop him, he'll not stop until all of the ducks are gone or he tires of trying. If you want the dog to stop flushing when you deem it necessary, you must teach him to do so.

Stopping a dog once he is actively chasing ducks around is a bit more difficult than teaching most other commands because stopping midstream is contrary to the dog's natural inclination to pursue. The fact that the dog may be quite a distance from the falconer doesn't make matters any easier. This is where all the early training really pays off because the dog has already been preconditioned to obey. If the pup's obedience is in question, he can be kept on a leash or a check cord for a while. But in order to get value out of a flushing dog, the apron strings must be snipped. Having an adult dog that knows the routine can really help the pup understand what is to be expected. Pups will naturally take cues from an adult (pack mentality). If the older dog stops, the odds of stopping the youngster are greatly increased. I recently purchased a shock collar and have been experimenting with it on a young english setter – I must say, the results have been impressive. Still, one must bear in mind that a shock collar is a training and/or management aid only, not a training replacement. Don't kid yourself into thinking that you'll just put that electric wonder around Fido's neck and he'll turn into the perfect hound. The cold, hard reality of dog training is that you get out of it relative to what you put into it. The amount of time spent in the field with the pup will be reflected in his performance.

It is also important to try to make the time spent in the field a positive experience for the pup. If the pup is constantly being negatively reinforced (yelled at, spanked, shocked, etc.), especially around ducks and ponds, he may develop an aversion to the whole ugly affair. To dampen the enthusiasm with which the dog flushes is entirely counterproductive. Remember, the primary function of our duck dog is to flush ducks, he'll do a much better job when attacking the pond with a joyful, reckless abandon. In many instances it is that little extra bit of pandemonium caused by a half-crazed dog that spells the difference between a clean, epic flight and just another rat hunt. Reflushing ducks after they have been totally intimidated by one or more stoops from the falcon is very demanding and a hesitant dog is unlikely to create the kind of necessary sensory overload required to panic the ducks into making a fatal error. At such times, the more chaotic it is in and around the pond, the better.

I highly recommend teaching all falconry dogs to locate grounded hawks. At times it seems absurdly difficult to find kill sites, even after having seen the bird go down. Often, pinpointing a hawk's exact location from close range is faster with a dog than a receiver. In addition to divulging a hawk's whereabouts, a dog serves as a wonderful deterrent for an array of potentially deadly threats while sitting next to his feathered companion. More often than not, brook flights terminate on the side opposite from the falconer. If the dog can be sent across to guard the hawk, the falconer has a little more leeway in looking for the most practical spot to make the crossing.

Teaching a dog to "locate" is a relatively simple task. Each day when the hawk kills, the dog is told "Go falcon" (or whatever word/phrase you choose) and is guided to the site. Upon arrival, the dog is placed in a sitting position and given a stay command. With a little repetition, the dog will soon catch on and begin searching for grounded game-hawks when directed to do so. Some duck dogs will eventually learn to follow the falcon and automatically guard the falcon without having to be told. Needless to say, all falconry dogs must be totally trustworthy around falcons at all times. This is easily accomplished especially when the pup is raised in the company of hawks. Most hawks are quick to put the inquisitive pup in its place from day one. A little nip on the nose, accompanied by a gentle admonishment is usually all that is required to permanently establish the canine's rank in the pecking order. The pup also needs to be educated about livestock. It is not enough that he refrains from chasing livestock, he needs to show no interest at all. If a landowner even mistakenly perceives your dog to be a threat to his livelihood, your days of flying his land are bound to be short in number. As with all animal training, it is easier to prevent a behavioral disorder than to correct an existing vice.

Dogs are amazing creatures and when they learn to work cooperatively with the falcon, the results can be fantastic. Watching a hawk/dog team working synergistically clearly illustrates the compatibility of the two species. Some of the most dramatic duck flights I've ever witnessed were shallow water flights with the dog and falcon working in concert with one another without my participation. These flights resemble cast flights in that both falcon and dog are working together for a common goal. For the duck, there is no refuge; the falcon dominates the sky and the dog owns the water. As sure as the sun shines, the duck can't avoid both for long. For the falconer, these flights present an otherwise rare opportunity to just stand back and watch the flight unfold, unburdened with flushing obligations, free to absorb the action in all its panoramic glory. Priceless!

CHAPTER 6

Weight Management

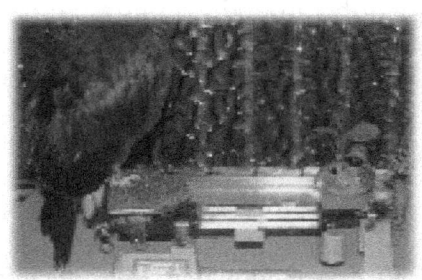

The year 1978 was big for me. I was sixteen years old and new experiences seemed to come with the scenery. I was a sophomore enrolling in a new high school. I got my first job and my first car. Though I had trained hawks before, for the first time I was actually flying a genuine game-hawk. Shiekra was a forty-eight-ounce passage hen redtail that I had trapped, trained and entered entirely on my own. She would hunt from the fist or she would wait-on, soaring along ridgelines on the warm updrafts. As Shiekra's head count rose, so did my pride and confidence. I was riding the wave of enthusiasm and invincibility that engulfs us as youth. I thought I knew it all, but I didn't know enough to realize that I was headed for a wipeout.

Toward the end of that fateful season, my father invited me to spend a week with him on the Gulf of Mexico. I agreed and made arrangements to leave Shiekra with another falconer during my absence. On the day of our departure I dropped off Shiekra, along with a supply of hawk food. Mexico was great; our entourage consisted of several families, two of which had daughters my age. Plenty of ocean, sand and girls—a paradise of sorts. Nonetheless, after one week I was ready to get back to California and retrieve my redtail.

Shiekra looked fine and hadn't been a problem though my "friend" complained that I hadn't left enough hawk food and he hadn't bothered getting any. I took Shiekra out hawking and found her to be less enthusiastic than normal. It appeared as though she simply wasn't hungry enough, so I shortened her rations for the day. The following morning, I took her hawking again and got a great slip, busting a bunny from cover just ahead. Shiekra launched and I gave her a smooth assist off the glove, yelling "Ho, ho!" at the fleeing rabbit. After a couple of wingbeats, the hawk just fluttered to the ground. I was instantly aware of what was happening, my hawk was too low. She hadn't had enough energy to pursue, and I felt as though I'd been punched in the gut. I had misinterpreted her performance the day before and had prescribed exactly the wrong remedy. Once I realized what I had done, I wasted no time and gave my hawk what it was she so desperately needed—food, and lots of it. I allowed her to gorge herself, which of course was the proverbial last nail in the coffin.

Shiekra's digestive system became overtaxed; because of her weakened condition she was unable to muster the energy required to process the meat in her jammed crop. As Shiekra's crop soured, her systems shut down. She died, and my world was changed. It is with a sense of guilt and shame that I make this confession and it is in the hopes of diverting inexperienced falconers from making the same avoidable (classic) errors that I made. The fact that I have learned from and am able to capitalize on these specific errors is a source of personal pride. No doubt, every game-hawk I have flown since this dreadful incident has benefited from the lessons I learned so long ago.

This event changed my philosophy and shaped my approach to weight management. It was the catalyst responsible for subsequent experimentation in flying hawks toward the upper parameters of response weight (and beyond). There have been setbacks, like the day my overweight tiercel Cooper's hawk just flew away, but over the years I have honed a system that has enabled me to develop powerful game-hawks and consistently intermew them while some other falconers seem to move from one tragedy to the next, year after year. I suspect that in many cases, the root of the problem may be traced to hawks being flown in low condition, predisposed to disease and other equally destructive forces. Looking back, the cascade of mistakes that I made then is now blatantly obvious, and had I done any number of things another way, the outcome could have been much different. I should have fattened the hawk up before going on vacation. I should have left more food. I should have left her with someone who would trouble himself enough to acquire additional food if necessary. I should have put the hawk on the scale immediately upon my return. I should have felt her keel. I should have been more observant and correctly interpreted the signals the hawk was sending. Lastly, I never should have gorged Shiekra in a weakened condition. It is far better to feed small quantities of easily digestible food frequently—making sure the hawk is putting over each meal. Live and learn!

Weight management is one of the most tangible and essential elements of raptor training. It is a skill that must be mastered by the falconer in order to fly an efficient game-hawk day in, day out. By accurately measuring and recording a hawk's weight at the same approximate time each day (after digestion of the previous day's meal is completed) the falconer can compare the hawk's performance in relation to weight, factoring in an array of other pertinent information, and draw some logical conclusions.

I am not a numbers person. I'm not fond of numbers and I don't retain them well either. Nevertheless, I do use a gram scale and I consider this to be the foundation of my weight management regimen. Throughout the winter, I fly three game-hawks and I weigh them religiously. These daily weights would be rather insignificant to me without some sort of reference, a means of caparison. As I've stated, I'm not good at recording this information in my brain so I use a journal. The journal not only allows me to keep accurate record of daily weights of each hawk, but it also allows me to incorporate other useful information such as weather conditions, temperature, type of quarry flown, field performance, etc. This gives me something solid and meaningful—another tool to help me keep my game-hawks in top form. I have used graph charts in the past and suggest apprentices use this format in conjunction with a journal because they clearly divulge weight trends as they occur. This helps make things slightly more foolproof for the sometimes-overwhelmed novice (I once had an apprentice confide that for a period of several days he had been misreading his scale to the tune of 100 grams, which of course is quite significant and in some cases could easily be fatal).

It should be pointed out that a raptor reaches a given weight in three different ways: coming up, going down or maintaining. Each of these three categories will represent different levels of energy, appetite, motivation and aggression. Therefore, it is important to recognize which of these three categories pertain to the raptor's weight, while comparing and evaluating field performance.

I tend to feed diverse food types because I catch a wide variety of ducks and other quarries as well. This complicates the regulation of food intake slightly. Obviously a teal breast has only a fraction the food content as that of a mallard, simply because a teal is so much smaller than a mallard. Fortunately, the falconer can use crop size as a means of estimating the quantity of food that is being ingested. Feeding a hawk a full crop will result in a weight increase, fasting will cause a decrease and any crop-size between these extremes will likewise have a predictable affect on the hawk's weight. Though this method of gauging the hawk's intake is less than exact, I have found it to be satisfactory for most of my applications. By weighing the hawk before I go hawking and comparing the current weight with that of the previous day's weights and factoring in an assortment of other variables, I can project which direction I'd like to head for tomorrow's weight. The mental computation is in grams, i.e., the weather has been warming, I think I may want to bring the hawk's weight down fifteen grams, then I envision the size of the crop that will accomplish this reduction. In so doing, I have a mental image of what the hawk will be eating before I enter the field. However, the field performance will directly affect the amount of food the hawk is ultimately fed. To use the example previously stated, I enter the field expecting to feed a meal that will decrease the hawk's weight by fifteen grams in order to compensate for her decreased caloric requirement in the warmer weather. After watching the hawk put in a stellar performance, I change my mind and opt to forgo the decrease in favor of maintaining the heavier weight in spite of the warmer weather. Should the weather turn colder, I'll be looking to increase her intake thus providing the additional calories she'll burn keeping warm. So it goes, day after day.

If the falconer desires exacting weight control, weighing daily rations is very useful. Several years ago I was subcontracted to temporarily run a bird of prey show at a theme park in Texas. I was provided with five raptors, each of which performed in five shows a day, seven days a week. There were no back-up birds, so I needed to have consistent weights everyday. By far, the most technically demanding aspect of the job was managing the merlin. Lure flying a merlin five times a day in the sweltering heat of a Houston Texas summer was a bit tricky. By weighing the merlin at least a couple times a day and weighing the last meal of the day, I was able to maintain a constant weight range within one and a half grams everyday.

If the falconer is feeding a stable diet of a singular prey species, he may achieve similar results by feeding exact known quantities. For example, through trial and error, a falconer may determine that his game-hawk will maintain a specific weight when fed a mallard leg, heart and liver. Though consistent, the falconer will still have to weigh his hawk daily and compensate for differences in temperature and the amount of physical activity the hawk enjoyed. These external and internal factors will influence just how the raptor will metabolize a particular meal. The particular kind of food fed to a hawk will also affect the metabolic rate, and various food items will contain different nutritional values. Any dieter will tell you that all foods are not created equal. To go one step further, even a particular food item, i.e., duck, pigeon, rabbit, etc., will contain a variety of digestible body parts that have a range of nutritional content. As a general rule, lighter colored meats have a lesser nutritional value, while darker meats have a higher value and as such will yield a greater caloric content. Some of the older falconry literatures referred to darker meats as being "heated," meaning nutritionally rich. Jackrabbit, a dark meat, will have a significantly higher food value than a cottontail rabbit, which is a light meat. Some of the austringers I'm familiar with that catch cottontails on a regular basis supplement their hawks diet with small birds. Regardless of the type of animal I may be feeding my hawks, I usually incorporate vital organs for their vitamin content. All ducks are dark-meated birds, and hawks can readily gain weight on a diet of duck if the falconer doesn't exercise some control when feeding. Healthy winter ducks tend to have large reservoirs of fat distributed throughout their bodies. Much of this fat is adhered to the underside of their skins. Large fat deposits are also found in the pelvic regions. Hungry gamehawks relish duck fat and, when left to their own device, may over indulge. The digestive system of raptors tends to react unfavorably when too much fat is ingested; I've seen falcons vomit their crop contents.

I had a bad experience once with an anatum peregrine I was flying. She had killed a mallard and I wasn't going to be flying her the following day so I fed her more than usual. I foolishly allowed her too much duck skin laden with fat. I had also fed her a duck leg with femur and tarsus broken. Sure enough, the falcon's system objected to the excessive amount of fat and she began to wretch. Unfortunately, the falcon's efforts were stymied; the duck leg was lodged in such a way as to preclude her from ejecting her crop contents. The anatum continued wretching, trying in vain to regurgitate. After two or three hours of strenuous effort, the situation deteriorated, the falcon became increasingly stressed, and her crop began to sour. I took her to the U.C. Davis Veterinarian Hospital where they quickly performed a crop extraction, manually removing the putrefying contents with a long pair of hemostats. Upon completion, the falcon was immediately relieved, and I learned a few lessons from the experience. I am more cautious about the amount of duck fat my hawks ingest. I do still occasionally feed duck legs (bones cleanly broken/no sharp splinters) and necks, because I have found that hawks that are subsisting on a diet of big ducks or other large game birds or mammals, are usually ingesting little bone material. I do avoid feeding much bone on big crops. Usually a raptor will vomit its crop contents, when necessary, of its own accord. Nonetheless, there are occasions when a manual extraction can mean the difference between life and death and I made a point of learning the technique for myself.

I've never been a proponent of hard-washed meat, i.e., meat that has had all the nutritional value leached out through a prolonged period of soaking and/or rinsing in cold water. In theory, a course of washed meat was fed to hawks over a period of time to induce weight loss while still keeping the raptor's digestive tract functioning. This regimen was/is considered preferable to starvation. The old axiom, "Washed meat and stones maketh a hawk to flie but great casting and long fasting maketh her die," (Lathams *Falconry* 1615 pg.23) seems to have been universally accepted and probably has greater application in regards to passagers. Though I do use "light meats," I have not found it necessary to resort to the distasteful (literally) washed meats with the eyas. I've found that the imprint need not be reduced in weight prior to free flight and can be flown initially at about hard pen weight. The term hard pen refers to the completion of feather development in the eyass.

Game-hawks flown throughout the season should not require washed meat either. Postmolt is where the intermewed eyas is most in need of weight reduction. My records indicate that my imprint falcons are reduced an average of approximately 4 to 5 percent below molt weight before resuming flying. This reduction is easily accomplished over the course of about ten days by simply cutting back slightly on daily rations. As a means of enseaming (purging excess internal fat), some falconers administer rangle (small, smooth stones). It is understood that some raptors intentionally ingest rangle. I've made it a point to have rangle available to them, especially toward the end of the molt, and I've noticed a couple of falcons take advantage of the stones then cast them the next day along with other indigestibles. I am, however, averse to forcing rangle down a raptor's throat, as was Ronald Stephens (*Observations on Modern Falconry*). I suppose one could cleverly hide rangle in meat in order to get the hawk to swallow them without having to "manhandle" the creature, but I am perfectly content to let the hawk decide for herself.

As stated, I am a firm believer in the scale, nonetheless I

believe the use of a scale has in some ways allowed the modern falconer to be too lax, to rely too heavily on a fixed number that can and should fluctuate in harmony with changing conditions. The scale is but one of several indicators and if used solely, in isolation of the other indicators, the falconer has missed the boat in terms of weight management.

In proper context, the weight of a hawk is not indicative of the hawk's condition; it is merely a reference number and virtually meaningless without corroborating evidence. Even same-sex siblings can fly at markedly different weights. It is the hawk's state of physical health, attitude and performance that largely dictate the hawk's food requirements. Changing weather patterns usually necessitate a change in the hawk's dietary needs. A switch of terrain may also require weight manipulation. If I plan to fly my falcons in tight, forested mountain conditions, I generally want an edge on their appetite. If I'm going to hunt sage grouse with hybrid tiercels, I again want an edge to enhance aggression on such large quarry, however these grouse are found in a notably colder region, so this must be factored in as well. Being hungrier in a colder climate does not necessarily require reduction. In cold weather, raptors require additional fuel (food) to maintain body heat and weight. You have undoubtedly noticed a slackening in your appetite in warm weather and an increase when you're exposed to the cold. Thermoregulation is the process of maintaining body temperature.

Cold-blooded reptiles thermoregulate externally; their body temperatures fluctuate depending on external factors. Solar radiation is a snake's primary means of elevating body temperature. Many a chilled snake has been squashed while basking on roadways. They are drawn to the open road where they are exposed to the direct rays of the sun and are additionally warmed by the heat retention of the asphalt. During the heat of the day, reptiles retreat to cooler, shady areas to avoid overheating. Warm-blooded animals thermoregulate internally, maintaining a constant body temperature in spite of fluctuating external temperatures, using metabolic processes. This is reminiscent of heating a home. In the winter, I burn wood in a wood stove to generate heat, which warms my house. When the weather gets colder outside, my wood stove requires more fuel (wood) to compensate for heat loss to colder outside air and to maintain a constant indoor temperature. Similarly, raptors require additional fuel in increasingly colder conditions to maintain status quo. Do keep in mind there will be huge differences in the metabolic rate of various species of raptors as a result of their particular evolutionary history. Body fat plays a role, and certainly raptors in "thicker" conditions are better able to withstand frigid temperatures.

In addition to weighing hawks, I manually check the keel in order to gauge musculature and fat volume. Though obviously less precise than a scale, day-to-day checks of the keel will divulge a great deal about the actual physical condition of a hawk. Raptors have the ability to rapidly metabolize fat along the keel, and subtle or even dramatic differences may be felt from one day to the next. Thousands of years ago this tactile method was likely the primary means of determining a static hawk's physical condition. By feeling along the ridge of the keel and along the edges where the pectoral muscles connect, the falconer can get a sense of what his game-hawk feels like in a variety of physical states. This also makes it possible for the falconer to reach in and feel any type of raptor with which he has experience and assess the raptor's general condition with some measure of accuracy.

This technique is useful in many ways. One such way is in working with a fresh passage. The generally accepted formula for weight reduction in passage birds is approximately 10 percent from trap weight. However, if the falconer is incapable of determining the hawk's physical condition at the time of capture he is disadvantaged. For all he knows, this hawk may have come to his trap in or near a state of starvation. It is not uncommon for passagers to develop some form of sickness shortly after capture. It would be reasonable to assume that many hawks are infected prior to capture. I once trapped a passage tiercel redtail with an acute case of pox that, in spite of my efforts, proved fatal. Nonetheless, I think it is also reasonable to speculate that a lot of the hawks that become symptomatic shortly after capture were not ill before capture. They may have been thin, perhaps on the edge of good health when they blundered into the trapper's net. A falconer ignorant of the "tactile" method of determining body fat is out of luck. It will do no good to know that "so and so's" bird was trapped at "such and such" weight. These weights are meaningless in terms of this particular hawk's health. There is simply far too much variation among individuals of a species to rely on a categorically designated weight criteria. To reduce a thin hawk's weight is tantamount to intentionally compromising its health, for then it is automatically predisposed to contract disease from exposure to past, present and future contaminants.

A further complication to the passager's health is the effects of stress after capture. It is well known that organisms under high amounts of stress tend to be immuno-suppressed. This, combined with excessive weight loss, has undoubtedly been the deadly cocktail served to more than a few passagers. At the other end of the spectrum, a hawk trapped in a state of high condition may require a reduction of greater than 10 percent to generate initial response. It would certainly ease one's anxiety when having to reduce a hawk beyond the 10 percent mark if by tactile examination we had an assurance that the hawk was still metabolizing body fat. As a sponsor, I need to be able to ascertain the physical condition of the hawks being trained by my apprentices. The typical apprentice often stumbles hard while attempting to enter his passager. Keel assessment helps me critique my apprentices' weight management while in the field and allows me to make intelligent suggestions.

I intentionally fly my eyases on the heavy side. In most instances an accomplished game-hawk need not be flown sharp (thin) to ensure good effort and continued productivity in the field. Properly managed game-hawks thrive on hawking, and once in the groove need not be coerced with excessive hunger. I believe this is key and one of the reasons I have had great success intermewing game-hawks year after year. A hawk flown on the light side may not only be less vigorous and less resistant to viruses, but also be more prone to accident out in the field. I can imagine many scenarios in which an overwhelming appetite may override the hawk's better judgment or common sense, increasing the odds of injury. What's more, game-hawks injured while in low condition are less resilient to any traumatic injury.

Behavioral clues obviously play a big role in the scheme of weight management. Both in and out of the field, the hawk's demeanor, posture and actions continually transmit information as to its physical and mental state. Proper interpretation of these visual and sometimes audible clues is imperative. Thoughtful, consistent observation permits the falconer to ascribe meaning to the subtle as well as obvious mannerisms. This is not an exact science. Individual raptors will exhibit different levels of tolerance, enthusiasm, excitement, aggression, anger, etc. This is further compounded by the fact that different species of raptors and age classifications influence mannerisms. Generally, imprints top the list as being most demonstrative; usually, when an imprint is hungry you'll know it. Next in line would be the nonimprint eyas, followed by the hacked eyas, passage and then the haggard. Sometimes the raptor's behavioral messages are obvious. Other times the behaviors are more convoluted and difficult to decipher. Occasionally the hawk will send false signals, note the imprint's behavior when being fed at home. Even at the upper end of her response weight she acts ravenous at home. Sometimes I get fooled into feeding the hawk more than I had intended, then I pay the price the following day when the not-so-hungry hawk performs well below her potential. If this same hawk, at an identical weight, were to be flown and fed in the field instead of at home, her mannerisms would be significantly different—a lot more mellow.

I find it easier to manage the weight of a hawk being flown daily as opposed to one that is flown sporadically. The activity that takes place in the field is very telling as to the hawk's true desire to eat (appetite), particularly when the raptor is an experienced game-hawk that understands its predatory role. When my game-hawks fail to take quarry under favorable circumstances, I usually feed little or nothing (another benefit of flying hawks thick). The following day I marvel at the ease and expertise by which they then take quarry. This is very noticeable in my Harris. When he's not quite motivated, he will consistently just miss jack after jack, giving the impression that they are difficult for him to catch. On the other hand, when the hawk is properly motivated, he appears to be magnetized to his quarry and often takes the first jack seen, giving the impression that he can easily catch them at will.

When my falcons are hungrier, they bate more frequently, which can ultimately lead to leg and foot problems and feather damage as well. Flying falcons thick tends to mellow them out on the block. This is also a good reason to fly the game-hawk in the morning if possible, and I've found it beneficial to feed molting hawks in the morning as well. Once fed, raptors are less anxious and may spend the afternoon bathing or preening rather than bating. I like to fly falcons six days a week, and on the sixth day I feed heavier than usual. On the seventh day I rest and feed the falcons minimally, perhaps a duck wing as a tyring. I don't really like to fast falcons and have found that falcons are more relaxed after having dismantled the tyring than they are when not given anything. My Harris, with his much slower metabolism, is usually fasted once a week with no signs of ill effect. After a day of rest, my game-hawks are ready physically and psychologically to go back at it hard, and so am I.

Many falconers talk about a quite specific, static flying weight and strive to maintain this magic number throughout the season. I have never felt comfortable relying on this philosophy. Raptors are not machinery; they are living organisms subject to external and internal elements that continually affect their minds and bodies. How can we possibly assign a perfect weight in August or September and expect that weight to remain static in spite of changing weather conditions with the onset of winter, especially in areas that experience dramatic changes in temperature? Clearly, to do so is to be very short sighted. I periodically raise the weight of my game-hawks until the performance level begins to decline, then methodically reduce the weight until the desired field performance reemerges. This cycling continues off and on throughout the season, shaping the flying weight parameters in ever-changing conditions, always striving to keep the game-hawk in a groove where field performance is powerful and predictable. In some ways a finely tuned game-hawk can be compared to a professional athlete at the top of his or her game. Physical conditioning is paramount; confidence is vital. Weight control is a wonderful tool but it is not a panacea to solve all that ails.

Occasionally, weight reduction is precisely what is necessary to achieve a certain goal or perhaps to make a specific point. However, in some instances weight reduction will only exacerbate existing problems. This is especially so when working with falcons and the chained behavior of waiting-on, or when any raptor doesn't have the capacity to grasp the lesson in the fashion that it is being presented. Certainly hawks can be starved into submission and made to jump through hoops, but I am not convinced that starvation is synonymous with training. A hawk with a healthy appetite and a hawk experiencing a condition of starvation are two separate beasts. When we find it necessary to reduce the hawks weight below that which we consider to be the norm (such as when entering to large quarry), we look forward to the hawk making the transition so that the weight may be put back on. When reducing a hawk's weight, it is important to remember that the hawk's fat content will affect the rate of weight loss. Raptors with higher fat content require less food to maintain body weight. While monitoring the weight loss of a fat hawk, you will notice the hawk losing weight at a fairly steady rate as it augments its fuel by metabolizing internal fat reserves. Eventually, as this fat supply diminishes, the hawk begins to drastically accelerate the rate of weight loss. The falconer must exercise extreme caution at this point; raptors that are allowed to slip past this level will begin metabolizing muscle mass, which is entirely counterproductive, and it becomes increasingly difficult to build the hawk back up. Through experience and observation, a falconer can learn to develop a hawk into a powerful, athletic killing predator without resorting to harsh food deprivation. Consistent game-hawks are habituated to successfully capture quarry; once habituated, hunger is less important and weight is incrementally increased. Falconers that are interested in maximum performance will want to fly a hawk with a thick breast in as high condition as possible. These are the birds that have the ambition and stamina to launch and sustain strenuous attacks.

Many years ago, I flew a tiercel kestrel that would kill and cache birds, eating only the brain. This behavior is occasionally seen among trained merlins as well, catching and killing multiple birds without feeling the need to consume them. Obviously, these falcons are cooperating and killing in a very high condition; their motivation is something beyond hunger. Certainly raptors have the capacity to hunt and kill without much (or any) appetite and in excess of what is required to maintain body weight. I recently had the good fortune to locate a Cooper's hawk (*Accipiter cooperi*) nest, one quarter of a mile from my house. The nest is 100 feet from the road, down the side of a hill, and at eye level. This convenient location has made observation easy and informative. I was impressed with the hen's dedication to the eggs and then the developing eyas; her vigilance was inspiring. Meanwhile, I found the tiercel's dedication equally impressive. He took on the role of provider, hunting to support himself, the hen and their four progeny. Like some phantom, the tiercel slipped through the forest killing, then delivering bird after bird. If, as falconers, we could tap into this mental capacity with our game-hawks, we would be flying hawks at their peak of performance and weight management would become unnecessary.

A few years ago, I had an enlightening experience while hawking pheasants with my gyr/peregrine hybrid Shaman. A rooster busted wild and Shaman took up chase, tailing him out of the field and over a hill and across an interstate highway. The dog and I paused, waiting for the falcon to return, but he did not. I went to my truck, flipped on the "box" but got no signal from Shaman's transmitter. I drove to a nearby elevated overpass but still picked up no signal, only dead air. I crossed to the opposite side of the highway, checking the general area where the two should have been and still no sign or signal. I spent the next hour driving, searching and worrying, never once picking up a signal. Since it would have been out of character for Shaman to leave the vicinity, I decided to do a more thorough investigation on foot, near the area where the pair should have crossed the highway. Four hundred yards from my truck, I began to pick up a faint signal and to my horror it appeared to be emanating from the highway itself. I had a sinking feeling, expecting to find Shaman's remains strewn across the asphalt. As I got closer to the highway, the signal strength continued to increase, seeming to confirm my fears and I braced myself for the inevitable.

Suddenly I spotted Shaman, not in the roadway, but above. He was 400 feet up and getting higher by the second, ascending effortlessly on thermal air rising off the blacktop. I couldn't help but notice the enormous size of his crop; Shaman had obviously killed the pheasant and gorged to his satisfaction. I tried to lure him down but he just kept circling higher and higher. The prospects of a fully cropped falcon riding a full on thermal early in the day had me feeling more than a little uneasy. I dashed for the truck, hoping I could coerce Shaman down with a live lure before he disappeared into the sky. To my surprise, Shaman tucked his wings, slanted across the sky and arrived at the truck before me. He wasn't looking for a handout; he'd had more than his fill with the pheasant he had killed. Shaman was ready to go home.

To those who have never experienced this type of relationship with a falcon, I may sound a bit anthropomorphic, but I can assure you that the man/falcon bond can transcend the bounds of hunger. The fact that Shaman, an extremely experienced and efficient predator, prefers to come home with me for reasons other than need was complimentary and educational. I couldn't help but reflect upon a past conversation I'd had with the president of a wildlife rehabilitation organization. She was of the typical antifalconry variety and though she obviously knew nothing about falconry she felt compelled to inform me that my birds "never really fly free." You know what I say? Bull shit!

CHAPTER 7

Pitch

Pitch is defined as the height from which the falcon waits-on in expectation of being served. I have seen ducks, including mallard and pintail, flown down and killed in tailchases covering three-quarters of a mile or more without benefit of pitch on the falcon's part. However, these lengthier, successful horizontal pursuits are quite unusual, and for this I am grateful. The ducks that I have seen flown down in this fashion were likely inferior for one reason or another, otherwise this would not be such an unusual event. Perhaps the tenacious gyr with her extraordinary speed may be an exception. At any rate, the prospect of my falcons doggedly following ducks in linear flights has little appeal to me. A falcon stooping waterfowl is a beautiful thing, and falcons killing in close proximity are far less likely to be harassed, injured or killed.

Falconers sometimes use the term "killing cone," which describes the area within which a waiting falcon can stoop game effectively. It is a relatively simple concept—the higher the pitch, the larger the circumference of the killing cone. It is not difficult for a falconer with some field experience to visually compare the height and position of the falcon in relation to a pointer solidly locked on game birds of one sort or another, and thereby gauge whether or not the quarry is within the falcon's killing cone. The water becomes muddied (pun intended) when we switch from upland game to waterfowl, specifically because of the water itself and the quarry's propensity to use it. If a peregrine with a 100-foot pitch has the ability to cut down a pheasant within a specific killing circumference, it would stand to reason that a peregrine with the same 100-foot pitch could take ducks from a body of water of similar circumference. Were it this simple, we could easily judge the approximate circumference of a pond or lake and mathematically compute the necessary pitch required in order for the falcon to dominate the ducks in question. In reality, however, ducks are not mere figures in a mathematical equation, they are sophisticated, intelligent animals that, above all else, intend to survive.

Water has played a huge role in the duck's evolutionary bid for survival and you can be sure that they have an innate understanding of how best to use it in order to evade predators, including falcons. One of the biggest challenges and rewards of duck hawking is understanding how best to manipulate ducks so as to make them vulnerable to the attack of the falcon, and pitch certainly plays a prominent role here. Falcons like other animals, including you and me, are habitual by nature. Any repetitive task that we perform will likely be done in the same sequence or fashion day in and day out, i.e., brushing our teeth, toweling off after a shower or answering the telephone. When a falcon engages in hunting, the task of taking a pitch is habitual. Flown under the same set of circumstances, duck hawks will generally work from approximately the same pitch day in and day out once they have become proficient duck killers.

I would like to look at how various degrees of pitch will influence the duck hawk's ability to compete under a variety of circumstances. For these purposes I categorize pitch as follows: 0–300 feet = low pitch; 300–600 feet = moderate pitch; 700+ feet = high pitch. To begin with, we'll consider the pros and cons of flying a low-pitched duck hawk. This would certainly be a specialized falcon, capable of flying in rather unusual locales including tight cover. This falcon would require less in terms of training and conditioning. A low-pitched falcon would cover a smaller territory and would be less inclined to rake after distant quarry. Flying at lesser pitches, this falcon will be traveling at a fraction of terminal velocity speed, which may help to avoid injury caused by collisions with fences, trees and other obstacles in a tight environment. The negatives of flying a low-pitched duck hawk are rather obvious. These specialized hunters will encounter great difficulty on most sets involving anything but a minimum amount of water. Ducks that are taken by falcons with low pitches are usually pounded or bound to just after takeoff, which means that the ducks themselves will not be flying full tilt either. Because of this and a general lack of an aerial quality, this flight style is not usually highly sought after. Perhaps a shortwing would be better suited to the type of environment that would encourage us to consistently hunt ducks in this manner.

Most duck hawks are probably flown at moderate pitches. This pitch range will allow the falcon to take advantage of a wide variety of waterfowl habitats. Less specialized than either the low- or high-pitched duck hawks, the moderately pitched falcon is the epitome of versatility. Moderate pitches are usually the product of on-the-job training, meaning these falcons have personally identified an effective height to successfully take ducks from the typical sets flown. Therefore, these falcons don't require intensive pre-entering training. Once these falcons are waiting-on they may be entered without delay. Because the falcon chooses these self-adjusting pitches, there is less required by the falconer in terms of flight style management. The falcon will usually maintain a sufficient standard within the pitch range that will allow it to consistently take ducks within certain limits. Though these falcons may be slightly more prone to check than the lower-pitched falcons, they are probably going to be rather tight flyers and easier to control than high-pitched falcons. Moderately pitched falcons realize that position is paramount; they cannot afford to be wide on the flush because they will not have the height to make up much distance. The moderate pitch allows these falcons to fly somewhat confined ponds—a typical farmyard setting. Moderate pitches allow the falcon to hammer ducks in areas where the distance between ponds is short. The moderate-pitched duck hawk will, however, find really big water frustrating.

Flying a high-pitched duck hawk has much to offer but there are difficulties, drawbacks and inherent risks. In order to make a more solid point, I will address falcons flying at 1,000 feet or higher. There are some major benefits derived from flying these big-pitched falcons. Certainly one of the most influential reasons to fly sky-raking falcons is purely aesthetic in nature. I suspect that most of us who fly falcons do so in part because we love the aerial aspect. Much pleasure is derived from watching the falcon actually fly, not just the stooping portion. Some of these big flying falcons pump up spiraling in tight circles directly overhead, others cut huge swaths out of the sky traversing large tracts of land as they mount, while others fan their tails and effortlessly ride thermals into the upper atmosphere. Regardless of how they achieve such lofty spaces, the falconer not only appreciates the ascent, but is simultaneously energized with a powerful sense of anticipation and expectation. To witness a falcon stooping from tremendous heights is a multisensory event that feeds one's soul. It is visual intercourse, culminating with an explosive climax. Ducks that are flushed cleanly under huge-pitched falcons have the opportunity to reach the full potential of their powers of flight. Watching a duck get drilled at the edge of a pond and seeing one crumpled 100 feet up out over open field are not one and the same.

Aesthetics aside, there are also huge tactical advantages with big height. A high pitch equates to a large killing cone with the falcon in full command of a huge swath of earth far below. Height also translates into velocity, which appears to enhance accuracy. Long stoops generate ample inertia for multiple attacks, should the first attempt fail. Perhaps the most significant tactical advantage is psychological in nature. The pitch and positioning of the hunting falcon directly affect the decision-making processes of waterfowl—make no mistake, a duck's mindset is crucial when flying big, deep sets. Ducks are intelligent creatures as anyone who has spent much time hunting them can attest. Their senses are acute and they have an impressive ability to remain composed and make lucid choices in the midst of chaos. Ducks instinctively recognize falcons and the threat they represent, they also fully comprehend that this threat is all but insignificant so long as they remain on water. Taking to the air with a falcon overhead would be tantamount to playing Russian roulette—given a choice, it just doesn't make sense and it is bound to hurt. The bigger the water (the farther you are away from the ducks), the lesser the impression you will make on them. On big water, all the yelling and rock throwing in the world will often be ineffectual at flushing ducks with the falcon dangling above. Compensate this with an extremely high pitch. The higher the falcon (the greater the distance), the less intimidating the falcon becomes, and things begin to balance out. When ducks feel less pressure from falcons, they are far less likely to consider flying under one as being suicidal.

On an outing a while back, a small group of mallards entered the field we were flying and flew directly under the falcon who was more than 1,500 feet up. A hen was struck 100 feet above the plowed earth. They obviously either failed to see the falcon way up there or, more likely, misjudged his intent. The higher the falcon's pitch, the smaller it appears, and it becomes increasingly difficult for the duck to assess the falcon's intentions let alone trajectory and speed. Ducks don't fully appreciate a falcon's ability to cover vertical distance while traveling at terminal velocity, and depth perception becomes a factor. When we look up at a flying falcon, we are viewing its largest surface area. A stooping falcon viewed from below presents a radically smaller surface area. The effect is enhanced with tucked wings. It is kind of like looking at the flat side of a piece of paper and then turning the paper viewing only the edge. This is why it is extremely difficult to visually relocate a high-flying falcon once it has begun its stoop even if we avert our eyes for only a moment. Even as the falcon is rapidly accelerating, it gives the optical illusion of getting smaller, which usually means getting farther away rather than closer. These critical few moments make all the difference in the world. The time lapse between the falcon initiating its stoop and the ducks coming to the realization that they are under attack will allow ducks to really pick up steam and perhaps even to emotionally commit themselves to a clean departure, or at least it may cause ducks to err in calculating their ability to turn and beat the falcon back to water. Sometimes, you'll detect some indecision among a group of just-flushed ducks, as they struggle to decide whether to turn and come back to water or to keep going. If the ducks ponder a hair too long, the falcon will get its shot. Often the ducks will opt to just keep heading out in the hopes that the falcon will target somebody else.

A falconer can also make good use of tremendous pitch by allowing the falcon to fly wide, that is, to fly out of position. This can be tactically advantageous at times because, as mentioned, the farther away the falcon is, the less threatening they appear. A falcon that is really high can cover ground in a manner that has to be seen to be appreciated. Some falconers prefer these panoramic stoops to the conventional vertical stoops by falcons that are in position. Ducks that may otherwise be impossible to flush, can often be coerced into flying when the falcon is well out of position.

Flying big-pitched falcons on a smaller sets is a beautiful thing. Flushing ducks from a tiny pond with an ultrahigh falcon allows the falconer to spend less time trying to get the ducks up and more time watching the attack unfold. The falconer also stands a greater chance of staying dry because these easily orchestrated flights are usually straightforward and tend to terminate with a clean impact well away from the pond. It is quite rare for a duck thus struck to regain the pond, which, conversely, is a regular occurence when low-pitched falcons are pounding them at the waters edge.

Finally, there are certain circumstances where a higher pitch will decrease the falcon's risk of injury. It is not uncommon to find fencing near at least one side of a pond. When ducks are flushed under sky-high falcons, the likelihood that the ducks will be well into the sky and away from the perimeter of the pond when the falcon intersects with them decreases the risk of a fence strike by the falcon. Also, some falcons prefer to headshoot their quarry. My hybrid, Omen, is one such falcon. It is amazing how efficient a smallish falcon can be while striking large quarry on the back of the head. These headshots are not only extremely effective, but also minimize the risk of self-injury to the falcon while impacting these large targets. Headshots are made possible by vertical positioning of the falcon over quarry; the falcon stoops through its prey maintaining this vertical trajectory. This is not easily accomplished when quarry is flying "on the deck," which is why most headshots occur well up in the sky.

As noted, there is much to be said of these ozone-scraping pitches but there are also inherent risks and parameters under which these flights may not be suitable or even possible. Wide, open spaces are prerequisites; tight spaces just won't suffice. I have flown fields that were simply too small for the falcon's height. Under these circumstances, quarry may be knocked down in undesirable locations. In some cases, high-pitched falcons may be repeatedly avoided by ducks taking refuge in any adjacent waters after the flush. High-flying falcons may experience greater temptation in the form of check (unintended quarry). Not only can these falcons visually scan huge tracts of land but they can also launch lethal attacks after check, taking them considerable distances from the falconer. Sometimes the lofty falcon need not rake in order to kill unintended quarry. I've seen various targets fly right through a field, oblivious to the deadly falcon cruising high above.

High-flying duck hawks are not hatched but created. Good results require a concerted effort on the part of the falconer in terms of training and conditioning. There are various methods and tools available to assist the falconer in this endeavor, some of which appear quite imaginative, such as teaching falcons to follow a pilot/falconer up into the sky using ultralight aircraft and conditioning falcons to climb after balloons, kites and model airplanes. I even heard a rumor in the 1980s that some falconers were using cocaine as a means of stimulating falcons ever higher, though I suspect this was founded more on jealousy than factual information. Of course, historically, our European predecessors did manage lofty falcons trained only with lure and live game (not bagged). These falcons were usually passagers however, and I must wonder what percentage of these were truly high flyers and what percentage fell into the more moderate pitch ranges, which would have certainly cut down on the loss rate without the benefit of telemetry.

I think really high-flying duck hawks can be trained through practical experience—flushing ducks and making the slips ever more demanding until the falcon is having to fly very high indeed in order to succeed. However, there is a possibility that as the eyas learns early on to kill ducks from lower pitches, she may not be inclined to fly high on the easy sets later. At any rate, where I live ducks don't come into season until well after the eyases are on the wing, and even if that were not the case, I would still opt to extensively condition them before exposure to the duck hawking arena. The first ducks my eyases encounter are mallards because until the migration gets under way, they are what is available here on the types of sets conducive to young falcons. Mallards are a tough customer and it takes a great deal of aggression (particularly for smaller falcons) to initiate and sustain a lethal attack against them. The period of time used to train and condition the eyas may also be used to work toward an elevated level of confidence and aggression without having to resort to extreme hunger as incentive.

Since I am not much of a gadget person, I have shied away from the mechanical training aids and rely on homing pigeons, occasional bagged game birds and waterfowl, and I incorporate a fair amount of thermal training early on. The emphasis is on teaching the falcon to ascend to great heights and stoop vertically in order to cut quarry out of the sky. These techniques provide results that compare favorably to anything I've seen. Regardless of how the falcon is schooled on upper atmosphere etiquette or how they are entered to quarry, there is still work to be done in terms of flight management. Producing a stylish and high-flying duck hawk and maintaining this level of art are not one and the same. Without thoughtful attention and careful management, previous efforts can be undone in short order. Duck hawking has the potential to reinforce pitch and style, but it also has the potential to rapidly deteriorate into a ratty affair. Providing good slips and properly orchestrating flights will keep the falcon on track; this will at times require restraint on the part of the falconer and requires placing quality ahead of quantity. Remember, it is much easier to reduce a falcon's pitch than it is to teach them to go higher after they have become habituated to killing ducks from lesser heights.

In the final analysis it becomes readily apparent that there is no right way or wrong way to take ducks with falcons, but certainly there are tactics that will prove more efficient, more visual or perhaps simply be more fun. There can be no specific numerical pitch that would best suit all varieties of waterfowl and the various habitats in which they're found, let alone suit each of our own personal preferences. However, with an understanding of the relationship between a falcon's pitch and the particularities of each duck slip, we can cultivate behaviors that will allow us to orchestrate flights that leave us speechless and entirely absorbed in the moment.

CHAPTER 8

Pigeons

Pigeons are the cornerstones of my falcon training. They are excellent tools with which to teach the falcon several fundamental axioms. Proper pigeon use can teach the falcon (especially an unhacked eyas) pitch, position, trajectory, timing, footing and futility in tailchasing, all the while providing excellent conditioning. Having superior homing pigeons and knowing when, where and how to serve them to falcons are key. Falcons that are properly served good "homers" will also learn to read their quarry, anticipating its next move in an effort to cut it out of the sky. Pigeons are accessible, affordable, manageable and reusable. All pigeons are not created equal; genetics play a major role, so it is wise to begin with the best blood available in order to avoid teaching the falcon all the wrong things.

Pigeon racing is popular in many locales, so it is usually relatively easy to access sources from which to begin. Most pigeon racers produce an excess of birds each year and are forced to cull their flock one way or another. A well-timed phone call may provide the fortunate falconer with these excess birds, and they can be the building blocks for the falconer's own kit (flock). Superior racing pigeons are fast, agile, cunning, extremely evasive and can ascend at steep angles. In contrast, bagged game birds (even those kept in flight pens) present easy targets when served to a waiting falcon regardless of pitch. If, for one reason or another, the bagged game bird isn't knocked down or bound to on the stoop, they are virtually always flown down in a tail chase. Captive-bred, free-ranging waterfowl would probably fare better, but would require larger facilities and greater financial investment than homers, and they would still likely be knocked down almost always, once the falcon got the hang of it.

Proper conditioning of the homers prior to falcon training will give them the stamina, experience and confidence necessary to provide great training sessions for falcons. I provide my flock with a lot of exercise liberating them almost every day at my residence. I live in a rural setting, so the biggest problem I've encountered has been wild hawks. I estimate that I lose between ten to twenty birds annually to these hawks, primarily Cooper's. One afternoon, I was sitting in the livingroom with my family when a large plate glass window suddenly exploded, sending a shard of glass the size of a handsaw onto the shoulder of my son, Austringer, who was sitting on a chair next to the window. A very wide-eyed pigeon stood on the floor of the livingroom having escaped a brush with death itself in the form of *Accipiter cooperi*. I was extremely grateful that Aussie hadn't been gashed in the incident. Oh, the life of a falconer!

One particular haggard hen has been coming around for years and has proven especially effective. At times this can be frustrating. One summer, I imprinted and hand-reared a beautiful white homer to use in my lectures. I made the mistake of leaving him outside one afternoon when I had to run errands in town. I was none too happy to come home and find the red-eyed devil had made a meal of him in my absence. Nevertheless, these ongoing attacks have undoubtedly had offsetting benefits in terms of a natural selection culling process by the hawk as weaker, slower, less intelligent or resourceful homers provide the bulk of these kills. The homers that survive a summer of such assaults are primed for falcon evasion toward the fall.

For serious aerobic workouts, I condition my homers with road training. This is a very simple process. Homing pigeons have a very strong homing urge, hence the name. These pigeons will go to great lengths and distances to return to the place where they were raised. I take my birds about half a mile from my house on the first day, which isn't far considering that many of the youngsters will have already flown farther than this in flock formation during their daily liberation. Just the same, if I have older birds, I take a few of them along as well to help ensure things will go smoothly. Never take squeekers on the road as they are simply too young and the likelihood of them making it back to the loft is extremely low. (You know a young bird is a squeeker if it "squeaks" when you pick it up—simple.) After the initial drop-off, I continue daily releases of the flock, roughly doubling the distance each day. In short order the birds are very fit.

Keep in mind that a pigeon develops physically a bit faster than it does mentally. In other words, just because a young pigeon has reached a point of strong physical conditioning, it may not necessarily be mentally competent to be served to a falcon, particularly if the falcon it is matched with is a veteran. Just as our eyas falcons develop psychologically over a period of time, so do the homers. This additional period may be short and measured in weeks, but it is critical if we are to avoid intimidated pigeons cowering and being slaughtered as lambs to lions.

The types of fields where we serve our pigeons to our falcons will determine the pigeons' escape tactics. Pigeons are incredibly adept at surviving falcon attacks fair and square; however, pigeons are not averse to using any and all available obstacles. Their favorites include fences, power lines, vehicles, trees, buildings, farm equipment, ponds and so on. Some of these obstacles are used merely as shelter and others are used in an intentional attempt to kill the pursuing falcon. Fences and power lines rank at the top of the list of things to avoid when training falcons with pigeons. Pigeons will time their deadly maneuvers under and through wires at the moment the falcon intersects with them. Occasionally these proactive tactics backfire for the pigeon, as on the occasion when one such hard-pressed pigeon tried to run my tiercel peregrine into the side of a barn, but slightly misjudged and effectively committed suicide via the barn wall.

Aside from the safety factor, there is good cause to serve homers in open areas, because only then can we expect them to rely upon their tremendous agility to avoid the stooping falcon and then power up into the sky, ascending above the falcon in order to escape. If we serve homers in areas with refuge, such as trees, and the pigeon beats the falcon to cover before the completion of the stoop, we have in essence taught the falcon to either lower her pitch or not bother stooping at all. Also, when pigeons utilize trees, etc., for shelter, they are far more likely to be killed if the falcon continues to pursue. This gives the falcon ample incentive to tailchase if the stoop proves unsuccessful and may ultimately lead to the falcon killing long distances from the falconer, which is always disconcerting. At the very least, tailchasing falcons are far more prone to becoming lost. Additionally, falcons that learn to kill horizontally are less likely to expend a lot of energy mounting to great heights when they have already proven pitch unnecessary. Pigeons served to falcons in areas devoid of refuge know they must rely solely upon their aerial abilities, avoiding the stoop and outclimbing the falcon, in order to survive; they are far more likely to succeed utilizing this tactic rather than ratting through cover. Our falcons then learn to stoop from great heights generating tremendous speed and take their best shot. A really high pitch will allow the falcon multiple opportunities to stoop the pigeon before the flight flattens out and the pigeon begins to outclimb the falcon. These strong homers may be followed several hundred vertical feet before the falcon concedes defeat. This is where conditioning (physical and mental) on the part of the homer pays off, giving them the strength, stamina and confidence to contest the sky with the falcon and leave her in their wake. Thus, a falcon that has been fairly outflown quickly realizes that its best, and perhaps only, chance of slaying these nimble rockets is a well-timed stoop.

Tailchasing is somewhat more likely to occur with the faster falcons, notably gyrs and gyr hybrids. Falcons that are unsuccessful in their tailchasing efforts are negatively reinforced by the simple act of failure. We can further enhance the benefits of this negative conditioning by positively reinforcing the breaking off and returning behavior of the falcon by producing the lure and feeding or by allowing the falcon an opportunity to remount and serving another homer. There is huge potential for setting great behavioral precedence at this juncture. If the falcon has stooped, missed, tailchased and then returned unsuccessful, we can allow her the opportunity to remount and perhaps reach an even greater height than the initial pitch and then serve a handicapped pigeon that she is almost certain to kill. It does not take long for a falcon thus served to realize that its energy is better spent ascending in anticipation of a huge (perhaps fruitful) stoop than to continue those futile, horizontal tailchases. Flying a falcon in thermals during this period of conditioning will make it incredibly easy for the falcon to stoop pigeons from massive heights.

When serving pigeons destined to be killed in order to reinforce a behavior or really drive home a lesson, I prefer not to use recognizably inferior pigeons (young, weak, slow, etc.) as this would be "dancing on the rim of fire"—hoping the falcon will kill cleanly, but knowing there is a greater chance of the falcon killing in a degenerative or lackadaisical manner. To avoid this I use strong, conditioned homers that have been visually handicapped. By placing masking tape on the pigeon in the form of a visor, I can effectively obstruct the pigeon's view of above and behind. A pigeon thus impaired will fly completely naturally with one important exception, they will not evade the attack of a stooping falcon simply because they will not see it coming. What this means for the falcon is an all but unavoidable opportunity to deliver a clean, devastating impact and fully realize the significance of the waiting-on tactic. Pigeons that are flying recognizably impaired will sometimes elicit a casual response from some falcons, particularly those with a lot of experience flying pigeons. Under these conditions some falcons will stoop below and behind the homer, bleeding off most of its speed and gingerly bind. I don't like to encourage this behavior. I like to see a serious, committed effort on the part of the falcon, whether hawking or training. If, for some reason, the falcon chooses not to strike at all, the pigeon is very likely to outfly the falcon and the falconer has lost no ground.

Another consideration having to do with field selection is the terrain itself. I have come to appreciate the use of hills for training purposes. Just as our falcons take advantage of height so will our homers if given the opportunity. Falcons are less likely to kill pigeons thrown from hilltops than pigeons thrown on flat ground. Remember, the goal of training falcons with pigeons is not to teach the falcon to kill pigeons but rather to instill desired behaviors and establish a hunting protocol. Pigeons thrown from hilltops will immediately have height to work with as they travel away from the hillside. As the falcon approaches in her stoop, the pigeon will respond by inverting into a stoop of its own, picking up more speed just before the falcon closes; more importantly, the now-vertical pigeon has the ability to turn very radically in any direction it chooses. By contrast, a pigeon thrown on a flat surface cannot generate as much speed and is limited directionally, being able to turn only to its left or right. Also, if homers are thrown in an area that requires them to fly over nearby hills in order to get home, they are more likely to climb in earnest after evading the stoop instead of taking a flatter line. This is to the pigeons' advantage because their wingload allows them to outclimb the falcon. This is also to the falconer's advantage. All falcons can be expected to continue to pursue pigeons as long as they have any height advantage at all. Many falcons will pursue pigeons for great distances as long as they are flying level with the pigeon. Few falcons will go far tailchasing pigeons that are above them and ascending at a steep angle, provided they haven't flown down inferior pigeons previously. When the falcon does break off, she will be up in the sky, which may also be advantageous.

If for any reason you anticipate the possibility of a homer bailing out into some form of unavoidable cover, you may find it beneficial to serve two or more pigeons simultaneously. Pigeons that are not alone in the sky are under somewhat less pressure; there is a safety in numbers mentality. The last thing any pigeon wants to do under these circumstances is to draw attention to itself by leaving the formation of the flock. This is the very depiction of flock mentality and natural selection in motion. Any member of a group that isolates itself from the group while under attack from a predator will be viewed as deficient and the most easily killed, greatly enhancing the odds of attracting the predator's full attention. Consequently, when multiple pigeons are served, they are less likely to disappoint the falconer by bailing. Sometimes, after the falcon has stooped and missed a particular homer, you can actually see the pigeon mentally juggling the idea of ratting out or pulling back into formation with the others. Usually they will opt for the formation, hoping to lose themselves in the crowd, whereas a solitary pigeon may well succumb to the pressure and bail. The byproduct of simultaneously serving multiple pigeons to an inexperienced falcon is that the falcon must learn to select a singular target from a group—something that will be a regular occurrence for the would-be duck hawk.

The time of day we serve pigeons will directly affect the flight style and performance of the falcon. Most pigeon training takes place during late summer and/or early fall, when the weather is warm or hot with possibly mildly cool dawn and dusk periods. We will discuss these related issues in the chapter titled Weather.

Knowing precisely when to and when not to serve pigeons to a falcon is not an exact science but will have such enormous ramifications that it is difficult to overemphasize its importance. Every time we fly our falcons, they are learning or reaffirming tactical concepts. Hungry falcons quickly become habituated to things that work (provide food); likewise, falcons can be expected to abandon a behavior that consistently proves futile. If the falconer has a vision of the types of behaviors he does and does not wish to see in his falcon, he can then construct a mental framework of how to best accomplish the task. A falconer's ability to master this concept is imperative. Great falcons are invariably flown by great falconers because they have refined their training techniques so as not to impede but rather to enhance the natural ability of their charges.

I usually recommend allowing an eyas the opportunity to kill at least one pigeon before actual field training begins. This will generate a bit of enthusiasm, aggression and encouragement for the falcon when serving homers in the field. This also gives me a sense of security, allowing me to fly young falcons free without a sharp edge to their appetite and avoiding a lot of repetitive lure and creance work, which I detest. I feel that belaboring the lure training is a possible impediment to instilling the predator concept and aerial hunting style of a recently fledged falcon. A falcon that has killed and enjoyed at least one pigeon before liberation will likely respond to a live lure early in its training should all else fail—though I have yet to resort to this.

Once the actual field training begins, I insist that my falcons kill pigeons only from the stoop. Initially they may be served pigeons while the falcons buzz around snatching at grasshoppers, and they will always be outflown. When the falcon has even a little height during these first sessions, a pigeon is released under her and the falcon will quickly realize that her height makes her more competitive with the homer. The falcon will recognize that only when she is above the falconer (not necessarily directly) will pigeons appear, because now we are no longer serving them horizontally, only vertically. With each passing day, our falcon is getting stronger on the wing and is learning to maneuver in the air to come closer to its target. Each day we should try to withhold the presentation of the pigeon until the falcon has improved upon the previous day's pitch, and we should be serving the falcon only while it is actually pumping its wings and, hopefully, ascending. With any luck, by about day ten the falcon has already learned a great deal about flying, maneuvering, pitch and is starting on footing. She may have killed one or two pigeons as reward for markedly improved pitch (I usually have a partially "sealed" pigeon on hand for just such occasions). About now, I like to begin thermal training, because it is the fastest, easiest way to get the falcon really high while still focusing on stooping. The chapter entitled Thermals will cover such flying in detail.

As we proceed from one day to the next, we continue to see progress both physically and mentally. In short order (if we have kept errors to a minimum) we have instilled in the minds of our falcons the types of behaviors that produce positive results, and they have abandoned those behaviors that went unrewarded. If, on the other hand, we provided incentive or even encouragement of negative behaviors, our progress may have been retarded or worse. A case example of a mistake that

I made (which in retrospect seems so obvious I am reluctant to admit) should be a clear indication as to how quickly and easily we can foster the wrong message to the eyas. It was early on in the training of my first gyr x peregrine hybrid tiercel, Indy. I had started flying the young hybrid in a small valley flanked by heavy tree cover. Upon releasing the falcon, he quickly took to the trees. Now I reasoned that sitting in a tree was not good, so I tossed a homer to motivate him into the air. To my surprise, not only did he get motivated but also he managed to fly the pigeon down through the trees and kill it. Embarrassingly enough, it took several episodes of this before I caught onto the fact that the falcon was conditioning me! In short order he realized the nature of the game and it went like this. I drive him to the valley. He flies to the nearest tree, patiently waits for me to produce a pigeon. He flies it down, kills and eats. I pick him up, we go home and repeat tomorrow. What could be simpler?

I sometimes get the impression that it is easier to teach falcons the wrong things than the right things. Correcting an error such as the one just noted may be relatively simple if the falcon can be flown in an area devoid of perches. If, however, the falconer does not have the luxury of flying on totally open ground this "little mistake" could be a difficult, time-consuming obstacle to overcome. By constantly assessing how our training procedures are shaping the falcon's behavior, we can stay on top of whatever may arise and make adjustments accordingly. This process is constant and does not stop even after the falcon has been successfully entered and is consistently taking quarry. Each falcon is different and catering to each falcon's individual needs is part of the artistry of falconry.

Another issue pertaining to pigeon usage is the question as to how many homers we should serve the falcon during any particular session? I don't believe there is a simple answer, but if we discuss some of the typical components of a session, we may shed some light on the decision-making process. Remember, we are not training with pigeons to educate our falcons on how to catch pigeons, but rather to instill specific behavioral qualities as well as to develop fundamental skills—both aspects are equally important. While the eyas is learning about mounting, waiting-on, pitch, position, etc., so to is it developing musculature, aerobic capacity, timing and footing. All of these factors plus external considerations in terms of weather/atmospheric conditions and the falconer's schedule play a role in determining how many opportunities a falcon may get to stoop on released pigeons during a particular day's training session, as can be seen by the following examples.

Imagine you are working with a young falcon and she had been progressively taking higher pitches just about every day until she hit the 600-foot mark. Perhaps you have wanted to get more height out of her, but each day for the last week, she has shown no desire to exceed the 600-foot mark. On this particular morning however, the temperature has dropped a few degrees lower or perhaps you are able to get out a bit earlier; in either case, the air is slightly colder/denser and the falcon finds this to her liking. She responds by mounting with brisk wingbeats to 900 feet, a marked improvement on her previous efforts. This may be an ideal time to serve her a partially sealed pigeon to encourage her to repeat this behavior (increased pitch) on the next outing. In contrast, if the eyas has been taking 600-foot pitches but on this particular day due to dull, dead air and/or lack of motivation (too heavy) she stops ascending at 300 feet and hangs lazily in the air, we may consider her effort not worthy of positive reinforcement in the form of any pigeons being served at all. In both situations the falconer is adjusting the number of pigeons served in the best interest of future performances.

Now let us look at a somewhat different set of circumstances. Say, for example, a falconer has recently pulled his competent, intermewed game-hawk out of the molt. Her average working pitch is 350 feet, which is well suited to their particular hunting area. The first several flights of the new season are a bit taxing on her, as she is thoroughly out of condition, and she does mount to her standard pitch of 350 feet. With this falcon, the greatest benefits to be derived from the pigeon sessions will be physical in nature in the form of aerobic conditioning and target practice. The more pigeons she can stoop at, while still maintaining the integrity and enthusiasm of her flight style, the sooner she will be in top flying condition and ready to compete with wild, strong quarry. I personally enjoy using thermals during this period of reconditioning. Thermals allow the falcon to stoop at however many pigeons we have the desire (or time) to throw, because the out of shape falcon can ascend with minimal effort, get in a lot of practice all the while getting an excellent workout briefly chasing pigeons and searching for lift in between elevator rides to the upper atmosphere. It also happens to be a lot of fun.

There are two more considerations I'd like to point out in relation to how many times to serve pigeons during a session. One school of thought suggests that if the falcon is served only one pigeon per outing she will put forth her best effort each time she is put up, for she is aware there will only be one chance. This philosophy is valid. I have, on many occasions, seen falcons flown that I suspect were trained in this fashion because after missing the released pigeon, they immediately come butterflying back to the trainer fully anticipating lure presentation. I was left with the impression that the falcon almost considered the pigeon stooping a mere formality before the lure was granted. I wonder how these falcons would respond under game-hawking situations—would they throw in the towel and look for the garnished lure after the first unsuccessful attempt at game or would they switch their behavior and remount after missing or knocking quarry into cover/water on the first stoop? It would seem that the former, the conditioned response, would be the likely choice. I prefer a game-hawk to remount after such occurrence and am often rewarded with a second stoop superior to that of the first and a heavy game bag. To this end I opt to train falcons to remount after a first failed attempt and do so by providing multiple opportunities to stoop pigeons during most training sessions.

The means by which we serve the pigeon to the falcon is critical. I have always relied on a forceful underhanded throw that projects the pigeon out and up at about a forty-five-degree angle. This approach has the pigeon up to speed very quickly, which of course is desirable. Any tact that impedes the pigeon's ability to achieve almost instant maximum speed and orientation will increase the mortality rate of the pigeons, particularly when a falcon's lower pitch allows her to take advantage of the pigeon's slow start. This is counterproductive to the entire concept of proper pigeon usage. I avoid any effort to disorientate the pigeon by dizzying, etc. I don't plant pigeons in cover and kick them out either. Not only would there be the possibility of a pigeon coming up prematurely, etc., but a pigeon trying to break cover is severely disadvantaged as it has difficulty getting up and free of cover cleanly. The result is a pigeon that is often barely on the wing before the falcon is upon him—not the desired effect.

It is good practice to serve the falcon when she is ascending, avoiding serving immediately after she stops climbing. Otherwise, the all-too-eager-to-stoop falcon will associate a cease in climbing as a trigger to the serve. The message sent will be the sooner you stop mounting, the sooner you'll be served. In order to prevent the falcon from stooping prematurely, release pigeons as quickly as possible with a minimum amount of commotion or any repetitive behavior that will tip off the falcon with visual or audible cues that she will be quick to learn and equally quick to capitalize upon. Otherwise, the falcon may cease to mount at the slightest familiar gesture. All falcons will be looking for any hint of an imminent serve and will begin to stoop preemptively if a pattern is detected. Last year I was photographing my tiercel Omen as he stooped homers in preparation for a pigeon article I was working on. It didn't take him long to realize that as soon as I began to fumble with the camera, that a pigeon would be forthcoming. This distraction caused him to cease climbing and frustrated me.

Falcons that learn to preemptively stoop pigeons will do so while hunting wild quarry as well. Often the quarry will really take advantage of this flaw in the falcon's style and withstand the falconer's flushing antics until the falcon has lost virtually all pitch and most hope of killing. Then the quarry departs, dragging the foolish falcon off on a tailchase as the bewildered falconer curses the dog. Avoid this by not tipping your hand with repetitive body language. If the falcon does stoop early, wait her out; teach her to stoop only when quarry is on the wing by withholding the serve, even if it means no serve at all. Be careful here or you may find yourselves afraid to look up at the falcon, to move or even breathe for fear she may interpret this as her cue to stoop. Counteract this by overexaggerating movement if necessary. Bombard her with false cues and stick to your guns. Don't serve unless the falcon is performing the behavior you want to reward.

Be aware that serving experienced falcons that are in position at heights less than approximately 300 feet seriously increases the mortality rate of homers. Pigeons are very vulnerable when served to falcons that are low and close enough to hit them before they are fully underway. It doesn't take many such kills for the falcon to adopt a low pitch/pigeon killing strategy, which once again is counterproductive if the intent is lofty pitches.

I should point out that those falconers living and flying falcons in areas with heavy feral pigeon concentrations may experience a higher incidence of check (chasing of unintended quarry), as these pigeon-trained falcons may be highly motivated to engage wild flocks whenever they are encountered. Whether there is a significant difference between these falcons' reactions and those falcons not trained with pigeons, I can't say because I have trained all of my falcons with pigeons and am unable to draw comparisons. Nonetheless, I'm happy to report that Omen, now in his fourth season, has never raked on feral pigeons and will only stoop them if they fly directly under him.

It has been said that pure gyr strains are simply too physically endowed for homers to be used effectively. I have zero experience here having only trained gyrs for the Middle East market and not Classical waiting on falconry. For the last couple of seasons I have been flying a ¾ jerkin and he has not been able to fly down my homers. Perhaps of greater concern is the gyr's vulnerable immune system. Pigeons are capable of transmitting disease to falcons including frounce and avian herpes virus, to which gyrs are particularly susceptible.

I haven't had any instances of pigeon-transmitted disease with any of my falcons including my gyr hybrids. I did have one incident a couple decades ago when my goshawk contracted frounce from a wild-trapped pigeon I fed her, a practice I have long since given up. I don't feed wild pigeons to any of my raptors. When I feed pigeon from my flock, I remove the entire digestive track from beak to vent except for the liver. I also visually inspect pigeons especially the oral cavity before using as food. Sanitary housing conditions and a good diet will help keep the flock healthy. The details of pigeon housing and husbandry goes beyond the intended scope of this book and the reader is encouraged to seek additional materials written by expert pigeon racers.

CHAPTER 9

Thermals

The earth feels like an oven and I am being baked, as the thermometer soars above 100 degrees Fahrenheit. It seems odd weather to be flying any falcon, let alone a gyr hybrid, the gyr being an artic falcon. I release Indy into the solar-heated atmosphere and watch him swat the pointer with the exuberance of youth and cockiness that denotes the eyas. Indy has been off the creance only nineteen days and, literally, everything is still new to him. Indy forgoes the dog in favor of a more abundant quarry packaged in a more manageable size, the illusive grasshopper. Hundreds, no, thousands of grasshoppers blanket the field, providing Indy with no shortage of winged targets. I wonder how a grasshopper must feel being drafted by 820 grams of aerodynamic perfection? Eventually, Indy's attention is diverted to a more worthy opponent—a hapless turkey vulture.

The vulture has unwittingly cruised into our air space and is now Indy's plaything. The falcon greets this new friend with a barrage of low-level stoops, inflicting no damage but seriously cramping the vulture's style, forcing the massive scavenger to beat a hasty retreat. With inflated ego, Indy escorts his playmate out of his territory and then steps on an awesome thermal elevator. I watch the falcon spiral effortlessly into the sky, warm air pushing him higher and higher. At 1,000 feet, I release a homing pigeon and watch the falcon fold and roll into his stoop. The pigeon side shifts, easily evading the inexperienced falcon, then rats into a tree 150 yards out. Indy, now having the time of his life, gets back on the elevator and, in short order, is looking down on me from 1,500 feet. I release a partially sealed homer and Indy descends in an audible vertical stoop. The speed is intense and this intimidates the falcon, who intentionally avoids impacting his target. Indy throws up, rolls into another stoop, this time binding and taking the pigeon to the ground where it is released and quickly recaptured in a brief chase. I shade the panting falcon with my body and cool him with water from my spray bottle. I can't help sensing the unlimited potential of this barely hard-penned falcon and leave the field with a solid feeling.

Literature written in previous eras either neglected to mention anything about thermals or else offered brief admonitions warning of dire consequences to those foolish enough to actually fly falcons when thermal conditions exist. Anyone intentionally encouraging his or her charges to sail up and away into the wild blue yonder would probably have been looked at sideways. Oh, how times have changed! The twentieth century brought forth technology at a dizzying rate, some of which (surprisingly enough) has benefited falconry, and none more so than captive propagation and radio telemetry. My generation cut its teeth on transmitter-equipped, captive-bred eyas falcons, greatly reducing the likelihood of permanent loss of the hunting falcon to a rate below that which could have been imagined by our predecessors, who largely flew passagers and always without transmitters. In those days, maintaining visual contact with the falcon was vitally important. Today, the notion of flying falcons from out of sight pitches is no longer folly. Falcons can be monitored via telemetry once beyond binocular range, and this ability has opened the door to exciting possibilities. Thermals are now used as an effective tool for both training and hunting with game-hawks. As with any tool, thermals should be used in a thoughtful manner to avoid mishaps and achieve positive results.

Just what are thermals? They are vertical currents of rising air. Thermals are usually the result of solar-radiated earth heating ground level air to temperatures above that of sections of adjacent air. Warmer air is less dense and therefore rises. This air punches through the colder air and forms a thermal updraft. These formations have been described as columns as well as bubbles of rising air. My impression of thermal structure is that it can be columns, bubbles or a combination of columns with occasional belches of warmer air masses forcing their way through the funnel. One can get a visual reference by observing rising smoke.

All thermals are not created equal; various weather, atmospheric and geological conditions influence this irregular phenomenon. Thermals tend to be most active during periods of unstable air. Areas of dry, dark earth that are devoid of vegetation are impacted to a higher degree (in terms of temperature) by solar radiation than areas with dense growth. Certain aspects in the landscape often dictate where thermal air will erupt through dense, cooler air, so thermal locations tend to be consistent. Falcons flown over familiar ground learn these locations and will head straight for these areas when flown during periods of thermal activity.

It has been suggested that birds can actually see thermal columns, and perhaps they can. Certainly, the human eye detects distortions in the air created by solar radiation, probably most often noticed as we drive on a heated asphalt surface. As we scan the road on a summer day, up ahead in the distance the road appears to shimmer. Whatever the case, all trained falcons can learn to locate and utilize thermals.

Some raptors are more efficient at utilizing thermal lift than others as a result of wingload. Turkey vultures have evolved as very efficient consumers of thermal lift, which is their primary means of locomotion. My gyr hybrids easily outclimb wild prairie falcons in powered ascents, but under the sole influence of thermal lift, the lighter prairie reigns supreme.

I've found that the affect of thermals on falcons also varies in relation to the location of the falcon within the thermal column. It is not unusual for a thermal to have little or no pull until the falcon is approximately 200–400 feet up. As the falcon spirals up the thermal column, the rate of ascent is increased. Initially, a particular thermal may elevate the falcon at a rate of ten feet per revolution at the bottom of the column. By the time the falcon reaches 1,000 feet, she may well be ascending at a rate exceeding 100 feet per revolution. It is simply amazing to watch a falcon in such lift speck-out within moments.

The height to which thermals rise before mushrooming or flattening out varies and is dictated by atmospheric conditions. I've seen some thermals that appeared to top out around 1,300 feet and others that seemed to rise indefinitely. Thermals lose a measure of continuity in windy conditions and wind wreaks havoc on a falcon's position. There often seems to be cleaner thermal activity earlier in the day before afternoon winds pick up. I usually work thermals between 10:00 and 11:30 a.m. in the late summer and progressively later as the days grow shorter. Throughout winter in California's Sacramento basin, thermal conditions can be few and far between; nonetheless, I've noticed that, occasionally, the air is conducive to extremely high pitches. Tremendous lift conditions often follow on the heels of a passing storm and are associated with low barometric pressure, blue skies and huge cumulo-nimbus clouds. The sky almost seems to suck the falcon upwards. The sight of a falcon back-dropped by this dramatic skyscape is powerful and inspiring.

Thermals are an effective means of flying falcons from extraordinary heights. Given an opportunity, falcons will utilize lift and revel in this environment. Thermals are the easiest and fastest method that I am aware of to teach falcons to wait-on and stoop from the upper atmosphere. I marvel at watching falcons just learning to fly, hooking a good thermal and then riding the elevator out of sight. Eyases must feel exhilarated performing their first stoops from breathtaking pitches. The velocity generated from these heights provides the falcon with a real shot at those oh-so-fast homers, and this is encouragement enough for the eyas to mount again and again for another opportunity at a pigeon. Intermewed falcons may be pulled out of the molt and put directly into thermals. The immediate results are towering stoops in spite of the falcon's current state of physical conditioning. This tack allows me to work falcons back into hunting condition, while recommitting them to big pitches. I am able to kick back and relax a little, knowing that I can serve the falcon when I choose, and if the falcon is still visible I can watch the entire stoop, something only occasionally possible in the realm of duck hawking. These are ample incentives for me to continue thermal training and watch stoop after stoop originating somewhere near heaven.

There are those who claim that thermals make for a lazy falcon, creating an unwillingness to mount without benefit of lift. This has not been my experience, perhaps because I do not train with thermals exclusively. I use thermals first and foremost to habituate the falcon to stoop from great heights. A falcon that has been properly habituated to hunt only from great heights will seek out pitch regardless of weather conditions, within reason.

Thermaling does come with certain risks and drawbacks, some of which are exacerbated under actual hunting conditions. Flying falcons in thermals does require a lot of open space. It makes little sense to attempt to teach the falcon to stoop from exaggerated pitches if cover or terrain prohibits this method from being successful. Also, falcons are far more likely to make contact with other raptors while thermaling, simply because there are more birds in the sky. My falcons have shared thermals with other falcons, hawks, eagles, harriers and vultures, some of which are more troublesome than others. My falcons interact most frequently with red-tailed hawks. Sometimes, these hawks will position themselves above and wide of the falcon, occasionally stooping the released homer but most often waiting for an opportunity to pirate a kill from the falcon. My falcons are well aware of the buteos and will forsake the kill in the wake of an incoming red-tail. Woe to the red-tail that takes to the air with the falcon's hard-earned prize, making itself a target for the incensed falcon who may pummel the thief in a relentless assault until, at last, it drops its stolen booty or reaches the sanctuary of cover.

On one occasion, I had recently pulled Indy out of the molt and released him into a thermal. When he was 1,300 feet up, a female prairie falcon showed up and immediately crabbed with him. They locked feet and both falcons began to plummet from the sky. This was not the typical attack of a haggard prairie falcon in a territorial dispute, rather it was a foolish play by an impetuous eyas in well over her head. As I watched both falcons disappear from view behind a large hill, still bound together, I was concerned but not terrified—not until I glimpsed a haggard hen red-tail streaking across the sky in a near supersonic stoop headed toward the entwined falcons. I wondered if the recklessness of the young prairie falcon would cause the demise of my treasured duck hawk. I ran toward the top of the hill but was forced to slow to a walk several times due to the steep incline. After six or seven minutes of huffing and puffing that felt like an eternity, I crested the hill and trotted down the other side to where I suspected the trio would have intersected. Suddenly, up ahead, the startled red-tail jumped up out of the tall grass, making a hasty departure. I cringed at the thought of what I would find ahead in the grass. As I approached, I saw the ravaged prairie falcon, which, upon seeing me, took to the air in an awkward, sideways fashion, seriously injured. She limped her way into the nearest tree as I resumed my search for Indy. There he was in the sky, riding a thermal, quite unscathed. Perhaps luck was on our side that day, but, no doubt, the lessons learned by these predators in their struggles to survive during their lifetimes gives them a decided advantage over their younger counterparts, who often meet untimely ends before many of life's lessons have been learned.

On another occasion, I was thermaling a 480-gram tiercel peregrine named Tino. I stumbled across a burrowing owl, which the falcon was all too happy to catch. When I arrived on scene it was a bit confusing as to who actually had whom; it looked like a draw. I separated the two combatants, neither of whom had sustained injury, and placed the owl in a cavity under a large boulder and proceeded to walk away feeding the tiercel as I went. I hadn't gotten far before the owl was back on the wing. The poor creature was immediately caught by a red-tailed hawk that had been aloft in a thermal. The hawk was, in turn, immediately assailed by a haggard hen prairie falcon, causing it to release the owl. Competition, natural selection, survival of the fittest—it's all there. The more time we spend in the field practicing falconry and observing wildlife, the more we begin to understand and appreciate these dynamics. Sometimes these events are subtle and at other times, quite graphic. Certainly whenever and wherever thermals are encountered uninvited guests should be expected.

Thermaling can dramatically increase the risk of falcons raking after distant and unintended quarry. Superhigh falcons can see for miles, and they are able to launch attacks covering vast distances in moments. The same may be said of the falcon that powers up into the sky *sans* thermals, but there is a distinct difference. Falcons that are muscling their way into the sky usually have an immediate agenda. They are focused and generally spend less time in the air, which helps minimize the risk of falcons raking after check. Falcons in thermals are often in the air for extended periods and are usually flying with less urgency. They have ample opportunity to visually scan surrounding areas while riding the airwaves, thus increasing the odds of exposure to check. Best to fly thermals in areas with a minimum potential for check, or plan accordingly.

My falcons have demonstrated a crepuscular tendency and appear to experience a biorhythmic low in the afternoon, especially the types of solar-heated afternoons that are most conducive to thermals. This may also affect the responsiveness of the falcon, particularly if she is flying at the upper end of her flying weight. Flying an unmotivated falcon in no-lift conditions will likely result in a lackluster performance. Flying an unmotivated falcon in thermal conditions can easily set the stage for long-distance tracking excursions. Under actual hunting conditions, thermals can be a strategic boon or bane. Waterfowl generally do not flush prematurely or disappear during the interim between the moment of casting the falcon off and the moment of flush, provided the falconer avoids making an error. This allows the falconer to consider thermals as a viable means of waterfowling if he or she so chooses. The same cannot always be said of upland game birds where premature flushes or birds creeping off are more common. Our friend the ringneck pheasant tops the list of troublemakers along these lines. A falcon that flies wide and takes more time to come into position is apt to be disappointed as the falconer moves past the locked

Wild anatum peregrine in thermal. Note the fanned tail, providing increased surface area for maximum lift.

oming in hot, with out-stretched et, a falcon prepares to impact arry.

The homer shifts and the falcon slides right on by.

A second-year falcon's age is divulged by the immature brown shoulder feathers after an incomplete moult.

Duck hawks find coots irresistable targets.
Photo: Vahe D'Ala

Dramatic skies such as this often produce extraordinary lift.

Beauty, grace, and uncanny intelligence place the pintail in a class unto themselves.

Releasing a homer from the top of a hill encourages the falcon to stoop vertically through her quarry, rather than stooping behind and leveling out before intersecting quarry.

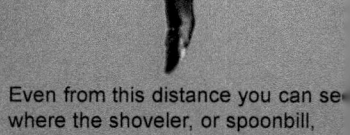

Even from this distance you can see where the shoveler, or spoonbill, gets its name.

Peregrine getting into position on incoming flight of ducks and geese.

Road training homing pigeons.

[Ho]ming pigeon struck by falcon survives the hit and then proceeds to out-fly the falcon and return [to] me.

Authors son, Austringer, doing the honors-catch and release.

Pigeon pursuit, pulling Gs.

Lookout! Coots will use their beaks defensively, always targeting eyes
Photo: Vahe D'Ala

Thermal training is a great way to re-condition sluggish falcons after the moult. *Photo: Sydney Mulligan*

Slightly off camera lies another mallard having been killed in one of these rare "two duck stoops."

r x peregrine tiercel, Shaman, pounds a hen pintail.

glish pointer "Jessy" working scent. Pointers can locate and point ducks knocked into cover.

Female goshawk taking hooded merganser.
Photo Leonard Rue III

Head study of female European goshawk.

LEFT: Explosive acceleration, extreme maneuverability and intense aggression are all hallmarks of the goshawk.

appy Hawker, Scott Timmons, having some success.

Black and beautiful, dark birds are easier to keep track of in the sky.

awking teal in the desert.

Photo by Cassi Roy.

When selecting a duck hawking dog, it's important to choose a breed you'll enjoy both in and out of the field.

Large ducks which are not killed or injured in the sky are capable of mounting a serious defense on the ground. Falcons are vulnerable to attack by other predators while engaged in these violent struggles.

Closing in fast.

The obligatory rouse before takeoff.

Immature gyr x peregrine on hooded merganser.

Three-quarter jerkin subdues mallard.

The author. Beach hawking with English setter pup. *Photo: Scott Timmons*

Start 'em young. Author's son Storm checking out the catch.

Mallards

Drake Wigeon
Photo: John Hendrickson

High Sierras pond hawking.

Drake mallard foraging in the shallows.

An average mallard can outfly most falcons in level flight.

Barrow's Goldeneyes *Photo: John Hendrickson*

Bufflehead pair *Photo: John Hendrickson*

This gorgeous line-up of snoozing mallards was photographed on the California coast.

Relaxed, well-adjusted falcons enjoy bathing.

Ringneck ducks (aka ringbills) usually flush very well.

al flights have the potential to work the hawking team to exhaustion.

Prairie portrait
Photo: John Hendrickson

Some pictures truly are worth a thousand words.

Strong homing pigeons can out climb most falcons and will do so provided they are thrown in a barren landscape.

Wide-open spaces are ideal training grounds for falcons. *Photo: Sydney Mulligan.*

LEFT:
Besides being excellent quarry, the beautiful wood duck is often found in picturesque settings making for an extraordinary falconry experience.

Thermal training the eyas-loads of fun under the sun. Don't forget to take along a spray bottle.

RIGHT:
Bright-eyed, preening falcon-a literal picture of health.

White jerkin-big, bad and beautiful.

OPPOSITE PAGE:
White gyr on a rock.
Photo: John Hendrickson.

BOTTOM:
Large and in charge, this three-quarter jerkin molted at thirty-eight and a half ounces.

Tiercel sonoran Harris hawk.

"Catching rays" on the beach.

Author launching Omen, tiercel gyr x peregrine hybrid.
photo: Sydney Mulligan

Omen spending quality time in a productive wetlands.

LEFT: The canvasback is considered to be the world's fastest duck and is certainly one of the strongest. This drake nearly marched right back into the pond with falcon in tow.

Dan Konkels' idea of a "proper mews."

BOTTOM: The difficulty in catching teal lies entirely in the flush.

Ducks in large groups are much easier to flush, and rightfully so, as the larger the number, the smaller the odds of being the one targeted by the falcon.

Drake Wood duck
Photo: John Hendrickson.

American Wigeon *Photo: John Hendrickson*

Grassy fields and sheetwater are a very enticing combination for "grazers" such as widgeon.

Catch and release, it's a beautiful thing. *Photo: Sydney Mulligan.*

A Pintail duck. *Photo: John Hendrickson.*

Pintail nest.
photo: John Hendrickson.

By targeting a duck's head, a falcon is less likely to sustain injury in a high-speed collision or, subsequently, on the ground because there is no confrontation.

Peregrine on rock. *Photo: John Hendri*

up pointer in expectation of an imminent flush but finds the pheasants have long since left.

So, how does one actually teach a falcon to thermal? The procedure is so basic, the act so natural, that it may be summed up in one word—exposure. Falcons develop the ability to thermal as easily as a baby learns to smile. If flown in lift conditions, the falcon will go up. It may take a few minutes or it may take a few hours to get the eyas into her first thermal. Be patient and let her explore. Should the falcon prefer not to fly in the heat on her own accord, toss a pigeon now and then. Eventually she will set her wings and let the updrafts push her high into the atmosphere where she will appreciate the cooler air above the baking earth. I bring along plenty of water for myself and a spray bottle for the falcon. Once the falcon has experienced her first thermal, she may be expected to utilize this form of lift whenever possible.

Selecting thermal locations carefully will help ensure good lift conditions and minimize some of the inherent risks. Uneven ground appears to enhance thermal formation. Hills and ridgelines are likely places for good lift. Hills are very useful for initial training because the falcon can be launched from the top. The elevation will help ensure that the falcon will feel the drafting push of the thermal column, which will be more active higher up. Often, the falcon will tip as she hits thermal air and is visibly bumped upward. The falcon will respond instinctively by cupping her wings, and fanning her tail, which increases surface area, in order to achieve maximum lift. By watching the tail of the falcon, one can get a good idea of when and where she is encountering thermal air as she soars. Observing wild raptors can clue the falconer as to where thermals are prevalent and the energy they are expressing. Obviously, thermal training an eyas in locations inhabited by eagles or an abundance of check is a recipe for disaster of one sort or another. A little common sense will go a long way toward making thermals a positive adventure.

To never indulge in the grand phenomenon of hunting with a falcon as she soars wildly far above the planet, patient in her thermal, is to miss one of falconry's richest experiences.

CHAPTER 10

Orchestration

There was a time when I believed that the crux of duck hawking was the flush. To an extent, I still believe that. Upon deeper examination, however, I envision many aspects of flight management as equally relevant to the production of the duck flight as a whole. It is the skillful orchestration of interwoven elements that allows a flight to flow so smoothly as to give the impression of sheer simplicity. If someone was to witness such a flight without benefit of knowing the inherent difficulties involved, he or she might easily misinterpret such a well-conceived and implemented flight as mere happenstance. When in fact, the strategy and execution involved was the culmination of a great deal of effort. In order to illustrate my point I'd like to describe a flight that took place last season.

It was a Sunday morning, the weather wasn't great but it wasn't bad either. I drove past one of my favorite fields and spotted two separate rafts of mallards in a large, oblong puddle. An excellent slip by any measure, and I knew I'd fly it later with Shaman. But right then I was headed just a few miles further down the road to a cattail pond. In most respects, the cattail pond is ideal. Situated between open pasture and rice checks, this pond gets plenty of waterfowl traffic. With ample cover, it attracts ducks with great magnetism. So long as the pond isn't overexploited, the presence of ducks this late in the season is almost a certainty, and since I was the only one even occasionally hunting this pond, burnout wasn't an issue. In fact, it had been two weeks since I'd last flown it, so I was extremely confident that it would be holding ducks. I decided to fly the pond "on spec," rather than risk a premature flush.

I ran through the usual preflight telemetry protocols and slipped a semisealed pigeon in my hawking bag, just in case the ducks weren't there. My two English pointers crawled through the tubular gate as I climbed up and over with the tiercel gyr hybrid, Omen the Headhunter, on my fist. Stepping into the pasture, I headed straight toward the pond some 350 yards away. If I'd had any lingering doubts about whether or not the set held ducks, they were quelled by the sight of mallards, winging in from the rice field then splashing into the pond. By then I had already begun removing Omen's leash, swivel and jesses. I paused before striking the hood braces as another group of mallards flew over the set. The small flock splintered and a couple of ducks splashed down, while another group went to the field, others cleared out entirely. I waited no longer, unveiled the falcon and held him in the air. Omen took to the air unceremoniously, stroking hard from the very onset. The Headhunter meant business.

The dogs and I strolled along at a leisurely pace allowing the falcon plenty of time to ascend as we made our way toward the set, still 300 yards away. Omen just kept cranking, never missing a beat as he spiraled ever higher into the overcast sky. Throughout his ascent, Omen never once intimated through his actions that he had any interest whatsoever in either the pond or the ducks it held. By the time the dogs and I were within 200 yards of the set, Omen was in a commanding position, halfway between the pond and us. When we were within 100 yards of the pond, the falcon was 1,600 feet up, still halfway between us and the ducks, and still cranking for more. This was also the point at which the dogs and I became visible to the ducks on the set, and at that moment eight of the mallards took their leave. It was just that simple. There was no running, yelling, waving or anything else. The sight of the dogs and me from 100 yards out was sufficient to send the flock on their way. Undoubtedly, these ducks had been shot at once too often and were hell bent on getting away from the dreaded biped.

At 1,600 feet the falcon was small but still clearly visible to the sharp-eyed mallards, yet it appeared as though the ducks had considered the falcon a minor threat, almost an afterthought. For sure, they hadn't paid Omen his due respect. The ducks flew hard, at a steep angle, unmistakably intent on a clean departure—no circling back to the pond today! With the ducks fully committed, I felt comfortable enough to take my eyes off them and just concentrate on the falcon. It took a few moments to pinpoint the projectile far above the earth as it hurtled toward the mallards in a stoop of mythical proportions. The Headhunter had missile lock and a clear line of sight on the imperiled ducks as they traversed open field to the north. The stoop was that of a graceful arc, the falcon gaining momentum as he went. As the gap between predator and prey closed, the angle of the attack sharpened so that the last several hundred feet were vertical. Omen intersected with the tightly knit band of mallards approximately 100 yards beyond the pond, some 200 yards from where I stood. He sliced through the flock, which by then was eighty feet up in the air. Omen's attacks are usually accentuated with lethal, surgical precision, and this one was no exception. There were no sloppy trajectory corrections in his stoop and no decrease in velocity before or immediately after the strike.

The sound one associates with the impact of a falcon body-slamming a mallard is noticeably absent. From a distance, one could easily get the impression that the attack has been unsuccessful. But in the millisecond it took Omen to begin his bottom turn, well below the flock, a hen crumpled, her skull crushed. The Headhunter, true to his name, had delivered yet another devastating headshot. I watched as the separation occurred. One duck's lifeless body fell headlong toward the earth, while seven others flew fast and strong, never looking back. The hen's body came to rest in the grassy pasture and the falcon calmly winnowed down to his kill. I checked the sky for any sign of incoming raptors, so did Omen, all was clear. The enormity of the encounter I'd witnessed was overwhelming and I knew without a doubt, I'd experienced something larger than myself. After collecting Omen and his prize, we headed back across the pasture and it occurred to me that nowhere on the planet will any human witness a finer sight than what I'd just seen—state of the art, classic through and through.

This kind of falconry exemplifies simplicity, and on the surface it may appear as though my contribution to the flight was minimal. But laying the groundwork in order to achieve and maintain such levels of artistry is labor intensive. Technically, the orchestration of this flight began the day I picked up the twenty-one-day-old eyas from Dave Jamieson's project in Reno, Nevada. All of the socialization, training, conditioning and entering procedures were precursory elements without which the end results I've come to expect would not have been possible. Omen's flawless performance was no accident or fluke, it was the reflection of prior experiences and encounters carefully sculpted over the course of his career. A lot of linear thought and preplanning went into creating the falcon's desired behaviors. Personally, I prefer to shape the falcon's flight style rather than letting nature take its course. By consciously choosing to shape behaviors and orchestrate flights in a desired manner, a falconer can dictate the kind of falconry that will be experienced. It is much easier to establish a desired flight style from the get-go than it is to change things later on, especially if the falcon has had some success the old way. Once a desired flight style has been established, consistent, well-orchestrated flights will maintain *status quo*.

Throughout the hawking season, the orchestration of any given flight begins immediately upon conclusion of the last flight. In order to adequately prepare for the next hunt, the last flight need first be evaluated. This postflight evaluation will provide a wealth of information without which it would be difficult (at best) to orchestrate the next. The evaluation deals with several issues. Topping the list are weight management themes. In order to make good use of weight-related information, at least this portion of the evaluation must take place immediately upon conclusion of the flight, before the falcon has been fed. Thus, we are not just feeding the falcon based solely on today's weight or performance, we are also feeding her an amount consistent with what we would like to have happen tomorrow. Attentiveness, strength, determination and aggression all must be assessed in order to manipulate the falcon's weight as deemed necessary.

The falcon's performance in its entirety should be analyzed, paying close attention to any negative behaviors or backsliding. If you saw something in today's performance that you didn't like, make plans to ensure that it doesn't happen tomorrow lest it become habitual. Finally, the falcon's confidence/skill level is gauged, thereby helping determine what type of slip should next be flown. In so doing, we have already laid the foundation for the flight yet to come. We've got the falcon's weight nailed, and if we haven't preselected a specific pond, we've at least decided what we are looking for. Perhaps we have chosen big water to ensure the falcon's failure, should she not take a high pitch. Maybe we've selected an easy set to shore up the downtrodden falcon's confidence. If the last hunt was "ratty," something that can be flushed cleanly would be a good bet. Additionally, the postflight analysis will help determine which tactics we'll adopt throughout the upcoming flight. Perhaps we kept the falcon on the wing too long and she raked, next time we'll be looking to flush sooner. If the falcon balked on big ducks today, we'll surely be looking for only big ducks tomorrow. There are times when it is in the hawk's best interest to not kill in order to "show her the light." Flushing can be used as a tool in itself, but must be used judiciously. Flushing ducks in a moment or in a manner which precludes her ability to kill, may terminate an undesirable behavior. Sometimes, not flushing at all is the only way to avoid reinforcing bad behavior.

From a tactical perspective, deciding when, where and how to flush ducks is largely determined by uncontrollable external factors, i.e., pond dimension, location, numbers and species of ducks, weather conditions, etc. The nuts and bolts of these tactical elements will be discussed elsewhere. For the time being I'd like to address some behavioral aspects from a conceptual standpoint. Following is an example of common behavior. A falcon learns to wait-on at pitch over a set, the falconer flushes, whereupon she stoops at the fleeing ducks—so far, so good. Eventually, the falcon learns to begin her stoop at the first wingbeat of any duck below. Not long after that she's stooping before the flush, jumping the gun as it were. This seemingly innocent little quirk can become quite pervasive and a real headache. All too often, what ends up happening is the falcon begins her stoop so prematurely that no duck in its right mind wants to fly under her. Thus, the odds of getting a clean flush, or any flush at all, are severely hampered. In the meantime, while the falconer is trying his hardest to flush (in spite of the falcon), the falcon blows her entire pitch on a pointless stoop at ducks with no intention of leaving. In a similar behavioral disorder, I've seen falcons take a pitch over a pond and then set their wings and rapidly lose altitude. In an attempt to minimize the negative effect, the falconer runs toward the pond hoping to flush the ducks before the falcon has lost all height. From here, things only get uglier. Rather than letting these little flaws take on a life of their own, better to nip them in the bud or prevent them from occurring in the first place through logical flight management practices.

In the case of the prematurely stooping falcon, one counter measure would be to flush only when the falcon is not stooping. Ideally, ducks should be flushed while the falcon is actively climbing. This not only avoids the premature stoop pitfall but also simultaneously reinforces the falcon's ascent. When she climbs, ducks are flushed. When she doesn't climb, ducks aren't flushed. This simple procedure puts the falconer back in control of the flight, as opposed to having the falcon calling the shots. The choice is yours, but if you don't decide, she will.

To date, I haven't seen anything in print that specifically deals with the biggest vice duck hawking has to offer—the "rat hunt." Maybe one of the reasons why is that the term itself is hard to define and subject to personal interpretation. We probably all could agree on some points, for example the flight I described at the beginning of this chapter, nothing ratty there. What about a flight that requires a remount and a second stoop? I've seen plenty of those in which the second stoop was from a higher pitch and more dramatic than the first. I wouldn't call that ratty, would you? How about a third stoop or a fourth? Is the number of stoops or their height the deciding factors? Perhaps the criteria should depend upon how wet the falconer gets. Maybe we could develop a grading system: dry feet = not ratty, wet shirt = ratty. But then that leaves a lot of middle ground, what if we are wet to the knees? Sure, I'm kidding with this, but the point is valid. The term rat hunt will always mean different things to different people. Heck, some people might enjoy a good ol' rat hunt just as much as anything else. The truth be told, I've enjoyed quite a few myself.

When I started duck hawking, I was just happy to catch a duck, style or not. I was really gung-ho back then and would take to the water like a fish if need be in order to make the flush happen. While my enthusiasm hasn't waned and I still get wet more often than not (they don't call it wetlands for nothing), I have come to realize that in some ways my extraordinary efforts have at times been misplaced. I suppose I underestimated the intelligence of the falcons I flew. Even today, my older falcon Shaman stands as witness to the error of my ways.

I wouldn't even care to estimate the number of ducks Shaman has pounded over water before they had a chance to clear land. It seems like such a simple concept—let the ducks clear, then, and only then, stoop. One thing for certain, if Shaman followed this basic doctrine, I would stay dry a lot more often. Once a duck has been hit, it is much harder to reflush, which in turn means I'm far more likely to have to plunge in. Who is managing whom here? I used to wonder why in heaven's name would Shaman keep pounding ducks back into the water when he could just hesitate, let them clear and catch them cleanly? Naah..the fault is mine. The only one not using their head here is me. Why on earth wouldn't the falcon pound away when the dogs and I just keep putting or pulling the ducks back out? These flights can get quite ratty indeed. As far as Shaman sees it, his job is to prevent ducks from escaping via the sky. To be sure, the duck that is foolish enough to try to slip past him has got another thing coming! The rest, though, is up to the dogs and me. The real bonus for Shaman is that no matter who comes up with the duck first, he'll end up with it in the end—he can't lose.

These are the kinds of things that can happen when you let falcons manage their own flights. The sensible thing for me to do at this point would be to just stop coming to Shaman's aid when he knocks a duck back in, and in some instances I have. It would be an interesting experiment if nothing else to see how long it would take such an entrenched behavior to fade. I suspect that the biggest hindrance would be me, not the falcon. I'm still addicted to the kill and I'm not entirely ashamed to admit it. When a duck has been knocked down one time too many and won't get back up, I'm not always above reaching in and pulling the duck out and serving the falcon. I am, I should point out, also likely to immediately remove the duck from the falcon in exchange for a reward, then liberate the duck. So you see, it's not so much the kill that I'm addicted to, it is the catch. Falconry is after all a hunting art.

What about style you say? Yes, what about style. It's a big question and there is so much gray area that a definition, let alone an answer, is illusive indeed. Some of the absolutely most stylish flights of any kind I've ever witnessed in twenty-five years of falconry involved Shaman, ducks on sheet water and dogs. These flights demonstrate the tiercel gyr x peregrine hybrid's capability and maneuverability like none other. They also provide me the visually unique opportunity to just stand back and watch the falcon and the dog do their thing. These flights typically involve several successive snappy wingovers and hard driving stoops, which one of my friends has described as the yo-yo effect. The aerial ability of this fine falcon is certainly well displayed throughout, as the dog repeatedly puts the ducks up and the falcon repeatedly puts the ducks down. Compared to the classic one-stoop duck flight, there is ten times the opportunity to observe the relationship between predator and prey skydancing with marvelous aerobatics. For me, the most remarkable thing about these extremely dynamic flights is the way the falcon dominates his quarry, sometimes herding large flocks over the surface of huge puddles—truly impressive. These flights have a class and style of their own and are some of the flights I look forward to most each year. Even so, for the last three seasons I've been adhering to an alternative flight management policy with my younger falcon Omen. His flights are all orchestrated with the explicit intention of killing from one long, dramatic stoop. And in fact, most of his terminate on the first stoop because his tremendous pitch allows ducks to clear so well. If the first stoop isn't successful and the ducks pile back in, or there are others yet to be flushed, I'll pause and wait for a remount. When the falcon remounts to his pitch, he is rewarded with another flush. If the flight begins to deteriorate for any reason, I'm much quicker to terminate the slip and I don't pull ducks out of the water for him. Micromanaging Omen's flights has produced some impressive results in the field, more than compensating for the extra effort required.

If dogs are used, they too must be factored into any flight management scheme. Their biggest contribution to duck hawking will be helping flush. Unlike upland game-hawking, where pointers are somewhat self-governing as they course fields searching for birds to point, duck hawking dogs require additional guidance. Obviously the timing of the flush can't be left up to the dog. When well managed, dogs are an invaluable asset to the duck hawk team.

The orchestration of a duck flight of course includes management of the ducks themselves. Through one means or another, it is the falconer's responsibility to provide the falcon with suitable opportunities to attack airborne ducks. Manipulating ducks into lethal situations will be further detailed in the Field Craft chapter. It should be noted that there are infinite variables associated with hawking ducks, therefore the manner in which slips are orchestrated need be as fluid as the water upon which ducks float.

CHAPTER 11

Field Craft

If there is one thing that separates duck hawking from all other falconry genres it is the water. Ducks use water as a primary means of defense when attacked by falcons; therefore, in order to be effective, most duck hawking strategies will have to include tactics that preclude ducks from maintaining or seeking refuge in water. Until a person has had the opportunity to witness ducks reacting to the presence or attack of a falcon, this may not seem too difficult, especially to those who have hunted waterfowl with shotguns. Flushing ducks is rarely, if ever, problematic for the gunner. Try flushing with a falcon overhead and suddenly everything changes. Ducks have a long evolutionary history with falcons and they have a firm grasp on predation and natural selection concepts. Consequently, flushing ducks can be technically demanding and any tactical errors in the falconer's technique will ultimately be paid for in the falcon's performance.

Most duck hawks make no attempt to deceive ducks by masking their presence or intentions. Thus, any ducks floating on a pond beneath a waiting falcon are operating under the premise that the falcon would pose a serious health risk if they chose to exit the pond. This predisposes ducks to not want to share airspace with the falcon. The challenge for the falconer, then, is to overcome the duck's innate flight inhibitions. In most instances this is accomplished through intimidation, making the pond less desirable than the air. Under optimal conditions, this may indeed be a reasonably simple achievement, and optimal generally refers to lesser amounts of water. In the case of small bodies of shallow water, ducks can definitely be flushed, one way or another. Note the word shallow, for ducks can at times be impossible to flush from even small bodies of water deeper than the falconer can easily wade. As one might expect, ducks are adept at submerging in order to elude would-be flushers if the water depth permits. In most instances, ducks resort to submersion after having been stooped at, at least once. This brings up a point of major concern. It has been said, "You never get a second chance to make a first impression." This is relevant to duck flushing in that the first attempt to flush is almost always the falconer's very best opportunity to get the ducks up and away cleanly. If, after the first flush, ducks pile back in avoiding the onslaught of the raging falcon, they will have learned two things: first and foremost, they will confirm that the falcon does indeed mean to kill them. Secondly, they will have learned that piling back into the pond is an option that you (the flusher) could not prevent. This isn't meant to imply that ducks can't be reflushed. Under many circumstances they can. But they can't be flushed as easily as they could have been the first time around, and with each successive botched flush they become less likely to make a clean break, so long as the falcon remains in position. This, then, is perhaps the quintessential rule of flushing: make a good first impression!

Keep in mind, the larger and deeper the water, the less vulnerable ducks feel. If a falconer is standing at the shoreline of a massive lake and ducks are rafting at the opposite end of the lake, it will be very hard to convince any duck that it would be in its best interest to fly under the waiting falcon. Any duck that has graduated from basic survival skills 101 (and by midwinter they all have) isn't likely to consider the falconer, from such an exaggerated distance, nearly as big a threat as the falcon directly above. The bigger the water, the more convincing the flusher need be.

Flushing ducks is part theatrics. In some respects it is a performance, and body language plays a critical role. When I'm flushing a tough set, I try to leave no doubt in the duck's minds that I intend to kill them; I am their worst nightmare incarnate.

The crux of duck flushing is to convince the ducks that you present a greater threat to their survival than the falcon. In those "iffy" sets where the ducks may or may not cooperate, the flusher need be most persuasive. Ducks must believe that the man can, and will, kill them if they don't get up and go. Those who do this well will reap the rewards of a clean flight and a heavy game bag.

Probably the biggest card the falconer has up his or her sleeve is the element of surprise. If you were to covertly observe a group of ducks that were on a midsize pond and then introduce the falcon, you would notice that the ducks wouldn't get too alarmed. Ducks know that the falcon poses little threat to their existence as long as they remain on the water. If you were to then show yourself from a little ways off and slowly approach the pond, you would see an immediate change in the duck's behavior. They would become much more nervous. The reason being, they would then be face to face with a real dilemma. Ducks instinctively fear man, and their natural impulse when approached is to take to the sky and put distance between themselves and the "hairless ape." But with a falcon in the air, ducks must choose. In terms of self-preservation, ducks are very capable of making wise choices indeed, and a wise choice under these circumstances equates with not flying under the falcon. The more time ducks have at their disposal to mull over such equations, the less likely they are to err and try their luck with the falcon. The element of surprise may be used in an attempt to circumvent the duck's decision-making process. Ducks taken completely by surprise by an aggressive flusher will react on impulse. Suddenly they have an immediate threat, which takes precedence over the falcon that had previously represented only a potential threat. When startled, ducks may flush cleanly without even giving a second thought. Often when ducks are flushed but not overly panicked, they will make a compromise. They'll get up all right, but they'll fly the length of the water never fully committed to leaving. If the falcon waiting above is of the sort to hesitate her stoop until the ducks clear, she may yet beat them at their own game. All too often, however, the falcon takes the bait and begins her stoop. This, being what the ducks suspected all along, comes as no surprise to them. They then easily thwart the falcon by splashing back in. By truly catching ducks off guard with an explosive flush, one can seriously impair the ducks' ability to plan such maneuvers in advance.

Flushing ducks isn't exactly rocket science, and everyone seems to have their own style. As a general rule, it is better to go overboard on the flush rather than risk insufficient intimidation the first time around. I try to inundate the ducks with sensory overload, using psychological, visual and acoustical methods. Remember, the objective is to disrupt the duck's capacity to rationally evaluate the crisis it suddenly faces. I flush most ponds armed with rocks. In fact, since some ponds don't have rocks lying around, I keep a bucket of conveniently sized rocks in the back of my truck. There have been innumerable instances when a well-thrown rock has made all the difference. Rocks being thrown create the illusion of being an extension of the man and have a profound effect on the duck's psyche. If a falconer just stands on the shoreline, there is a quantifiable distance between himself and the ducks. The ducks take comfort in this definable separation. If, however, the falconer creates watery explosions in close proximity to ducks, they don't feel the separation and believe themselves to be much more vulnerable. Put bluntly, well-thrown rocks can scare the hell out of them.

Rocks are also very useful in helping establish the direction of the flush. Rocks thrown behind ducks will get them moving in the opposite direction. When ducks are flying laterally over the surface of a pond, an additional rock or two splashed directly in front of them will greatly encourage them to stay on the wing and not bail. Thus, it often pays to have two or more rocks in hand while making the final approach. Depending on the difficulty expected, you may consider stashing a few extra rocks in your hawking bag as well, ready for use if need be. Better to have a couple of extra than not enough. Looking for additional rocks at a pond where there are none in the middle of a duck flight is frustrating to say the least. In a pinch, I've used just about whatever I could get my hands on such as clumps of mud, sticks, old beer bottles and cow pies. Years ago, I met a hardcore duck hawker who preferred to use a slingshot and marbles. He stated that he never flew ducks without them—considering the fact that he had a pocket full of marbles at the time, I think he meant it. I've heard of others going a step further and using firecrackers and guns to scare the bejeebers out of ducks. While I don't doubt the effectiveness of explosives and firearms to frighten ducks, I do find it somewhat distasteful, besides which, I suspect that many of the landowners who appreciate the lower profile I generally keep, would promptly "show me the door" if I took up such antics. Furthermore, the idea of conditioning a falcon to the sound of actual gunfire, as if it were the dinner bell seems a bad precedence that may ultimately lead to her demise. Nonetheless, I do at times handclap, which often triggers a panic response in ducks. By and large, however, when it comes to making noise it is the traditional falconer's yell that I invoke to ring terror in their ears.

Flushing ducks is every bit as visual an affair as acoustical, and then some. Aside from the mere approach of man, ducks are further intimidated (or not) by what they see the man do. Aside from running toward them (not from a distance), yelling at them and hurling rocks at them, I also wave my arms. Sometimes I swing a jacket or a hawking bag over my head. The motion of large swinging objects can really unnerve ducks. I've heard of others eliciting a similar response by rapidly opening and closing an umbrella pointed at ducks. My assumption would be that in either case these visual ploys stimulate a response associated with that of eagles.

In North America, both bald and golden eagles prey upon waterfowl. I have seen impressive video footage of a golden eagle stooping and knocking a buffelhead out of the sky in very falconlike style. Unlike falcons, baldies (closely associated with aquatic habitats) are adept at plucking ducks right off the surface of the water. Hence, when baldies course low over the water, ducks routinely get up and fly off in advance of the eagles' approach. Thus, any undulating objects as the above mentioned, that stimulates the ducks' "eagle response," may achieve the desired results.

Sometimes ducks require additional incentive above and beyond these methods. Sometimes it comes down to just how far the falconer is willing to go. Most men will stop their forward rush just at the water's edge, and this immediately registers as a barrier to the ducks. Yes, rocks can help bridge the gap, but sometimes rocks won't cut it. When ducks see a man stop short, reluctant or unwilling to immerse himself, they are reassured of their relative safety in their liquid realm. On the other hand, when a man hits the water running and continues, even just a couple of strides, looking as though he intends to run over the top of the ducks, it can shatter their confidence. They no longer feel as though water is sanctuary after all. This is why dogs are so beneficial to duck flushing; they dive in and invade the duck's place of refuge. Thus, dogs can do much of the wet work, and when dogs are used the falconer stands a much better chance of flushing ducks while staying dry in the process. Even so, the man willing to get his feet wet will surely flush some ducks that won't otherwise budge. How bad do you want it? When you consider all of the effort that goes into creating and maintaining a fine duck hawk, I for one, am willing to soak my boots in order to serve a diligently waiting falcon. If the only thing holding up a flush for a well-placed falcon is me getting wet, you can pretty much figure I'm going in. Sometimes there's just no other way.

A good soaking in a southern climate on a warm day is no big deal, but when things are chilly it takes quite a bit of commitment to take the plunge. Unfortunately, the colder it gets, the less inclined some dogs are to help out. Rather than going in after ducks, they tend to run around the perimeter barking at them. I suppose one could argue that my dogs have shown more common sense than I have on occasion, but then again, the dogs aren't particularly concerned about keeping the falcon happy either. I remember a specific occasion when I was working in the Mammoth area of the Sierra Nevadas in the dead of winter. I came upon a fairly large lake that was iced over except for a small portion of open water at one end. There were quite a few divers on the water and when I put the falcon in the air, they knew they were in for some trouble. Those ducks didn't want to budge. I tried to coax the pointer into the water, but had no luck. I even tried to push the dog forward into the water, which usually works, but he was having no part of it on that frigid day. I knew if I could get a duck to go, it would be easy picking, but the only way to get them up would be to go in and do it myself, which is what I ended up doing. Ironically, after I'd gone in, the dog figured he might as well also. We did get the ducks moving and the falcon did catch one, but in the process I nearly froze certain portions of my lower extremities right off, or so it felt. Afterwards, I asked myself, would I do the same thing tomorrow if need be? I decided I probably wouldn't, but there's no denying that if I went a couple of days without a slip and I was faced with a similar situation, I would. How bad do you want it?

The level of difficulty in regards to flushing sets varies widely depending on several factors, many of which the falconer has little or no control over. The amount of water is one of the most significant aspects. The species of ducks and their numbers will also play a critical role. Bigger flocks are more cooperative; it is a safety in numbers mindset. The length of time a specific duck (or group) has spent on a particular body of water will likewise have an impact. The more intimately familiar ducks have become with a certain pond, the more difficult it can be to pry them off the surface of the water. Meanwhile, ducks new to a pond will be much more easily manipulated. One variable the falconer does have control over is the falcon, namely her pitch, positioning and proximity.

In the past, I typically approached a set as closely as possible without flushing the ducks before releasing the falcon. This seemed like good strategy since less could go wrong when the pond was close at hand. This also eliminated the ugly syndrome I'd encountered when the falcon would lose serious amounts of altitude while I ran toward a set to flush ducks from farther out. There was, however, a negative side to this method. Falcons that were released very close to a set tended to intimidate ducks unnecessarily. This in turn made flushing them more difficult. I have since found that when falcons are released well away from the set and mount to appreciable heights before coming over the ducks, they are far less intimidating. Under these circumstances, the ducks are more inclined to flush cleanly.

Aside from proximity, the positioning of the falcon can make or break a slip. Ducks are much more cooperative when falcons are wide as opposed to directly above, especially when the falcon is at a lower pitch. They'll regularly take advantage of a falcon's misjudgment in positioning, taking off when the falcon is too far out to make up the distance, thus insuring their escape. Notice how some ducks refuse to flush in spite of our best efforts, until the very instant the falcon is sidetracked and momentarily out of touch. Then, all at once, the ducks erupt from the water to take their leave. For this reason, whenever the falcon is too far out of position, great care must be taken in order to minimize the risk of a premature flush. Crouching down behind cover may make the difference between the ducks staying put or not, in which case the profanity flies as surely as the ducks themselves. This innate escape behavior on the part of the ducks may be capitalized upon with a well-timed execution of an out of position flush, but one in which the falcon can make up the distance. The higher the falcon, the more ground she can make up, thus the easier to orchestrate. Nonetheless, this tactic can be very effective at even modest pitches if timed right (obviously faster falcons are capable of compensating for greater distances than are slower ones). Similarly, flushing out of position is virtually a natural byproduct of flights with multiple flushes in quick succession, where ducks are exiting the pond as staggered, splintered groups in chaotic panic. These flights usually terminate when a duck swings just a hair too wide and the falcon chops it down. Sometimes, instead of continually flushing the set, it is possible to flush a portion of the ducks when the falcon is wide—if she can make up the distance, fine, if not, that's okay too. If the falcon engages one group of ducks in a brief tailchase, the falconer then has something to work with. With the falcon's attention elsewhere, all flushing attempts cease; if need be, all flushers drop out of sight in order to prevent the remaining ducks from leaving prematurely. The timing of the next flush is dependent upon how far out and up the falcon goes before breaking off from the pursuit.

The remaining ducks, having seen their peers take off, become emboldened. Probably a combination of, "If he can do it, I can do it," along with, "Oh damn, I don't want to be the last duck on the pond!" Regardless, they are more inclined to cooperate after having been left behind by the others. If the falconer calculates the timing reasonably well, the falcon should be able to intercept them. The relative speed of the duck species involved should be considered, keeping in mind that divers will take longer to get up speed. This technique is enhanced when there is another body of water nearby. You can pretty much count on the first group of ducks flying toward the adjacent water if given half a chance. It is a very good bet that the second group will follow suit. This makes the timing of the second flush less critical because the falcon will then definitely intercept the second group somewhere in between the two ponds while on her way back to the first—it's just a question of where.

A variation of this tactic involves putting a falcon up where ducks aren't, but where they will be. Whether it is a known flight corridor for ducks (at a specific time) or if a remote assistant intentionally flushes ducks toward the falcon, the desired results are the same. Unsuspecting ducks will be flying toward and, hopefully, under the waiting falcon. A lofty pitch will dramatically increase the odds of ducks entering the falcon's killing cone. Whenever ducks are even temporarily unaware of the falcon's presence or location, they are at a huge disadvantage. Stealth is a way of life for many raptors, yet falconers by and large underutilize stealth in their orchestration of flights. Admittedly, it is difficult to mask the presence of a falcon circling overhead. Even so, there are occasions when stealth can and should be used as a means of facilitating a clean flush. Ducks in steep-sided ditches can sometimes be flushed without them even knowing a falcon is in the air. The same can be said for ducks in overhung or tree-lined ponds. Wild falcons use visual obstructions to their advantage, why shouldn't falconers? Orchestrating a midday slip so that the falcon stoops "from out of the sun," will make it tough for ducks to see what is going on up there.

Rather than always following a set blueprint, keep an open

mind when lining out a slip in order to fully exploit the set to the falcon's advantage. Devise a flight plan before releasing the falcon and include a contingency should things go awry. Here's an example that simulates a common gun hunter's tactic. Under certain circumstances, ducks may develop a strong attraction for a certain pond, so much so that when flushed they will return to their beloved pond within a few minutes. Gunners will often flush flocks of ducks off "potholes," then quickly set their decoys and take cover. As the previously flushed ducks begin to filter back in, the shooter will enjoy multiple opportunities to have a crack at inbound targets. I haven't personally gone so far as to flush a pond first and then put the falcon on the wing. I have, however, taken ducks that have returned to a pond minutes after having been flushed under a falcon. Thus, if the likelihood of ducks coming back to a particular pond is high, an unsuccessful hawk can be kept on the wing in the hopes of slamming a duck that just couldn't stay away. Once again, a lofty pitch will dramatically increase the odds of ducks entering the falcons killing cone. This method can be a very satisfying way of salvaging a slip that wasn't panning out. Do be careful to avoid keeping the falcon on the wing too long, lest she become bored and rake, or tire and land. Remember that the way you orchestrate a flight will leave an indelible impression on the falcon. This is of immense importance to those falconers interested in maintaining a specific standard or flight style.

Whenever ponds require a lengthy, exposed approach by the falconer, there is a temptation to make a dash for the pond in order to cover the distance as quickly as possible. This type of approach has two very negative side effects. Running toward a set (not to be confused with running at ducks near or around the perimeter of the pond) will almost certainly tempt the falcon into a pre-emptive stoop. This then establishes a pattern that will surely result in a degradation of the falcon's pitch prior to the actual flush. Furthermore, running at the set may indeed get the ducks up, but quite often it fails to get the ducks out! When a falconer flushes a duck well before reaching the pond, he has little leverage in preventing them from piling back in, which they are very prone to do when flushed in this manner. By the time the falconer finally arrives on scene, the ducks will have already bailed once and, in all probability, the falcon will have lost significant pitch. Use a little psychology to better the odds. Approach sets in a steady, slow, nonchalant manner. Act as though you don't know, or care, that ducks are there. If you don't walk directly toward the ducks, they are more apt to believe in the ruse and you will stand a much better chance of the ducks remaining on the set until you have come within reasonable flushing distance.

Sometimes, however, the ducks are going to get up prematurely anyway. If they do, that's okay. You've got two options and the best course of action will depend on how big an influence you can be from the remaining distance between you and them. A lesser distance and a smaller pond translates into more influence, whereas a longer distance and larger pond translates into less influence. It is wise to compute these details in advance and throughout the approach in order to act decisively when the time comes. Perhaps even draw an imaginary line at the threshold of what is and is not too far out. If the ducks jump before you have reached the threshold, it may be best to just ignore their actions. If they're going to dump, they're going to dump. If you react to them by yelling, running, etc., it may just make things worse by instigating the falcon. If you squat down, let the ducks do what they are going to do and don't encourage the falcon, the ducks may quickly settle right back, in which case even if the falcon went for them, she probably didn't get far. She's also more likely to remount if you haven't gone wild. Let her remount, regain all of her pitch, and maybe she'll go even higher while you proceed forward slowly and deliberately. If you keep a watch on the ducks' body language out the corner of your eye, you should be able to predict when the ducks are getting ready to take off.

Individual ducks don't want to be the first or last to go. They become increasingly fidgety on the water as they mill around one another prior to take off. Use this information to better time the execution of the flush. An assessment of the ducks' body language may also yield subtle clues as to which direction the ducks would like to bolt. Given a choice, ducks will flush in the direction they feel offers the best hopes of self-preservation. Sometimes for the sake of the falcon, they need to be steered in another direction. The direction of the falconer's approach can often dictate the direction of the ducks' departure, but the ducks' determination to fly in a specific chosen direction should not be underestimated. If, by chance, the ducks' preferred direction happens to coincide with that of the falconer, things are made simpler. Flushed ducks typically like to fly toward the next nearest water when available. So long as there is ample distance in between for the falcon to make a strike, the best chance of orchestrating a clean flight may consist of flushing the ducks that direction. Obviously, the falcon's pitch will determine just what ample distance is.

Great care should be taken to not disappoint a high-flying falcon. Prevent ducks from reaching the next pond before the falcon can get down, lest she abandon her lofty ways. If the falconer has a field assistant, he can be positioned where he can intercept the ducks just prior to their arrival at the second pond. So long as the assistant is well concealed, the ducks should flush as easily as ever. As they approach the second pond, the assistant suddenly leaps into action with a mighty commotion causing the ducks to flare from their would-be sanctuary. This affords the falcon the opportunity to make good use of her pitch.

Weather (wind in particular) will also influence the direction of the flush, both in terms of what the ducks want and what's best for the falcon. Weather is such a tactically significant factor as to warrant a chapter of its own. In a nutshell, ducks prefer to fly into the wind and not only because it assists in their lift off. Ducks either consciously or, more likely, instinctively appreciate the dynamics of wind shear. The average falcon will fare better stooping downwind, though an accomplished falcon with a grasp of the mechanics of positioning can take ducks flushed into a strong wind.

I have found that the desirable direction of a flush is usually dictated by either geography, positioning of ducks on the set or where the greatest hazards lie. Even then, it's not always cut and dry. Consider the following. Many ponds have a dam on one edge. Ordinarily, the least conspicuous approach (element of surprise) is by way of the dam. Using this method, the ducks will be pushed toward the opposite end, this may well have the ducks flying directly over a tributary, which can really put a wrench into an otherwise potentially clean flight. In order to avoid this, the ducks could be approached from the tributary end instead; that would result in the advantage of sending the ducks out over the dam. Ducks thus knocked down are unlikely to get back up over the dam to regain the pond before the falcon is upon them.

Sometimes the best possible approach comes from neither end of an oblong-shaped pond, but rather from somewhere in between depending on where the ducks are. The idea being, the falconer attempts to cut the ducks off from the main body of the pond by approaching and angling toward them to push them out whichever end is closest. The location of ducks on almost any set is critical to the direction of flush and, therefore, to the approach as well. Getting ducks up over land as soon as possible is usually preferable to flushing them over the length or width of the pond; the longer ducks are flying over water, the more time (and opportunity) they have to consider bailing out. Based on this premise, it would seem wise to push them toward the nearest edge of the pond relative to their position. Using this formula, ducks are approached from the opposite side of a pond in order to send them over land not water. This method works fine on small to midsize water. However, on big water sets, the gap between the falconer and the ducks on the opposite side can be prohibitive. Lobbing rocks that don't even reach the halfway mark and yelling at ducks that can barely hear you isn't particularly effective. Sure, you could approach them from the other side, but then you will be sending them back across the expanse of all that water—again, not particularly effective. Thank heaven for dogs.

When flying big water, dogs are a godsend. With dogs falconers can approach big water sets from the far side and still be effective. A dog will either swim directly across, which should push the ducks out the other end, or the dog will run around the perimeter of the water and be on top of the ducks in short order.

Now, the ducks are pinched between the dog on one side and the falconer on the other. As the dog jumps in and swims toward them, the ducks are in an awkward position, and quite often the result is a clean flush.

Unfortunately, when hawking in the twenty-first century, all too often the direction of a flush will be dictated by one form of hazard or another. The three leading causes for concern are all man-made and potentially lethal to the duck hawk. These are fences, power lines and roads. Of these three, power lines are the hazard I most fear. When you stand on the road and look up at power lines against a blue sky, there is good contrast and they appear to be visually obvious. But when you look at power lines against the backdrop of a hillside, which is similar to the backdrop a falcon sees from up above, there is far less contrast. In fact, the lines can be darn near invisible, and multiple wires can easily impede depth perception, making a collision a very real possibility. One should always carefully consider flying a set with power lines anywhere in the vicinity.

Fences are the most common man-made hazard my falcons encounter. While it may be impossible to always guarantee a duck flight will go in a certain direction thus avoiding collisions, it is wise to flush in the safest direction possible and skip the sets which present an unacceptable risk. Never assume that a falcon that hasn't been introduced to fences will avoid them.

Sometimes, when flying tricky setups, the best hopes for a flush is to first move the ducks to a more vulnerable location on the set. If you anticipate or encounter difficulty flushing the ducks in a normal fashion, they may be alternatively bumped or herded into a more conducive location. Many bodies of water are very irregular in shape. Herding or bumping is best done with a slow, judicious approach. The object is to maneuver the ducks through controlled manipulation and not to panic them (not yet anyways). Some ponds neck down considerably at inlets and/or outlets. Many such tributaries provide good vegetative shelter, which ducks readily take advantage of given a chance. By approaching indirectly and not making eye contact, ducks milling around the entrance to such tributaries may slip right on in, believing the falconer hasn't yet detected them.

With any luck, they may even paddle a little ways up or downstream to better conceal themselves. This is their undoing, for they have willingly isolated themselves from the pond and are ripe for harvest. Sometimes herding takes the form of one or several subdued flushes (bumps) wherein ducks are "leapfrogged" to a desirable section of the pond where they can be pinched into a corner and cut off from the main body of the pond. These sorts of manipulation may well require the falconer to exercise extreme aggression to finally execute the flush when the ducks are in the desired location. In this situation, the willingness of the falconer to get his feet wet often makes all the difference, because the previously bumped ducks have felt the presence of the falcon breathing down their necks. Their natural inclination would be to continue hop-scotching around the pond and not leave at all. If the falconer can place himself directly between the cornered ducks and the rest of the water, he can send them packing in spite of their better judgment. Even if the ducks renege, the falconer should still be able to force them to swing wide. As they fly around him, the ducks may be over land just long enough for a well-positioned falcon to make the hit and close the deal. Using a dog or a team of flushers can really augment the herding tactic by enabling the falconer to work both sides of the water simultaneously.

When manipulating ducks into a flushing position, keep in mind that puddle ducks and diving ducks don't take off in the same manner. Whereas puddlers can take off vertically, divers need a running start in order to generate enough speed for lift off. Therefore, divers can't be corralled at the very end of a pond and expected to fly straight away out over land. Plan accordingly and leave divers sufficient space to get airborne, otherwise they'll turn and head back over water or, worse, dive.

There may be occasions when the falconer wishes to flush selectively, rather than flushing the entire pond. Such is the case when hoping to fly multiple falcons in succession, or perhaps the set contains a mixed flock and the falconer would prefer to flush only a select species. More often it is a matter of which species the falconer doesn't want to flush, i.e., coots! Rather than flushing the pond in its entirety, selectively flushing the pond with dogs held in check may mean the difference between an awesome pintail flight and just another coot slaying.

Once ducks have lifted off, a falconer's natural inclination is to look at the falcon and watch the stoop. The reality is that "lift off" by no means guarantees that the ducks are going to fully cooperate, and a slip that begins with all the hallmarks of an epic flight can turn on a dime into a fiasco. I learned this the hard way with my first peregrine.

I was looking for a quick afternoon flight while on my lunch break and was pleased when I found ten wigeon on a nearby pond. I cast the peregrine into the warm afternoon air and watched her fly to the base of Wolf Mountain, where she hooked a thermal and began to ascend. The thermal was really active, and in short order she was way up in the sky. At the time, I had never flown in thermals before, so I was both anxious and excited. When the falcon came over, she was 900 feet up; this was the biggest pitch she'd taken to date and much higher than the meager pitches to which I had been accustomed. I went in for the flush; the wigeon blasted off without any hesitation, rising at a fairly steep angle. I shifted my attention back to the falcon, caught sight of her in all her glory and watched, transfixed, as she audibly cut a thin sliver out of the sky plummeting toward earth. I was all but overwhelmed with excitement as I anticipated the climax, a climax that would never come to pass. Unbeknownst to me, the crafty little bastards had decided to double back and pile back into the pond. The falcon aborted her stoop, no hope of reaching them before they splashed in. I was disappointed to say the least. My anxiety was further compounded by the fact that the falcon was denied an excellent opportunity to reinforce a stellar performance. Knowing what I know now about ducks, particularly wigeon, the outcome of that flight isn't surprising. I also know now that the outcome could have, and should have, been avoided. I resolved myself that day never to be caught off guard in that manner again, and to the best of my recollection I haven't.

Unless the falconer takes countermeasures, ducks piling back in ahead of the falcon will be a common occurrence. Flushing ducks differs from flushing game birds. Game birds aren't in the habit of returning to the same patch of cover from which they were just flushed. Once game birds are up and away, the falconer is then free to stand down and absorb the action as the flight unfolds. Such is not the case in duck hawking. In the case of waterfowl, a high percentage of flushed ducks will attempt to boomerang back to the pond in order to escape the falcon. When this occurs, it is up to the falconer to intervene on the falcon's behalf. It is imperative that the falconer plans for this and act accordingly. Ordinarily, after the falconer has executed the flush, he must continue to monitor the duck's departure. I frequently yell and wave my arms at the ducks well after they have gotten under way. Primarily, this is an attempt to unquestionably convince them that they have made the right and only choice in leaving and deny them the opportunity to reconsider their plight. Additionally, I do it to create a distraction. If a falconer were to just stand back and complacently watch the ducks go, the ducks could then focus entirely upon the falcon and their reactions would reflect this. If, however, through distraction, the falconer can divert even a little of the ducks' attention, they are far more likely to either leave cleanly or at least hesitate in making the crucial decision in regards to returning. While that brief interlude of indecision may seem insignificant, in the high-speed world of duck hawking it can mean everything. Once the ducks fly past the point of no return, they have sealed their fate and the falcon will have her moment.

Much of the time, ducks will make a U-turn before reaching the "no-return zone," regardless of the falconer's performance. In some instances, a quick-footed falconer can get between the ducks and the water they so desperately crave. For this reason, it is beneficial to move with the flush in order to block the returning ducks whenever possible. Sometimes, the ducks can be waved off, even when the falconer isn't exactly between them and the water. Other times, it doesn't matter where the falconer is situated; the ducks are going to come in no matter what and they can't be stopped. This tends to occur more frequently after the falcon has struck a duck once already.

Several years ago, I was scouting a slip for Indy. I found a lone hen hooded merganser on a small, isolated pond. The pond was dammed on the southern edge, making for an easy, stealthy approach. As a matter of fact, everything about the slip seemed easy, maybe too easy. Indy flew around the pond and I'm sure he looked down at that little duck in that little pond and he, too, thought this one was as good as in the bag. With the falcon directly overhead and rocks in hand, the dog and I sprang over to the top of the dam and scared the holly hell out of the merg. She instantaneously paddled into a takeoff and flew straight away. Indy, a well-honed duck-killing machine, snapped into a stoop and smashed the little hen out of the sky. Ordinarily, this would be the end of the story, but not this time. Indy was so confident, he was a bit on the cocky side. Instead of executing a quick wing over to seize the duck on the ground, he leisurely pitched up on the outrun, thinking he had all the time in the world. The merganser had other ideas. Before rolling to a complete stop after being struck down, she was back on her feet and then into the air. This time, however, she wasn't flying away. She was flying straight back toward the pond—her only hope. I'm pleased to say that I wasn't just standing idly by while all this was going on. I had in fact anticipated this possibility, so it was by no means a coincidence that I was smack dab between the little duck and her sanctuary. I took a wide-spaced stance meaning to block as much of the pond's narrow edge as possible, all the while yelling and waving my arms at the incoming refugee. I knew the merg wanted in desperately and I didn't know if I could keep her out, but I was pretty sure I could force her to swing wide, maybe just wide enough to give Indy a chance to catch up before she bailed. Apparently I wasn't nearly as impressive as I'd hoped (or as Indy had been!) because that little hen just kept coming. You can't fully appreciate 650 grams of merganser until it smacks you square between the legs full tilt. Needless to say, I was doubled over in considerable pain as the merg entered the pond. There she would wisely remain, at least until dark. In spite of overwhelming odds, the little hen craftily bested us that day. She certainly earned all the respect and admiration I could muster.

Duck hawking is an in-your-face art in which the falconer is an active participant during the whole process. The more engaged the falconer remains as the flight unfolds, the better he will be able to affect the outcome. There are times when the falcon's best or only chance to score is to let ducks back into the pond. You'll notice that occasionally, ducks flying with good speed (perhaps even pulling away from the falcon) may still want to dump, rather than clear out. I suppose it is a lack of confidence on their part. They don't want to commit to the big blue sky with the falcon dogging them. Consider stepping back, taking cover and allowing the ducks to come in. If the pond is conducive, let the falcon remount and then reflush the duck. Follow this procedure for prodigies being conditioned to kill from lofty vertical stoops only.

When hawking duck out of ditches, it doesn't take long to realize that the duck's fundamental desire is to fly along the length of the ditch and plop back in when pressed by the falcon. The duck is more than willing to repeat this maneuver over and over until everyone is exhausted and ready to forget the whole thing ever happened. In order to avoid this *faux pas*, ducks need to be approached in such a way as to be driven straight away out of the ditch and over land. If two flushers are on hand, each man may simultaneously approach the duck from either side, thus pinching it between them. Whenever an assistant is used at the ditch, or anywhere else, it is necessary to fully instruct them as to just what should and shouldn't be done.

I was out hawking one day with three guests, one of whom was a falconer and the other two were not. I had scouted a small group of mallards in a favorite ditch and lined out a plan of action for my companions. I positioned the other falconer in some cover upstream of the ducks and instructed him to stay put until I executed the flush, at which time he would block any ducks that flew in his direction. In the meantime, I took the remaining two members of the party downstream with me. With the ducks positioned between us, the flush was a slam dunk in the making. It was warm and sunny when I released the falcon, which began to thermal as he drifted slowly in the breeze. I kept tabs on his progress and in short order the falcon was 800 or 900 feet and about a half mile down wind. "Great," I thought. "In a few minutes he'll really be up there, then he'll come over for the serve and my guests will be treated to a fine duck flight indeed!" It was just a matter of biding my time. Presently my attention was drawn back toward the ditch as all the mallards were breaking out in a panic. I glanced upstream and it was then that I saw my fellow hawker making his way downstream along the water's edge. I was dumbfounded to say the least. The departing ducks drew the attention of the falcon who was too far out of position to engage. Fortunately I had a homer on hand to serve the falcon. Afterwards, I questioned my helper as to why he'd flushed the ducks. He replied that he couldn't see me and was uncertain as to what was happening so he decided to make his way downstream and had not intended to flush them. Why he hadn't backed off of the ditch, I'll never know, but in his moment of impatience he spoiled what was destined to be a fine flight and a unique opportunity for the other guests.

I usually hawk alone (surprised?) and have found that a lone falconer can hawk ditches very effectively. Generally speaking, ditches that wind around are easier slips to orchestrate than straight ones. The key to flushing ducks from ditches is entirely in the approach. It is imperative to come up over the top of them, thus sending them directly out the other side. Otherwise, if the approach is made from the side, the flush will most likely result in the ducks being pushed farther up or down the watercourse. As usual, larger groups of ducks will be more easily flushed than singles or pairs. When ducks are initially spotted in a ditch, they need to be marked. Pick something, such as a boulder, bush or anything else, that will be visible from the angle of final approach. Note whether the ducks are currently stationary or if they are moving. If so, which direction and how fast? Even if the ducks aren't moving, it's not a bad idea to double-check their precise location just before springing them. Make every effort to pop up dead center. An exception may be made in cases where the ditch makes a sharp bend. In such cases the ducks may be approached from an angle and flushed toward the bend. Remember to flush ducks toward the outside edge of the curve. Ducks thus flushed will have a greater distance to travel, should they attempt to regain the ditch.

When ditch flushing, it is important to be prepared to move

laterally along the edge. Most ditches aren't so wide as to allow ducks to comfortably land directly across from a screaming human monster. So, a falconer moving quickly in the right direction stands a fair chance of waving off any duck that turns around looking to bail. Once a duck has returned safely to the ditch, the prospects of a positive outcome are radically diminished. You probably stand a better chance of jumping in and catching the duck in shallow water by hand than flushing it out of the ditch. But remember not to do too much dirty work for the falcon, as this sort of thing can quickly become habitual. Before you know it, the falcon will start thinking her job is to intimidate ducks back into the ditch so you or the dog can catch it for her!

Regions harboring large concentrations of waterfowl may provide somewhat unorthodox opportunities for the duck hawker. Many thousands of acres of the Sacramento Basin are covered with rice fields. Historically, after the rice was harvested in the fall, rice stubble was burned in order to speed up the decomposition process in preparation for the next planting. Unfortunately, the burning of fields has contributed significantly to the poor air quality in the valley. This condition has sparked legislation mandating a phasing out of rice stalk burning. Farmers have alternatively resorted to flooding their rice checks to hasten stalk decomposition. This practice has had an impact on ducks and duck hunters alike. Flooded rice checks provide very attractive feeding and loafing habitat to waterfowl. On the surface, more habitats and more ducks would seem beneficial to hunters, and in some respect it has been so. But with more habitat to choose from (much of it nonhunted), state refuges and private gun clubs alike have experienced a decrease in duck harvest numbers. Some of the hunter's farther south are none-to-happy either, as more water up north has apparently translated into fewer ducks to the south. From a falconry perspective, specifically in the basin region, large-scale field flooding has its ups and downs. Gunners, who are largely responsible for moving ducks around in the basin, have become less influential as ducks settle into the nonhunted zones. With fewer ducks moving around, the likelihood of fewer ducks finding and utilizing the typical sets falconers are scouting is high. I would also imagine that the potential for pond burnout would be significantly higher as well. In some respects, falconers have a leg up in that some farms that prohibit guns may be receptive to falconers. While hundreds of acres of wall-to-wall flooded rice checks may not be ideal slip material, they can be flown and at the same time, produce some truly interesting flights. They can also provide both falcon and falconer with a great deal of exercise. It's not so much the standing water that makes for tough travel, it is the gumbo that makes each step laborious and slow. Flooded checks are a bit of a paradox. It's not altogether uncommon to see hundreds, in some cases thousands, of ducks rafting on the checks. When you look at all those ducks it almost seems impossible to not catch one. Then you look at all of that water—hundreds of acres of standing water with only thin slivers of muddy earth separating one check from another. It looks like mighty big water, and it is. Nonetheless, ducks can be taken there.

My falcons have taken ducks in this environment in three different ways. A dog is very beneficial for two of these methods and all but mandatory for the third. Falcons, which are partial to binding, can do well, especially when they exercise a little patience. If, after the flush, the falcon can resist stooping the swirling mass of ducks, they may well ring up hundreds of feet beneath the shadowing falcon. The falcon can then weave through the flock and bind at altitude. This then gives her the impetus to make a controlled glide to either a berm between checks or the outer perimeter. Obviously, if the size ratio between falcon and duck favors the falcon, she'll be better able to manage such a maneuver. Falcons that can disable or kill ducks outright in the stoop will likewise do well, particularly if they're patient and let the ducks rise. The only other method I've seen falcons adopt hinges more heavily on the canine factor and is similar to a puddle flight except in this case the "puddle" is enormous. The success of this flight depends upon both falcon and dog working in tandem on a single duck. A dog's weight distribution keeps it from sinking too far into the quagmire, so it can run ten times faster than a man and fast enough to keep the pressure on a duck, provided the falcon keeps snapping off stoops each time the dog puts the duck up. When performed well, the flight eventually terminates with the dog running down the exhausted duck.

Whenever flying big sets with massive amounts of ducks, the falconer loses a measure of control over the falcon and the dog. In the case of the falcon, I wouldn't necessarily consider this a drawback. It is actually a lot of fun and very interesting to observe a falcon working the flocks, and you'll see things you won't otherwise see. Besides, there's little to be done about it any way. The dog presents a potentially bigger dilemma in that once he starts flushing, it will be difficult (if not impossible) to turn him off until he's either latched onto a duck, he finally runs out of ducks to flush or he exhausts himself. Dogs conditioned to respond to shock collar stimulus will be more manageable.

The areas where I do most of my hawking don't provide opportunities to hawk dry land ducks, as is more often possible in colder climates. Thus, while I thoroughly understand the dynamics involved, I've had little opportunity to have a go at it.

Several years ago, I had occasion to lecture in Rexburg, Idaho, for a few days in the dead of winter. I spent the first chilly night in the back of my four-wheel drive parked on the outskirts of a potato field. My snarling pointer awakened me at the crack of dawn. Somebody was tapping on my window and I figured I was in for a tongue lashing by an irate potato farmer. I quickly explained that I'd pulled over late the night before, just looking for a quiet place to spend the night. He looked at me a little puzzled, then asked if I'd like to have some breakfast. I said I would, and he directed me to his house. He said to tell his wife he had sent me and that she'd be happy to fix me up some food. I did as he said but felt awkward introducing myself to a total stranger—"Oh, by the way your husband said...." But the hospitality of the family was such that in no time I felt right at home. Their eldest son had gone off on a religious mission, so they had an extra bed and I ended up staying there for the next few days while I completed my lectures. Turns out, the farmer was a duck hunter and he was interested in watching a falcon fly.

He took me out to his pasture where he said we'd find some ducks. Sure enough, we found a small flock of mallards hanging out in a section of pasture that was covered in a thin sheet of ice. I opted to fly Indy, the more experienced of the two falcons I had with me. I flew the set as if it were a shallow puddle. I released the hybrid a long ways from the mallards so as to not alarm them. Indy took a respectable 500- to 600-foot pitch in the crisp winter sky. I slowly eased him into position directly over the earthbound mallards that were now more than slightly alarmed. The ducks held off bolting for as long as they could stand it, but in the face of my approach they had no alternative but to fly. At that point, the falcon rolled into his stoop. With wide-open pasture and no open water nearby, the mallards had nowhere to run and nowhere to hide. The whole thing looked very much like a done deal. Looks, however, can be deceiving. Halfway into his stoop, Indy just pulled up and the mallards sailed away. Something about that sheet of ice just hadn't looked right to Indy, so he called the whole thing off. Definitely not the climax I'd been hoping for but an interesting one nonetheless, and my host enjoyed the experience regardless.

Thus far we have discussed a variety of techniques for taking ducks whose locations are either known or their arrival is shortly anticipated. An alternative flight mode involves flying falcons over ground where ducks are assumed or hoped to be. This flight is most often referred to as speculative. Under the right circumstances, this method can be extremely productive and rewarding—so much so that I've dedicated an entire chapter to this sole technique.

It is my hope that by now the novice realizes that the methods for taking ducks are as varied as the ducks themselves. There is no right or wrong when it comes to art. However, in order to establish and maintain an effective duck hawk, she needs to be able to catch ducks with consistency. By assessing the tactical errors we make, we can apply our learned knowledge to further improve future attempts. Whenever I fly a pond for the first time, I learn a great deal about its particular dynamics. The mental notes I take better enable me to set up the next flight under similar circumstances. If something I tried doesn't work, I'll want to try something different the next time around. I enjoy experimenting with alternative or modified tactics always in an endeavor to enhance and perfect the art I so love. Likewise, I encourage others to continually "think outside the box" and find innovative ways to pursue quarry with skilled falcons.

CHAPTER 12

Speculation Flights

Technically speaking, speculation flights are those in which the falconer releases the falcon, in order that she may take her pitch, prior to actual knowledge that game is present. This is in contrast to the traditional flights at marked game, i.e., game that has been either seen or heard by the falconer or pointed by the dog, confirming its presence. At a glance, "spec" flights may appear haphazard in nature; however, under preferable circumstances, spec flying becomes an intelligently managed and highly productive tactic. Falcons are very opportunistic predators and spec flying is right up their alley. Well-managed spec flights can teach falcons loyalty and the rationale behind following the hawking party long distances, ever ready to capitalize on opportunities as they arise. At times the speculative tactic is the most viable option available, offering the best or only chance at flying game. Knowing when, where and how to use this tactic will mean the difference between outstanding spontaneous flights and entirely counterproductive debacles.

When I first began to fly falcons at ducks, I worked a conventional job; my hours were 7:00 a.m. to 5:00 p.m., five days a week. This schedule left little daylight during the work week throughout duck season when I was not confined to my job. Regardless, I flew great duck hawks, owing mostly to pigeon work (maintenance training) during the week and hawking on the weekends. Eventually I began to combine pigeon work with a speculative approach, flying some of the local ponds I had access to before work. I'd put the falcon in the air and if there were no ducks, I'd throw a pigeon; when there were ducks, I'd show up at work with wet shoes, bloody hands and a smile on my face. I rationalized that if I'm going to throw a pigeon before work, why not do it next to a pond? These flights were brief and could be over and done with in about the same timeframe as any training exercise, fitting well into my work schedule.

These days I have much more time available for hawking. Nonetheless, I still occasionally utilize a speculative approach. Some flights that don't start out as speculative evolve into a spec type format. Many waterfowl habitats such as wetlands, estuaries, streams and consecutive ponds have the potential to harbor ducks in a variety of locations. If for any reason the original set up fails, it is often most practical to elongate the flight, keeping the falcon on the wing while the remainder of the habitat is explored. Such flights often present the falcon with multiple successive stooping opportunities without having to call her down between attempts. In game-rich environments persistence usually pays off. Conversely, in situations where opportunities are few and far between or when flying in unfamiliar territory, the percentage rates of fruitful speculation endeavors fall markedly. Duck hawkers soon learn that randomly speculating ponds will provide only a fraction of the number of duck slips that could otherwise be flown. Great duck hawks require decent slips on at least a fairly regular basis. It is very demoralizing for a duck hawk to be repeatedly put up over empty ponds only to be called down to the lure. If a falconer is unable to locate quarry with reasonable consistency, he may need to re-evaluate his prey base and switch to an alternative falconry genre. If we expect the falcon to religiously crank up to pitch and maintain a desirable level of confidence, then we must uphold our part of the bargain and provide opportunities. Intermewed falcons can withstand somewhat more disappointment than the rookie. However, even the old campaigner is best not disappointed often or consecutively.

Spec flights are generally most productive on ground with which the falconer is intimately familiar. Some of the ponds I fly are virtually guaranteed to have ducks at certain times of the year. Even so, such ponds that can be easily checked to verify the presence of ducks are usually scouted prior to releasing the falcon. On the other hand, it makes little sense to scout a pond that you are almost certain will contain ducks if the prospects of a premature flush are high. Even when speculating sets that are all but guaranteed to have ducks, it is a good idea to formulate a contingency plan should things not pan out as expected. I prefer to carry some type of bagged bird that I can liberate should quarry fail to materialize. In so doing, I can fly with an assurance that the falcon will have an opportunity to stoop something, one way or another.

To say that we can mindlessly amble around tossing bags here and there is of course an oversimplification. An understanding of bagged game dynamics is an essential prerequisite to spec flying. Quality homers are truly difficult for any falcon to hit and harder to knock down. Thrown in the right environment, an occasional homer served to a falcon while speculating will keep the falcon interested and focused, indeed some gamehawks may benefit from stooping the occasional homer throughout the season. Properly served homers tend to enhance pitch without teaching the falcon to wait for an "easy" bag, thus ignoring game in the process. Homers are small and light, which makes it physically easier to carry them into the field. However, small targets may be the last thing the falconer would want to serve a would-be duck hawk, depending on the falcon's size, experience and aggression. Many ducks are large and as such can easily intimidate falcons lacking in any of the three preceding categories. In other words, if intimidation of the duck hawk is a factor, pigeons are likely to exacerbate the problem. If we fly a set or two and the falcon fails to kill, and then we serve a homer when no other quarry is to be found, in short order we can easily establish a pattern whereby the less-aggressive falcon becomes disinterested in killing big ducks altogether, opting for a less threatening pigeon serve instead. This, of course, is a recipe for failure and should be vigilantly guarded against. These types of falcons would be better served if mid- to large-size duck bags were utilized only, in conjunction with flushing wild ducks. If wild ducks are not consistently flushed under a falcon who lacks confidence, she may well demonstrate her willingness and abilities to handle any duck emanating from the falconer's bag and still remain completely ineffectual as a legitimate duck hawk.

Relying on homers for spec flights can also present problems due to location and terrain. There are many ponds where I am comfortable flying ducks, but I cringe at the thought of flying a pigeon there. Whereas most seasoned duck hawks won't bother tailchasing waterfowl long distances, many of them will follow homers quite a distance if the terrain is such that it encourages the homer to fly low to the ground rather than committing to the sky. The thought of protracted homer pursuits in some settings is not pretty and conjures bad memories. One such incident occurred five years ago and was the result of throwing a homer by a pond in heavily timbered mountainous terrain at dusk. What was intended to be a short duck flight escalated into a nightmarish escapade as my falcon, Shaman, and the homer I served flew out of sight into the hills and the fading light. Oh, did I mention that I had my four children and my (then new) girlfriend, Sydney, in the truck? Shaman didn't return, so I knew he had killed the homer. Tracking commenced but was hampered by the hills. After a lot of driving and hiking, radio telemetry guided me to within earshot of Shamans' bell, jingling as he rustled around getting comfortable. I honed in on the sound and the flashlight beam revealed the totally gorged falcon roosting in a pine tree. He wasn't coming down so I climbed the tree to retrieve the little darling, which at that point I really didn't mind in the least. It was 10:00 p.m. before I found my way back to the truck, aided by the headlights Sydney had thoughtfully left on for me. Unfortunately, the truck's battery had been sufficiently drained to prevent the engine from starting. Luckily, I was parked on a hill and was able to jump start it. By 10:30 p.m., the kids were eating fast food and had forgiven me. Sydney's chilly demeanor, however, left little doubt that Shaman and I were still in the doghouse. In retrospect, I think it is safe to say that Shaman was the only one who enjoyed himself at all that evening. It was some time before I convinced Sydney that this flight had been aberrant and normally things went much smoother. The moral of the story is always beware even when throwing your best homers, because they have a way of getting caught at some of the most inopportune times and places.

These days I compensate by partially sealing pigeons if I'm specking in a location or at times when a tailchase in unacceptable. Sealing pigeons, at least partially, may prevent them from dumping before the falcon can execute her stoop. Since sealing essentially negates the pigeon's ability to escape, the dynamics of the speculative flight are altered somewhat and can at times put the falconer between a rock and a hard place. If the set fails to produce quarry and the confident falcon is flying well, allowing her to smash the homer can be a great way to end a technically strong performance. If, however, the falcon flew poorly, it hardly seems fit to reward her inferior performance with an easy bag. Of course, we could call her into the lure, but this action carries consequences as well. If a falcon flies poorly, there is a reason. Sometimes her reasoning is justified; perhaps she recognized the set and, based on past experience here, she surmised that the likelihood of success was not good and therefore did not warrant much effort on her part. Calling her to the lure will surely reinforce her conviction that this set sucks, and in all probability she will not want to fly this set again. No big deal if it is an insignificant pond, a real hassle if it is one you really like to fly! Decisions, decisions. Avoiding this kind of mine trap is preferable. I always strive to fly falcons under circumstances that preclude me from having to make "least of the worst" type choices.

When specking larger areas, flights tend to last longer than traditional flights at marked game, so atmospheric conditions play an increasingly important role. In decent weather, falcons in peak physical condition can easily wait-on for extended periods and mount repeatedly. Obviously lousy flying weather, including heavy winds, precipitation or dead air, prevents the falcon from staying in position at pitch for as long. Thermal conditions permit falcons to remain airborne indefinitely and can open windows into imaginative hawking possibilities. At best, this kind of flying transcends the regimentation of conventional falconry, which can pale in comparison. The thermal falcon revels in her element as she soars at tremendous height, dominating vast swaths of earth below, stooping from all conceivable angles. Like an artist, she paints with broad strokes using the sky as her canvas. These spectacular flights require a lot of open ground and steady nerves on the part of the falconer since the falcon will be flying under less controlled circumstances. They also carry an elevated degree of inherent risks, lurking in the form of eagles, gun-toting morons and the seemingly ever-present temptations of check. The falconer must always weigh the benefits against the risks when contemplating a flight of this magnitude. Should he decide to go forward, the falconer will soon realize that maintaining the falcon's interest and faith is key. If the falcon becomes bored (due to a lack of targets) she'll eventually rake, searching for greener pastures. After only one or two such episodes she'll determine that you are dispensable, she'll not linger long in your presence and the wretched vice of self-hunting will have stamped a footnote in her mind.

The art of speculation is somewhat of a balancing act and as such requires a great deal of discretion. Surely there are instances when there is more to be lost flying on spec than to be gained, and it is in the best interest of the hawking team to forgo a day's flying if necessary in favor of a proper set up tomorrow. Perhaps the crux of speculative flights lies not only in having the common sense to know when, where and how, but also in knowing when to throw in the towel and call it a day. Certainly, spec flying has the capacity to produce an awesome falconry experience, blending ingredients such as intrigue, spontaneity and intuition in an uncommon manner. As the flight progresses, each step strings the nerves tighter; hearts pound as quarry rockets into the sky and excitement redlines as the falcon shifts high above in the atmosphere, metamorphosing into a lethal projectile.

CHAPTER 13

Weather

Throughout the course of a typical hunting season, most falconers will experience a wide range of atmospheric conditions. These irregular weather patterns are part of what make falconry interesting, challenging and, ultimately, rewarding. Understanding the affects of various weather systems and temperature fluctuations on the metabolism and field performance of a hawk is beyond desirable—it is mandatory. We earthbound *Homo sapiens* tend to view the sky as a one-dimensional element. Due to the transparent texture of the sky, it is easy to overlook or minimize what is going on up there all around us all of the time. When we begin to recognize the huge influence environmental factors have on our falconry, we begin to take notice, to study and to learn.

Imagine for a moment that you are a die-hard surfer and, therefore, have a deep interest in the ocean and more specifically waves. Now, as every surfer worth his wax knows, all waves are not created equal. Some days the waves are like gifts from Kahuna, the surf god himself, priceless jewels just begging to be ridden. Other days are not so good; you can hardly find a wave let alone catch one. After years of addiction, the surfing lifestyle penetrates all aspects of your life, and thoughts of mountainous blue water with hollow barrels fill your waking moments and invade your sleep. As you learn to master these slabs of hydro energy and begin to fully appreciate the finer waves, you become a connoisseur. While others may look to the ocean and see its beauty, you see its beauty and its potential. By listening to weather and surf reports and observing how the right combination of atmospheric elements and geography create the waves you crave, you are able to develop a strategy that helps you to maximize your enjoyment of the surf's potential. In other words, you learn where to be and when to be there, depending on conditions. In many ways, the sky is similar to the ocean. They're both fluid, they both affect and are affected by the weather. Season by season, day by day, minute by minute, changes are taking place. The sky is alive. As surely as the oceans can generate swells of epic proportion, so too can the sky serve up some tasty flying conditions. The connoisseurs of classical waiting-on falconry will revere the days of optimal weather conditions, because these are the days when we are most likely to see exceptional performances from our falcons.

To a certain extent, we are at the mercy of whatever weather the environment sends our way; but by making adjustments, altering when, where and how we orchestrate a flight, we can make the best of whatever weather we are dealt. Flying falcons under adverse conditions can provide an interesting diversion from the norm. Watching falcons interact with strong winds, for example, can be entertainment in itself. Watching falcon, quarry and wind all interacting together can be extremely dynamic. During windy periods, you will see maneuvers and aerobatics the likes of which you'll never see on a calm day.

One of the most bizarre duck flights I have ever seen occurred in midwinter, 1998. The weather was absolutely wicked, howling gale-force winds accompanied by rains made it difficult to stand, let alone hawk ducks. This was certainly not the kind of weather for right-minded falconers or weak-hearted falcons. I was flying a couple of intermewed gyr x peregrine hybrid tiercels, both in excellent physical shape. Shaman, the younger of the two, had managed to knock down a drake mallard at Cowboy Pond. By then, I was thoroughly soaked and motivated to quickly find another set for Indy, the older falcon, then get home and get dry. I opted to check the Chumash Ponds, a series of ponds scattered among sacred Chumash Indian burial grounds. My favorite of the lot is a small pond that is dammed on the south edge, which faced directly into the prevailing winds. Perhaps the spirits of the Chumash were smiling down on me or maybe they were laughing, either way I felt blessed to spot a hen mallard on this fine set.

I wasted no time getting Indy on the wing, and I didn't wait around long to execute the flush, knowing he would be unable to maintain his position for long while he fought against the hard-driving wind and rain. The dog and I went over the top of the dam, hoping to send the mallard downwind where Indy would have his best opportunity to catch her. In spite of our less-than-gentle persuasion, the hen decided to take her chances upwind. Initially she flew low to the water and was partially sheltered from the effects of the wind by the elevation of the dam. As the hen rose in order to clear the top of the dam, just a few feet from where I stood, she immediately felt the full brunt of the wind. While her forward momentum wasn't entirely halted, she was making only the slowest of progress though her wings churned furiously. Indy was able to stoop with what little pitch he had and, due to his excellent positioning, was able to make a clean bind over land, albeit in what resembled slow motion. Ordinarily, this is where the story would end, but not this time. This time things were just beginning to get weird. As I stood there, I stared in amazement as the two birds, now bound together as one, just hung in the air; neither flying nor falling, they just dangled there as though suspended by some invisible thread in the sky. Then, as if to further defy logic, they began to slide in a reverse direction, driven back by the brute force of the wind toward the pond. Now, I was no longer amazed, I was dumbfounded. I was seeing something I'd never seen before, nor have I seen anything quite like it since. Mother Nature may not have been breaking any laws, but she sure as hell was bending some rules!

I made some quick calculations and deducted that their current trajectory would inevitably deposit both falcon and duck smack dab in the pond. I guess Indy did a little math himself because he, too, seemed to realize that if he rode this one out he would be in for a good dunking. Then again, maybe the novelty of flying backwards was just way too unnerving for him. Whatever the case, he released his grip on the mallard and was quickly torn away by the wind. The liberated duck then began to fall, all the while being driven back toward the pond by the relentless wind. Luck (and the wind) were on the duck's side; she hit the dam, bounced off and was immediately blown back into the safety of the pond she had left only moments before. As for Indy and I, we had seen quite enough for one day and headed home.

Ducks can be taken in almost any weather, but the odds lean in favor of the ducks as conditions deteriorate. This is largely due to a significant reduction in the falcon's pitch caused by inclement weather. Taking ducks from a lesser pitch creates a dilemma for falconers rigidly managing a falcon's flight style. The fear being, if a falcon is killing ducks regularly from 1,000 feet and then is flown in poor weather, mounting to only 300 feet, and still manages to kill a duck, we may be undermining the "kill only at high pitch" concept for the falcon. If, however, the falcon is fairly beaten on this crappy day with her 300-foot pitch, we have basically reinforced the kill from a lofty pitch or don't kill at all concept. I would guess that flying falcons only occasionally in pitch-reducing weather would probably have an insignificant impact overall. However, if a falcon were unable to reach her pitch on numerous or consecutive days, there may well be a negative residual effect. So, why take a chance? Better to be safe than sorry and all that stuff. But out there in the field, extenuating circumstances seem to be the rule not the exception, and sometimes a lot of pressure comes into play when deciding whether or not to fly. Weekend warriors who spend weekdays conditioning their fine falcons and patiently wait for the weekend when they can really go out there and hunt, will find it difficult to skip a day of hawking when they have so few to begin with. Traveling long distances is always strong incentive to fly, weather be damned. Decisions, decisions…nobody ever said falconry was easy.

Pitch is habitual, which is to say that falcons usually fly at reasonably predictable heights from day to day, as dictated by previous and ongoing experiences. When a falcon is flown under circumstances within which success is enhanced by pitch, she will continue to mount well. If, on the other hand, she is flown under conditions that either prohibit her from reaching her pitch or succeeding from a lofty pitch, she can be expected to reduce her pitch accordingly. Once she has become accustomed to flying at lower altitudes, the falconer may have difficulty convincing her to resume ascending to previously established height. Ultimately, it will be up to the individual falconer to differentiate between what is acceptable hawking weather and what is not, based upon practical experience, flight style preferences and an appreciation for each particular falcon's capabilities.

Certain geographic locales are prone to specific predictable weather patterns and falconers must adapt to the conditions considered to be the norm for that particular area. Falconers living in the Pacific Northwest, for example, will probably be hawking in the rain on a fairly regular basis. Hawking waterfowl is by its very nature a wet affair, throw in some rain and things just get a little more wet. Ducks, having evolved in an aquatic habitat, are all but impervious to water, therefore their flight capabilities will not be compromised by rain. Falcons can shed water impressively, but sooner or later most falcons will be affected by prolonged exposure to rain. Some falcons are genetically better equipped to deal with moisture. The water resistance of the maritime Peale's peregrine is legendary. My falcons have all performed well in light to moderate rain, hail and snow. When it really starts to come down, I retire to the truck and wait for a lull. If the falcon to be flown is appreciably damp, I dry her with the heater vents in the truck before continuing the flight.

Wind is probably the most common environmental challenge regularly encountered by falconers worldwide. As wind speed increases from a gentle breeze into something more substantial, it will have a greater impact on hawking. When the wind really starts to howl, the balance of power shifts in favor of the quarry and the stronger the wind, the smaller the water over which the falcon may be effectively flown. In certain terrain, deflected wind may aid the falcon in ascending. A pond at the base of a mountain facing into the oncoming wind might be a great choice for a windy day. By and large, however, strong winds are going to have an adverse affect on the pitch of most falcons.

Another drawback to wind is an increased risk of losing a falcon in the field. I'm not insinuating that all falcons are predisposed to being lost on windy days, but even a rock-solid falcon can cover a lot of ground with the wind in her sails. Think of it this way, we get ten guys together to fly their falcons on any given day. Chances are, at least one or two of the falcons will rake off, maybe they'll come back and maybe they won't. Now let's suppose we get the same ten guys together again and they fly the same ten falcons, but this time the weather is punctuated by strong winds. It's a safe bet that more falcons will be lost on this day than on the previous get together. Not only will more falcons disappear but also they are less likely to return. They will almost certainly travel farther on windy days and therefore be more difficult to recover. To be sure, falcons are more likely to be permanently lost on windy days than on calm days. For those flying imprints, the risk is not as high as for those flying nonimprints, especially passagers. Nonetheless, any falcon is apt to experience something slightly intoxicating about feeling the wind in her face. If ever there was a perfect time for a to find mischief, windy days are it.

Sensible precautions are in order when flying in the wind. Sharpening the falcon's appetite beforehand will go a long way toward insuring her full cooperation. After all, she's going to have to work much harder in the wind, and if her appetite is borderline she may not be sufficiently motivated. Falcons will usually tailchase much farther when flying downwind, sometimes causing them to lose visual contact with the falconer. Will the falcon be willing to work its way back upwind? Let's hope so! Meanwhile, as the falconer stands there nervously swinging his lure he's asking himself three questions: "What was I thinking?", "What did I feed her yesterday?" and "How old are those transmitter batteries?"

When contemplating slipping a falcon on an especially windy day it is also important to consider the falcon's level of experience and physical conditioning. An experienced falcon in good aerobic condition will be better able to handle the elements, so it will be less of an inconvenience for her to come back upwind to find you, should things take a lengthy, downwind twist. There is comfort in flying on one's home turf when the weather turns foul. A falcon lost on familiar ground is more likely to be recovered than a falcon lost while flying in unfamiliar territory. It would be wise to schedule flights on very windy days in areas with a minimum of collision hazards. Obstructions such as trees, fences, power lines, etc., all become even greater menaces when the wind is strong enough to affect the falcon's maneuverability. I once lost a treasured falcon on just such a day, but it wasn't due to a collision with some foreign object. It was a fluke of sorts, but the high winds were definitely the contributing lethal factor.

I was once again flying Indy, my well-skilled hybrid. Throughout his career, Indy had taken hundreds of ducks, most of them mallards. He had killed pheasants and sage grouse as well. The thought of something as small as an average-sized homing pigeon posing a threat to such a falcon once would have seemed ludicrous, but that was then, before that stormy day. Sure, the weather was wicked; cold rain driven by hard winds made for less than ideal flying weather, but Indy had certainly flown in worse weather. But on this winter day something extraordinary was about to happen. I had just taken a mallard with another falcon and had gotten soaked in the process. And then I did something I very rarely do. I decided not to fly the other falcon, Indy, and just go home. I wanted to get the hell out of the weather and warm my bones by the fire. But then I began to have second thoughts because I so dislike bringing falcons home without having flown them. I reasoned a compromise might be just the thing. I'd drive up to the ridgeline, let Indy fly and burn up some energy, then toss him a homer, after which I'd hurry on home to the warmth of the woodstove.

I dropped the truck into four-wheel drive and we sloshed our way slowly toward the top of the hill. When I reached the top, I released Indy to the sky. He immediately began flying with an artistry that gave me cause to stop and recognize the grace and beauty of his performance. My whole life I have imagined how pleasurable and liberating it would be if I could fly. I watched in vicarious awe as the falcon slashed and carved his way across this windy backdrop with a simplistic, childlike joy. This singular flight stands as a reminder to me that falconry encompasses so much more than stooping and killing; falconry embraces life and the moment in a manner unlike any other.

After dancing with the wind for several minutes, Indy began to climb in earnest. When he had reached 600 feet, I let loose a partially sealed homer. Indy's stoop was tight and vertical, flaunting the polish and professionalism that had become his trademark. I didn't know it at the time, but something about Indy's stoop was wrong or, at least, was about to be. The pigeon swirled above, buffeted by the wind and hadn't gotten fully under control by the time Indy slammed into him with lethal force. The odd thing is the pigeon survived the impact, Indy didn't—not for long anyway. After the hit, Indy circled above while I bent to retrieve the pigeon, which had fallen into a shallow pond. When I straightened and glanced back up, Indy wasn't there. Then I saw him, just over there, floating on the surface of the water, wings outstretched, neck back, head up. It felt as though the world had stopped turning, hell had frozen over and pigs were flying, because what I was seeing was absolutely beyond my ability to comprehend. There was my falcon floating on the pond, and I could not for the life of me understand why. Sometimes when bad things happen, we subconsciously eliminate certain information or thoughts that we are unwilling or unable to immediately accept. I was in the midst of one of those moments, ever so briefly, before being slapped back to reality. Indy's head slumped forward and then submerged. I raced into action and pulled him from the water. As soon as I lifted him and felt his body, I knew things weren't good. I laid him on his back, unsure if he was alive or not. As I looked at Indy's listless body, I hoped for a miracle. Maybe I got one, maybe I didn't, but if I did receive a miracle it wasn't in the form of a spontaneous recovery or resurrection.

I buried Indy among the cedars and oaks below my house. I shed some tears and wondered what the hell had happened. Never once though did I ask, "What was I thinking?" I never felt as though I had acted with negligence or irresponsibly.

What happened to Indy was a fluke; an imperceptible yet fatal flaw in his trajectory caused him to improperly impact his target. Of course the wind played a pivotal role. I have no doubt that if it hadn't been windy that day that Indy wouldn't have died then. Nonetheless, I suspect that Indy would have died soon anyway. Not because he was in failing health or had poor eyesight or was even prone to bad luck. I believe that significant events in our lives happen for a reason. Often, perhaps always, these events promote growth. There's a saying that I like: God never shuts a door without opening a window. When tragedy is viewed from this perspective it becomes less a burden. I can't say that I'm glad Indy died, but if I had the power to go back and change things I don't think I would. With Indy's passing, I was given fresh opportunities to learn and grow. From a falconry perspective, it truly was a blessing in disguise, giving me a chance to work on new training techniques and hunting tactics. The results have been decidedly positive; I'm currently experiencing a level of falconry I've never seen before. Indy's departure was the catalyst for a significant evolutionary step in my art, my falconry. It's hard to see a tragedy here when looked upon in this light.

Lately, I've been more involved with the overall management of my youngest falcon's flight style. I do fly him on fairly windy days, but when the wind is really ripping, I usually won't, at least not yet. It's not that I fear for his safety, rather I'm interested in maintaining an established and preferred flight style specifically involving pitch. When I do fly in heavy wind, I try to level the playing field by flying smaller sets only. Ducks are well suited for flying in strong winds and are notorious for making intelligent decisions using the wind to their advantage whilst under pressure. When flushed, ducks prefer to lift off facing into the wind in order to achieve lift. They also prefer to fly directly into a wind when flushed under a waiting falcon. Which isn't to say that ducks can't be flushed downwind, sometimes they can, but ducks are driven instinctively to use the wind to their advantage. Falconry is a fantastic window through which to view evolutionary genius. The competitive interaction between two well-matched organisms is fundamentally what makes falconry interesting and challenging. Sometimes I find myself offering silent kudos to the quarry that narrowly escapes by using a combination of instinct, intellect and raw strength. Watching ducks use wind sheer against falcons is a testament of the evolutionary process. Wind travels faster (pushes harder) higher up in the sky than it does closer to the ground due to friction caused by irregularities of and on the earth's surface. Hills, rocks, shrubs and trees all create natural barriers that retard the wind's progress as it flows over the land. This is significant to classic, waiting-on type flights, because a falcon that is flying several hundred feet up in the sky will be acted upon by the wind to a greater extent than a duck flying low to the ground. The use of wind sheer against an avian predator isn't unique to the waterfowl family. That game birds, such as grouse, regularly fly into the wind to avoid aerial predation has been well documented throughout centuries of falconry literature. This kind of survival tactic isn't restricted to the bird community either and is commonly seen among some mammals. Jackrabbits obviously fully appreciate the effectiveness of this tactic. As the jack runs full tilt, ears flattened against its head, straight into the teeth of a fierce wind, its speed isn't visibly impaired. Note the poor hawk, wings churning like mad, literally left in the dust. On the flip side, an unlucky hare flushed downwind will be quickly overtaken by a hawk using the wind to generate blistering speed.

Once we duck hawkers comprehend the ramifications of wind, we have two options to consider. We can go with the flow and attempt to orchestrate flights factoring in the wind, or we can try to avoid hawking when the wind really picks up. Falconers residing in areas frequented by heavy winds will have little choice but to fly, wind or no wind. Obviously, the more a falcon is exposed to wind, the more competent she will become at coping with it and compensating for it. Falcons that learn to position themselves well upwind of the flush may take advantage of an otherwise difficult situation. If the falcon errs in positioning, the falcon may have little chance to connect with a duck in spite of pitch. Ideally, ducks are flushed directly downwind with the falcon waiting upwind. With this formula, if all goes to plan, the ducks are in serious trouble and impact will take place well away from the water. Even if ducks that were originally flushed downwind change their minds and decide to regain the pond, they're going to have difficulty. Their turning radius will be wider, they'll be moving slowly and they are then very vulnerable to an incoming falcon. A duck knocked to the ground on the downwind side of a pond is unlikely to gather itself and regain the pond before the falcon can wing over and claim her prize. Ducks that are flushed into the wind are more likely to try to return to the pond ahead of the stooping falcon. Aided by the wind, these ducks are able to turn more abruptly and, indeed, stand a good chance of beating the falcon back to the sanctuary of the pond. Even when ducks do commit to a clean upwind departure, they aren't going to be as far from the pond as they otherwise would be when the falcon makes contact. When ducks are knocked down in close proximity on the upwind side of a pond, they stand a pretty good chance of scooting back into the pond before the falcon can recover and wing over. When flying ducks on windy days, the timing of the flush and the positioning of the falcon become more critical. Do keep in mind that on seriously windy days, falcons will not be able to maintain their positioning for as long, so avoid delays. Most errors in executing the flush will work in favor of the ducks, which is as it should be. It does a falcon good to be beaten once in a while, exposing her flaws. I'd probably lose a measure of enthusiasm if my falcons always prevailed, and I bet you would too.

My all-time least favorite duck hawking weather is fog. While it is possible to fly shortwings in relatively heavy fog, flying longwings in dense fog is virtually impossible and unacceptably hazardous. Due to seriously reduced visibility, falcons can get disoriented and lost just as quickly and easily as you can recite the mantra, "What was I thinking?" Locating and retrieving a wayward falcon with such limited visibility is difficult at best. Every minute she spends on the wing, she is in grave danger of colliding with unseen objects. Lighter fog with a higher ceiling can be done, but the damp air wreaks havoc on a falcon's pitch. Falcons don't relish flying in these soupy conditions and generally do not perform at the peak of their potential. Often, fog will be unevenly distributed in a given area. Flying areas with patchy fog usually involves a little more driving as the falconer scouts for slips in acceptably clear air. In some instances, even though pond A is totally engulfed by the white muck, pond B a mile or two down the road might be free and clear, at least for the time being. Fog can move in or out of an area with surprising speed. Just the other day, I was scouting a pond about 300 yards from the black top. When I had first arrived it was foggy, but not enough to cause me to postpone a flight. I left the falcon in the truck as I trotted out to check the pond and quickly determined that it was currently occupied by mallards. I hustled back toward the truck, but to my dismay, even before I could reach the vehicle, the fog had consumed the field and effectively terminated the flight before it ever began.

Often, thin layers of morning fog are burned off by the rising sun relatively quickly. In such instances, a little patience can make a huge difference in the flight conditions if the falconer can procrastinate the flight even for just a few minutes. In the mean time (or as an alternative) the falconer may want to check areas of varying elevations. Sometimes a shift in elevation of even a few hundred feet can allow one to get down below or up above the white plague.

After several days or weeks of playing hit and miss with the fog, I really look forward to a weather system working its way through my area and clearing out the fog, at least temporarily. I long for the days of cold blue sky accented with high cumulus clouds and low barometric pressure. These are the conditions that enable, indeed encourage, falcons to fly at the pinnacle of their potential, setting the stage for some adrenaline-pumping falconry.

CHAPTER 14

Scouting

The most consistently challenging aspect of duck hawking faced by most falconers is in providing ample numbers of suitable slips for one or more falcons over the course of an entire season. The falconer that troubles himself to constantly locate ducks will fly consistent, superior duck hawks. Speculation flying plays an important role in the duck hawker's world but, generally speaking, the protocol is to scout for ducks and confirm their presence before releasing the falcon. It simply won't suffice to drive around and randomly put the falcon up over ponds in the hopes of flushing ducks not yet seen. In most areas, the ratio of ponds actually holding ducks would be too low to sustain the falcon's interest and enthusiasm. Due to the highly migratory tendencies of waterfowl, most duck hawkers experience sizable fluctuations in their local duck-population densities according to location, season and weather. Thus, finding ducks in a particular area becomes increasingly easy or difficult as the season progresses, depending on geographic region. The tremendous lengths hardcore duck hawkers go to in order to find sets when ducks are scarce is indicative of the rewards duck hawking offers. Were it not so, there would be little justification for the long hours logged behind the wheel, as well as the many miles of sloshing through muddy fields on foot scouting for ducks. The success of the duck hawk largely depends on the falconer's ability to consistently locate waterfowl in flyable settings without flushing them prematurely.

Scouting ducks is a skill and, as such, requires practice. I continually hone my skills, even during the off-season. Any body of water I drive by is visually scanned for ducks (surely a common idiosyncrasy among duck hawking fanatics). This helps the falconer learn what to look for and where to look for it, which, in turn, allows the falconer to scout habitat faster. During periods of minimal duck densities or when the falconer is short on time/daylight, it is crucial to be able to scout potential slips thoroughly and quickly. Duck hawkers soon learn to strike a balance, a rhythm that is conducive to checking as many areas as necessary and as time permits, without getting too sloppy. It makes little sense to spend fifteen minutes glassing a pond that is unlikely to yield ducks when there are a number of other ponds nearby that have yet to be looked at and daylight is fading. A familiarity with each site will greatly assist the falconer in this endeavor. Finding the right approach is key.

Some ponds are easy to scout—a splash of water on an otherwise barren landscape offering nowhere for the ducks to hide. Others are more challenging, providing ducks with a variety of hiding places both in and around the water. Ducks are masters of concealment, and at times it is literally impossible to detect their presence. Usually, when ducks have bothered to conceal themselves to this extent, they have either been under heavy hunting pressure recently and/or they have been alerted to your approach. It is always advantageous to scout any pond with a silent, visually obscured approach. If ducks don't know you are coming, they will not be hiding and should be more easily detected. Nonetheless, throughout the hunting season, ducks will often reduce their exposure by using some form of cover, even going so far as to shift to a nocturnal schedule, flying and feeding under cloak of darkness. In spite of my best efforts, every year I manage to prematurely blow ducks out of a few set-ups. Sometimes these errors are avoidable and other times the ducks are simply undetectable. Either way, when this happens I'll note exactly where the ducks came out of in order to better approach this set the next time. Meanwhile, as the ducks are leaving I'll quickly conceal myself, hoping I was only partially seen and hopefully by only one member of the flock. If the bulk of the ducks don't see me as they get up, they may think one member of their group has merely overreacted to an insignificant event. If so, there's a chance the group won't go far and it also decreases the odds of other nearby ducks getting sucked into a mass panic and leaving as well. By visually monitoring the departing ducks, I am occasionally able to see where they splash down next. If it is a flyable location, I'm in business. This tactic can also be used when ducks are initially spotted in unsuitable locations, perhaps too close to busy roads, power lines or high risk fence lines. At such times the ducks may be intentionally bumped (not terrified), and with a little luck they may splash into a flyable setting within visual range. Thus, a creative solution has been achieved.

While scouting for ducks, I'm not only looking for ducks present, I am also looking for signs of duck presence. Telltale clues, any indication that ducks may be frequenting this sight, include feathers, feces, tracks in the mud, etc. Stagnant water with surface algae may have faint trails temporarily etched in them, divulging the passage of some form of aquatic animal. When I do find indications that ducks have been using a particular site, I'll be sure to check there again in the near future.

Streams and creeks are sometimes very difficult to scout. Ducks will often utilize portions of these habitats that provide maximum available concealment. Including cut banks with overhanging vegetation that ducks can hide behind/under. I usually scout streams, checking at intervals, walking wide of the stream and cutting in toward the bank to glass the next section only when I've reached the farthest point that I could see from my last vantage point. In so doing, I reduce the likelihood of being seen or heard along the way. Streams with long straight sections can be more easily scouted; binoculars are worth their weight in gold in this setting. Bends in streams provide eddies of slower water and ducks are often found in these locations. Later in the season, ducks begin to splinter off into pairs; some species then seek smaller, more isolated water. Periodically scouting these previously unproductive locations can produce some outstanding setups late in the season.

The more ponds a falconer has at his disposal, the more

likely he'll keep his falcons "in ducks" throughout the season. This may sound like a simple proposition; unfortunately, this in not always the case. Waterfowling is very popular among the shot-gunning community. And usually where there is good duck hunting, there are plenty of duck hunters. Shotguns and falcons are incompatible, so public refuges and private duck clubs will be of little use to the falconer when gun hunters are present. I would imagine most gun hunters are ethical, responsible people just like falconers, but accidents can and do happen. I've had a couple of close calls in the field with my falcons.

My training field is a large tract of private land adjacent to a public wildlife area. Early one season, I was out thermaling falcons in the heat of the day—a little prep work for the upcoming season. I served a homer to a falcon that was riding heat waves high in the sky. The falcon missed on the first stoop, I watched through my binos as the falcon began closing again for a second pass at the homer when suddenly both birds were whizzing past a man that had entered the field. You can imagine how wild I went when I saw him raise a shotgun and level it at the two birds sweeping by. Much to my relief, the man didn't fire and lowered his shotgun. Later, he told me he was out hunting doves and would not have shot the falcon, having heard her bells. I felt lucky indeed.

If it is hard to control situations on one's home turf, it is really tough to do so in foreign territory. A few years ago I spent a couple of days in a small town high in the Sierras lecturing and visiting with friends. I was flying Shaman on some public lands when he unexpectedly began to power across the sky all businesslike, definitely in kill mode. One quarter of a mile out, I realized he was targeting a group of coots flying parallel to a small stream, and only then did I notice the camouflage-clad duck hunters stalking along the stream. One of the two hunters was in firing position just as Shaman pounded a coot to the ground. I knew I was too far out to influence the outcome and feared the worst. Once again, fate was on my side. By the time I arrived, Shaman was calmly plucking his coot in front of the amused hunters. They were actually pretty excited. One of them offered to carry Shaman back to my side of the stream, since he was wearing waders and I was not. Because the temperature was hovering in the twenties I gratefully accepted and later apologized for the pinholes Shaman left in his hand.

Speaking of duck hunters, the decoys they use seem to get more lifelike every year. Consequently, it is sometimes difficult to discern a spread of decoys from the real thing at a distance. Yesterday's decoys were primarily stationary, tied to their anchors, though in a breeze they would tack back and forth and bob on the waves. Today's generation of electronically equipped decoys can wing flap and vibrate (causing water rings), and one manufacturer even offers a remote-controlled robotic model. These days you have got to be careful, because that set of ducks you're glassing may not be quite what you had in mind. I've been fooled a time or two by the old ones, and the falcons weren't too amused. It's a tad bit worse when it is someone else's falcon you've found the "ducks" for, as I once did during a field meet. I have considered using decoys myself, placing them out at my favorite ponds in the hopes of luring ducks in during my absence. However, I'm of the impression that hunted ducks soon learn to associate these fakes with being shot at; so rather than benefiting, I believe the decoys would actually cause enlightened ducks to flare and avoid splashing in once they realize they've been duped.

One of the ponds I fly has been dubbed Cowboy Pond because they raise rodeo cattle there. It is a spring-fed pond, so it is always full, and I've had countless flights there over the years. In the past, the Cowboy attracted a fair amount of wintering wigeon, but it seems that an increase in the cattle population, resulting in a decrease in the available grasses surrounding the pond, has sent the wigeon elsewhere. Nonetheless, mallards still frequent this pond in spite of a high degree of nearby human activity. Part of the reason why this pond is so active is due to a small group of resident mallards. These mallards are wild but they've become educated about falcons. These ducks have intelligently chosen to ignore my flushing antics and remain on the pond. Meanwhile, the visitors (new ducks) can't take the pressure and provide the targets for my falcons. When we leave, the residents are still there and, like magnets, continually attract other ducks passing through the area.

We falconers have a leg up on our gun-toting comrades in that we can sometimes pursue ducks in areas where firearms are prohibited or landowners don't permit gun hunting. Falconers need to exercise caution and consideration when flying ponds near urban areas. Tame and/or hybrid ducks should be avoided. Usually they won't fly anyway, but if you take one incidentally with your falcon you are liable to run into some understandably irate citizens.

During the molt, off-season scouting can pay off by providing additional ponds when the next season rolls around. Keep in mind that ponds that are bone dry in the summer may be a Mecca for ducks after winter rains have transformed the land into a liquid habitat. Predicting exactly which ponds ducks will utilize can be tricky. Sometimes the ponds that ducks do and do not use seem to defy logic. No doubt the ducks do have their reasons. In wetland type environments the ducks may have many areas to choose from and can afford to be picky.

In desert environments just finding water can be challenging, but due to a lack of alternatives, when you do find water there is a good chance you will find ducks if they are currently in the vicinity. Livestock require water, so any place they're roaming the desert some form of water is sure to be nearby. Rainfall is a dicey proposition in the desert; often it is feast or famine. Heavy downpours can result in flash flooding, creating a temporary oasis and a visual contradiction. One year while touring the Arizona desert, I happened along a dirt road that was flooded by recent rains, the depth of which was sufficient to kill the motor of my four-wheel drive. On the bright side, the adjacent field was also flooded and my falcon and I ended up with a drake pintail for our trouble—not a bad harvest from a sandy desert floor.

Ponds come and ponds go, therefore I'm constantly on the lookout for new ones. Sometimes talking with people and doing a little networking pays off. I had an acquaintance that was a building contractor. He had just built a home that had a pond on some adjoining property, and when he heard I was interested in ponds, he gave me the name and number of the owner. I called the owner who invited me over and I was delighted to find a beautiful, productive pond. I flew the pond for several seasons before the friendly owner died, at which time his less-than-friendly sister took possession of the pond and immediately revoked my access. I checked back a year or two later and discovered that the property had changed hands once again. I contacted the new owner; he said he had always had an interest in falconry and wanted to know how much I'd charge to come out. Sound too good to be true? Well, there was a catch. After I assured him that it would be a great privilege for me to fly the pond, he said we'd have to arrange for any hawking to be done when his wife was not there because she was not fond of hunting. Such is life when hawking on other people's property.

Often the best ponds are those not visible from the road. Airplanes can provide excellent opportunities to view ponds that would otherwise be difficult or impossible to see. Nonetheless, there are subtle hints that may help reveal the presence of water to the earth-bound falconer. The topography of any given area will provide clues as to where water may flow and collect. Valley drainages, depressions and low-lying ground are all good places to investigate. Dams, dikes and channels suggest at least periodic water flow or retention. Two years ago, I found a new pond situated at the end of what resembled a dry riverbed. That year I flew both mallard and wood duck there, but last year the rains were insufficient and the pond remained dry all season long. Annual fluctuations in precipitation often result in dynamite habitat one year and desolation the next. While scouting for new ponds, pay attention to the vegetation; certain types of vegetation will only exist in areas with an abundance of water.

Sometimes the ducks themselves will lead you to their place of residence. One day, I was driving on a road that I had been on many times before, but this time I noticed a small group of mallards flying parallel to my truck some eighty yards into a field. I was amazed to see the ducks seemingly fly into the ground and disappear into the barren field. There was a house built on a knoll overlooking the field, and from this vantage point the mallards were clearly visible in a recessed drainage that snaked through the property. At the time, the landowner was busy hosting a party of pheasant hunters, but was receptive and interested in watching a duck flight, so I made arrangements to return at a later date. When I returned, the landowner had the pleasure of watching my hard-hitting peregrine x prairie hybrid, Omni, pound a mallard. And I've had the pleasure of flying this very productive set ever since. None of this would have happened had the ducks themselves not led me to their hideout.

When watching ducks splashing in, you can often get a very good idea whether or not there are other ducks on the set already. Winter ducks tend to be very tentative about coming in to any vacant pond, usually making several circular passes before committing to land. If the set is already occupied, however, the new arrivals will often pile right in indicating the set potentially contains numerous ducks. Other types of water birds can also provide useful information with great blue herons topping the list in my hunting area. The sight of a heron standing out in a field is cause for investigation because they are usually found in or near water. Herons are commonly found in the company of ducks, in fact some shot-gunners use heron-type decoys (confidence decoys) to further convince passing ducks that the pond is safe. Herons act as watchdogs, great blues are very tall and are often able to detect approaching danger well before the ducks. When herons are threatened, they fly off emitting a series of raspy alarm calls as they leave, alerting all ducks within earshot of imminent danger. Therefore, the heron is not only the duck hawker's ally, but it can also be a bit of a thorn in the side as they are flushed incidentally, sometimes unavoidably, while scouting ponds.

Duck hawking is somewhat unique in the art of falconry in that the success of the hawking team relies very heavily upon the falconer's hunting skills and his ability to stalk game. Early in the season before migrants filter into my area, slips can be more challenging to locate. I may spend hours scouting a number of locations before finding ducks. It is rather infuriating to go to such lengths only to accidentally bump ducks you didn't know were there. Sometimes this job is made much simpler by being able to view a pond from a distance aided by binoculars or spotting scopes. The farther away the falconer can remain and still confirm the presence of ducks, the less the likelihood of a premature/accidental flush.

Binoculars are absolutely essential hardware for the avid duck hawker. There are numerous manufacturers of binos and significant differences in design, performance and price. Performance is directly related to design, craftsmanship and quality of materials. Higher quality optics are sold at correspondingly higher prices. Superior quality binoculars will transmit light better, producing superior images in low light, i.e., dawn, dusk, shadowed areas— typical hawking conditions. They will provide finer resolution with less distortion, which cuts down on eyestrain. Prolonged eyestrain is very uncomfortable and probably harmful. Because I spend a great deal of time using binos, I buy the best pair that I can afford.

Most binoculars are marked with two sets of digits, the first of which specifies the magnification. A magnification of 8x is a very popular choice, but I much prefer a magnification of 10x. At this level of magnification, I can identify duck-sized objects from considerable distances. Hand tremor (shake) can be a factor at long ranges, compensate by steadying arms against body, trees, fence posts, truck, etc. Binoculars with a magnification of greater than 10x are prohibitive because they are so large and necessitate a tripod to avoid major tremor. The second digits of the binocular designation code refer to the diameter of the objective, or front, lens (known as aperture) and are registered in millimeters. The designated size dictates the amount of light that can enter the lens. The larger the aperture, the more light, detail and clarity provided and the wider the field of view (FOV). FOV is defined as the widest dimension of circular viewing area. It is measured in terms of linear feet at a distance of 1,000 yards. The smaller the FOV, the more difficult it becomes to locate distant objects, particularly if the object is moving. Some manufacturers offer compact binos, but the reduction in size drastically reduces the FOV. Personally I would rather carry a standard pair of binoculars than sacrifice the FOV in favor of the smaller compacts. I have been pleased with the apertures of both 42 and 50 mm.

There are two basic binocular designs: porro prisms (off-set barrels) and roof prisms (straight barrels). I much prefer the roof prism because they are less bulky, lighter and better able to withstand tough treatment. The design prohibits dust, fog and water from entering the barrels. Years ago, when I used porro-prismed, nonwaterproof binos, I would periodically have to disassemble them or send them back to the factory after I had gotten them soaked. Now, I can jump in ponds, fall in puddles and cross streams without worrying about submerging my roof-prismed, waterproof models. This has saved me a lot of time, anxiety and money in the long run.

Spotting scopes are effective at very long ranges; however, their ultrahigh magnification requires additional stability such as a tripod or window mount to reduce tremor to an acceptable level. They are most useful for scoping distant ponds that can be viewed from the vehicle. Sometimes a little elevation makes all the difference in the falconer's ability to view ponds from a distance, at such times anything that you can use to get far enough above the pond is an asset. Hills, boulders, trees, fence posts or the roof of the truck all present possibilities. If a pond can be glassed from inside the vehicle, so much the better.

Since many waterfowl excursions include muddy terrain, a four-wheel drive vehicle equipped with good traction tires is a huge benefit. One group of ponds I fly is located about one and a half miles into a habitually muddy field. I used to walk to these ponds (fitfully dubbed the Walk-in Ponds) and it used to take a long time just to get back in there to look for ducks. I didn't mind the walk when ducks were there, but it seemed like an awful lot of time to invest on a scouting run when no ducks were found. When I began to drive into this series of ponds I cut the time factor to a small fraction. In the world of duck hawking, time and mobility count! There's also a side benefit of getting your vehicle off the pavement and into the fields. Once, at this same location, I was exercising a peregrine less than 100 yards into the field with my car parked along the road. At some point I noticed another car parked behind mine but I didn't think much of it, supposing the driver had stopped to watch the falcon fly. A few minutes later, I saw a man squatting near one of my tires and the only thing I could guess was that he was letting air out of my tire, though I couldn't imagine why. I immediately began yelling and running toward the guy, whom appeared completely startled at my appearance. He stood, ran to his car and quickly sped off. From a distance my car looked okay, so I continued the session with the falcon. Afterwards I returned to my car and only then did I realize that the bastard had used a Slim Jim and broken into my car. He had emptied the contents from the glove box and had helped himself to the tools under the front seat. Fortunately, I scared him off before he had a chance to swipe the remainder of my possessions including a brand new telemetry receiver and the rifle I'd just bought. Apparently, when another car would drive past, the thief acted as though he were working on a disabled vehicle, so as not to arouse suspicion from the other drivers. All in all, the low life got very little for his efforts in spite of making off with my wallet, since it contained little (if any) cash and no credit cards. For me however, the loss was substantial, the wallet contained my driving, falconry and hunting licenses. More importantly, however, the wallet itself was a keepsake and one of my prize possessions, having been handcrafted in 1956 by my favorite uncle, etched with an eagle on one side and a duck on the other. Ever since, I've had disdain for leaving my vehicle parked along public roads while hawking. I much prefer to get my truck out into the field away from traffic and where I can keep an eye on it if at all possible.

When driving out into muddy fields, there are other considerations, not the least of which is the landowners who don't take kindly to ruts and gouges in their fields—better to keep to the established trails and tread lightly. It is also imperative to leave all gates as you find them, if you find a gate open that you suspect should be closed, consult with the landowner and offer to close the gate if necessary. Always avoid spooking livestock, the rancher's livelihood depends on the health of the herd and your continued access depends on your thoughtfulness. Always carry a jack and tow strap in case you do get stuck. A shovel and a set of tire chains wouldn't hurt either. Not getting stuck in the first place is always preferable and will save a lot of time, energy and, possibly, expense. A few years ago, I was out scouting for ducks in the rain and ended up in a field that I had permission to fly, but hadn't flown in years. I was surprised to find the pond had been bulldozed and no longer existed; the dirt road I was on had recently been reconstructed and had no solid base. My truck was buried to the frame and when I stepped out I sank to my knees in some of the deepest clay/mud you can imagine. Things only got worse from there. Unbeknownst to me, the land had since changed ownership and the new owner just happened to drive by, finding me mired. I explained the circumstances that had led to this misadventure and he seemed to be relatively cooperative, he even tried to pull me out with his truck, but it was no use. In the end, it took a heavy-duty tow truck with a winch to pull me loose to the tune of $100. By then the sun had long since set and the ducks would have to wait until another day.

With fuel costs escalating and time always at a premium, it behooves one to plan on scouting groups of ponds that are in close proximity to one another whenever possible. When arriving near a pond, a little common sense will help avoid an accidental flush. Don't slam doors, and if you have guests (or kids), keep them in the vehicle while you check for ducks. If they must get out, instruct them to stay out of sight and keep quiet. When hawking with other falconers, it is usually best to check your ponds for your visitors because your familiarity of the particular quirks of each pond will decrease the likelihood of bumping ducks. If, however, you are hawking on common ground, it is preferable to let each falconer check whichever ponds he intends to fly. That way, no one can blame anyone else for blowing his or her setup.

If you happen to see ducks on a pond you are driving past and they are relatively close, don't stop and stare—that's really unsettling for anything, ducks included. Rather, drive right on by as if you hadn't even seen them and only park when well out of sight. Ducks that are flown regularly may learn to recognize your vehicle, so plan accordingly.

When getting out of the truck to check a pond on foot, it is usually best to keep the dog and falcon in the truck. Dogs that aren't kenneled must be absolutely conditioned to respect unattended hawks no matter what. I've heard of a case or two where dogs left in a vehicle went temporarily insane and mouthed the hawk in the falconer's absence. I had an untidy experience with Shunka, the German shorthair hand-me-down. One day, while I was out scouting ducks, Shunka busied himself by burrowing a den where the back seat used to be. As if that weren't enough, he then set to work on the seatbelts, neatly cutting them in half with his teeth. I'm not sure when the delightful creature found the time to bark at the top of his lungs but he somehow managed.

When walking farther to scout distant ponds, you may want to bring the dog and falcon to avoid making the hike twice. Be sure to keep the dog in the rear when approaching the target area. Quite often, falcons get increasingly twitchy right about the time you're trying to sneak a peak at the water, typically venting with a series of hood scratching and almost always with their bell leg. The falcon can be kept off balance with a rotation of the wrist to forestall the inevitable bell ringing, but trickier setups call for a more sure-fire solution. A short piece of tape (electrical or masking), over the bell will effectively silence all ringing no matter how much the falcon scratches. By slightly folding one edge of the tape over on itself before sticking it on the bell, it can be easily removed with one hand prior to releasing the falcon.

When scouting, stealth is key. Occasionally ducks will come flying into a site that you're scouting. If you do a good job of blending into the scenery, the ducks may well splash in, otherwise they'll spot you and split. Surrounding vegetation, brush, trees, cattails, etc., may be used to advantage, whether hiding from incoming ducks or approaching a potential slip. Sometimes the falconer need crouch or even crawl to lower his profile and make use of short cover. Many ponds are diked on one or more sides, which makes for an easy approach.

Early or late in the day when the sun is low on the horizon, its imperative to scout from any angle other than facing into the sun. Otherwise the glare of the sun's reflection off the water surface will highlight you, while making it all but impossible for you to see anything. If you can approach with the sun to your back and avoid casting an obvious shadow, you will turn the tables on the ducks as they will be highlighted and simultaneously visually impaired.

Proper attire for duck hawking addresses not only the obvious camouflage issue, but the noise factor as well. Noisy fabrics or materials will stack the odds against a clean approach. When the ducks hear you coming, they'll either split or hide until you expose yourself and then bust out. Currently there are numerous outdoor clothing manufacturers catering to the hunting faction with innovative fabrics that are quiet, waterproof and camouflaged.

When scouting, it is important to try to pick a route to the pond that will create the least amount of noise possible, whether it be from branches catching your clothes or breaking twigs underfoot. Game trails often lead directly to the water's edge and eliminate having to bust your way through cover. When the ground is dry in the fall, tree litter can make one man sound like an army, avoid walking under trees at such times. Sometimes incidental noises can be used to mask an otherwise noisy approach. Routes that take us in close proximity to drainages, tributaries or perhaps just faster moving portions of streams can seriously compromise a duck's ability to hear. A similar masking effect may be achieved using passing autos, airplanes, trains and tractors. Ducks residing in ponds where cattle are grazed become habituated to the noisy approach of the cows, which works to the falconer's advantage as well. While making an approach, listen for the ducks to divulge their presence. Quacking, whistling and splashing noises are all "music to the ear." If all approach routes appear equal in terms of stealth, try to choose a path that will provide the best viewing angle of where you anticipate the ducks are most likely to be.

Ducks tend to hang out in the same general areas of their habitat from one day to the next; if you found them in the southeast corner last time, that's a good place to check first next time. Avoid coming up on ducks directly below you, better to check from across the pond if at all possible.

Remember, it is virtually always preferable to check initially from as remote a location as possible. Viewing ponds from farther away makes you less threatening and gives you a little breathing room. If the ducks do spot you, there's a better chance they won't blow out, depending mostly on just how far out you are, their current level of tolerance and just how they perceive your body language. As the hunting season progresses ducks become increasingly paranoid, and rightfully so! They don't like being seen, let alone noticed, and they will definitely feel threatened if they catch you blatantly staring at them. If they do catch you red-handed and they don't immediately take flight, it's best to not jump or act sneaky in any way. Simply avert eye contact and turn away. Act as casual as possible, giving your best impression of having not noticed them; make an easy exit, angling directly away if possible. If you are convincing, maybe they'll stay.

If you ever find yourself in a position where you are scouting a pond in totally open, flat country and you can't check the pond from the vehicle, it is useful to use an angle of approach that would take you past either end of the pond, as opposed to a straight-on approach. Otherwise, if there are ducks, they will become apprehensive if they see you walking directly toward them and they may well fly off before you've managed to actually spot them. Some ponds necessitate viewing from several angles, which may require multiple approaches. Begin with the angles that offer the best views of where the ducks are most likely to be. On windy days look for ducks on sheltered water, if they're still getting blown, they'll typically be facing into the wind on the downwind edge. When surveying a pond, the area surrounding the perimeter should also be inspected, because ducks will sometimes loaf and/or forage on surrounding edges. (Wood ducks, for example, are sometimes found perched in trees.) In fact, it is not entirely uncommon for ducks to materialize on a seemingly vacant pond while you conduct a brief surveillance. Sometimes submerged divers will resurface and miraculously transform an empty set into a slip waiting to be had.

Quite often, ducks are where you least expect them, so stay

alert. One day while hawking a small stream with a goshawk, I made a stealthy approach to an open pool of water that usually produced a slip. I was disappointed when I didn't see any ducks, but a few seconds later a pair of mallards came paddling around a corner and into view. I don't know who was more startled, the ducks, the gos or me. I let out a yell and the ducks rose from the water ascending at a steep angle in order to clear the cattails. The gos launched and immediately began to close the gap selecting the hen as her primary target. Feeling the pressure, the hen went completely vertical in an attempt to outclimb the gos. Unfortunately for her, goshawks do vertical very well, better than mallards. The two intersected twenty-five feet above the ground with the gos binding neatly to the mallard's breast in spectacular fashion. Thus, it often pays to stick around a minute or two and quietly watch, even if a pond appears deserted. Time is precious, especially when the sun is going down, but it makes no sense to be in too big a rush and miss seeing ducks or get sloppy and start blowing ducks out of ponds prematurely in an effort to economize time.

Probably the most critical moments of scouting occur just as you are positioning for a look. It is paramount that you expose as little of your body as possible, thus minimizing the chances of being detected by any ducks that may be present. Take care as you raise your head above or around whatever you are using for concealment because ducks will immediately be attracted to motion. Move slowly and methodically scan the pond as it becomes visible in small increments. It is not all that uncommon to spot a duck at exactly the same time it spots you. If you are mostly concealed, there is a decent chance that the duck will not be able to see enough of you to make an identification. In other words, the duck may know something is there but not what it is. By crouching, moving very slowly, the duck may hold its position. If so, retreat in absolute silence if at all possible. If the duck does blow off the pond, remember to drop and cover, especially the facial area. If some of the ducks go and some remain on the set, they must be handled very cautiously as they will be quite edgy.

Sometimes a falconer can get a quite good indication that

ducks are on a pond without seeing or hearing them. In fact, quite often the first signs come in the form of water rings. Though ducks are masters of concealment, they often give themselves away with the water rings they create while paddling their webbed feet, especially in still or slow-moving water. These rings travel across the surface of the pond and are very noticeable. Observation of water rings on ponds is a good indication of duck presence, yet rings are inconclusive because a variety of other animals, such as fish, beavers, muskrat, etc., create similar disturbances. I once saw rings in a small stream in which I'd never seen anything other than mallard, so I put the peregrine on the wing. With the falcon in position, I rushed in for the flush, yelling and throwing one rock for good measure. The supposed mallard turned out to be a coot. And to make things worse, the one rock that I threw, hit and killed the ill-fated creature. It is preferable to corroborate water rings with more conclusive evidence, unless further investigation is likely to result in a premature flush. In that case, knowing the history of the pond will help determine whether or not it is worth the risk.

In addition to water rings, the falconer should carefully watch for any kind of movement whatsoever. Unfortunately, when ducks are on high alert (as they're likely to be if they hear you coming), they'll usually be stationary and more difficult to discern among vegetation. Colors are very useful; the drakes of many species sport some brilliant, distinctive colors. Hens tend to be more drab and camouflaged but even some of the hens exhibit a bright, iridescent speculum (patch of secondaries). Occasionally, it is a tiny swatch of color seen between patches of cover that divulges a duck's presence. I've also found that the horizontal plane of a ducks' back is very prominent and recognizable. When ducks are in cover, virtually every line runs vertically (plants grow up), but even in heavy shadows, portions of the duck's horizontal silhouette stands out. Heads and necks also present a recognizable outline and when in tall grasses this may be the only visible portion of the duck's body. It's also a good idea to watch for eyes, if a duck has been alerted to your approach and is hidden, you can bet it is trying to keep an eye on you. In such cases an eye may be all you'll ever get to see. On some sets this is all you'll need to see because one duck of any species is sufficient. If, however, the falconer can do a little further probing without accidentally flushing them, the additional information can be quite useful.

Knowing the species, the approximate numbers and their locations will assist in determining how best to fly the set. If there are only a few ducks scattered here and there across the set, it is not a bad idea to be more specific with the details. In so doing, the falconer may be aware of whether or not all the ducks have left the set after the initial flush. That way, if the falcon fails on the first attempt, you'll know where to find the laggers.

When ducks are spotted, it's beneficial to assess their level of anxiety. Ducks will tell you very clearly whether they are nervous or complacent if you just take a look at their body language. At the height of the duck season, ducks tend to have an ultralow tolerance threshold; hell, they've been shot at a few times. Nervous ducks will exhibit an edgy/erect posture, they may freeze up and set silent, or they may chatter as they mill around uneasily, and most notacly, there will be a focusing of attention as they try to decipher the nature of the threat and a course of action. These ducks must be handled with extreme care as the slightest provocation may send them to the next county. Even after the falcon is in the air, caution is well advised until she is in a dominating position. On the other hand, ducks that are relaxed and/or oblivious to your presence will appear calm. They may be tipping or diving for food, they may be squabbling amongst themselves, bathing, dozing on the bank, etc. Any of these behaviors are ideal and these ducks are excellent candidates for a clean, explosive flush as they are taken completely off guard. After I have thoroughly surveyed a pond and its surrounding area for a couple of minutes and it seems to be vacant but I can't be entirely certain, sometimes I'll toss a rock in for good measure. More often however, even if a pond appears empty, I'll leave quietly, just in case a duck or two is completely hidden in cover. In so doing, the ducks will remain on the pond, perhaps until my next visit and in the meantime they may attract other ducks into the set as well.

After a few seasons of scouting ducks, a falconer will acquire a certain knack for finding them and develop an intuitive edge. The rewards of being at the right place at the right time are substantial, because there is nothing finer than watching a well-oiled duck hawk committed to her craft.

CHAPTER 15

Entering

The essence of falconry is game-hawking. Until the hawk has been successfully entered (capturing wild quarry), she will forever be something other than a game-hawk. Entering is a rite of passage—a sort of graduation for the eyas. This is the stage during which the eyas' relationship with the falconer evolves beyond a state of dependency into a quasi-symbiotic relationship. The same could be said of the passager as it transitions from its temporary state of dependency after trapping, back into the predator it once was. Under the best of circumstances the entering transition is straightforward and easy. Unfortunately, this is not always the case and it is this particular phase of falconry that causes the most stumbles for both novice and master alike, particularly in the genre of duck hawking. Austringers that are making a switch from flying shortwings to longwings for the first time will note an increased level of complexity in terms of entering. Falcons are generally expected to kill ducks from a waiting-on position. Thus, the longwinger is simultaneously concerned with the falcon's flight style in addition to the myriad of other elements related to entering. Entering is a bit of a paradox because nothing comes more naturally to a predator than killing, yet many a falconry bird has appeared anything but predatory.

In preparing for this chapter, I perused my library to reread what others have put down on paper about entering. Most of my falconry books are of European origin; thus, the bulk of the available information was primarily in reference to hawking red grouse. These authors each offered similar advice in varying amounts of detail. This advice, as sound as it may be in its context, creates a huge dilemma for the would-be duck hawker. Our European counterparts successfully enter their eyas (regardless of pitch) on young or molting grouse very early in the season. These grouse are far easier to catch during this early season window. As the season progresses and the grouse become stronger, wiser and more difficult to catch, the eyas, too, becomes increasingly adept at catching them. When we begin to compare red grouse hawking to duck hawking, we quickly realize that the apples and oranges concept applies. Entering an eyas to waterfowl presents an array of extenuating circumstances that complicate the entering process and necessitate a modified approach.

The fact that ducks can and do use water to effectively thwart attacks from aerial predators virtually negates the inexperienced eyas from killing ducks without the benefit of at least some pitch. An additional complication may occur with some falcons demonstrating an apparent indifference toward waterfowl. Most large falcons are turned on by game birds; even quite young eyases tend to exhibit a strong natural inclination to pursue game birds at first sight. Ducks are another matter; they simply don't have the same magnetic appeal for falcons that game birds possess. The fact that ducks are associated with water probably adds to the falcons' confusion and perhaps even creates an aura of distrust. Size can also be an issue. Big ducks can easily intimidate a callow eyas, making them all the more unappealing. Obviously, entering larger falcons to smaller ducks would alleviate at least this aspect of the equation. In reality, however, many falconers will have little choice in the matter and will be entering their falcons (large and small alike) to whatever ducks they have access to. In my area, mallards are the predominant, resident/early season ducks. So, until the migrants filter down, I usually fly mostly mallards or game birds.

Falconers that have access to early season coots may consider utilizing this species to bridge the duck gap. Coots are just about as unintimidating as imaginable and their powers of flight are pathetically feeble. Ordinarily the avid duck hawker for precisely the above-stated reasons avoids coots, but entering is an exceptional phase and at times calls for an unorthodox approach. In some instances, coots may be just the ticket. Personally, I would avoid killing more than a few of them before making the switch to ducks, lest the falcon become wed to them. In keeping with the desired flight style theme, it is desirable that coots only be flushed under the falcon when she is in correct killing position. Theoretically, when the falcon cleanly knocks down a coot on the first stoop from a good pitch, progress has been made. However, if the falcon doesn't have much pitch or the coots are flushed sloppily (either case resulting in a coot being flown down and killed by the falcon), her ever-evolving flight style may suffer from the very onset. We don't want to give the falcon the false impression that hawking waterfowl requires little effort.

Most American duck hawkers live far south of the major duck production centers of the northern praries, and therefore will be chasing many ducks that originated up north. By the time a duck hawker gets a crack at one of these migrants, the ducks are no longer pushovers. These ducks may have traveled many hundreds of miles and been shot at a few times, so they're not only in excellent aerobic condition, but they have acquired a certain degree of savvy as well. They'll leave an unprepared eyas in their wake. Most species of ducks are formidable quarry and are quick to capitalize on an inexperienced falcon's weaknesses. Large ducks are also capable of withstanding a substantial impact without being knocked down. However, if the eyas does manage to knock down a big duck, the falcon may yet be in for a surprise, since big ducks are quite capable of mounting an impressive defense on the ground. Young falcons are apt to be knocked senseless by the thrashing wings of a large grounded duck if she doesn't immediately take command of the situation. Clearly, entering falcons to waterfowl requires thoughtful preparation and a strategy that will bring the eyas to a reasonable degree of physical and mental preparedness.

While in the early stages of writing this chapter, I found myself struggling to articulate just how entering is accomplished. I think it would almost be easier to actually enter a hawk than to describe the process. Our human brains appreciate black and white issues, i.e., up/down, on/off, however in the abstract and fluid world of shaping behaviors, these delineated examples are more phenomena than norm. The difficulty in writing a comprehensive dissertation covering entering is that there are so many facets involved and there is no single right procedure. There are, however, common and consistent themes, things to encourage, incorporate or instill, as well as things to avoid. Entering is very mental in nature for hawk and falconer alike and is the most delicate period of training that the eyas will undergo. I do not wish to overcomplicate what can and should be an easy task, but it need be noted that much can go right and much can go wrong. What transpires during this critical phase can leave a long-lasting impression for better or worse. Entering is a time when the falconer is called upon to create every possible advantage to help insure the hawk's success.

To enter an eyas is to step through a threshold. For me, game-hawking is the element that creates the intense emotional gratification that makes all of the inconveniences of falconry worthwhile. Successful game-hawking is also beneficial to the emotional stability of the hawk. As of yet, the eyas has rarely felt anything so satisfying as when she experiences the fruition of her hardwired predatory drive. A mental maturation takes place as the eyas metamorphoses into the skilled hunter she was designed to be. Some of the annoyances that are occasionally associated with the improperly raised eyas (most notably mantling, screaming and misplaced aggression) will diminish as she begins to feel that she is in control of her destiny.

Entering a duck hawk isn't an astrological event, however proper alignment of tangibles such as weight management, physical and mental conditioning, weather and slip selection are imperative. Of these particular elements, slip selection is perhaps the easiest to control. It is essential that the falconer make wise choices pertaining to which slips should be flown and which slips should be avoided. In order to encourage the falcon and build her confidence, the most viable slips initially will be those that put the ducks at the greatest possible disadvantage. This usually involves minimal amounts of water. Possessing an intimate knowledge of waterfowl and knowing how various species of duck react in a variety of settings while under pressure will aid the falconer in orchestrating killer slips for the rookie duck hawk. This kind of knowledge may be partially acquired through literature, but nothing beats actual field experience. The novice would do well to accompany a skilled duck hawker into the field, since simply watching a duck hawk in action will teach the observant student volumes. Also, I've found that most people don't mind answering thoughtful questions about their field of expertise, if they are approached considerately. Overcoming my fear of appearing naive and asking pertinent questions has, at times, allowed me to access the kind of information that can take a lifetime to otherwise acquire.

When entering your new hawk, it is best to keep the hunting party to a minimum; unnecessary distractions are best left at home. During this critical stage, precision flushing is imperative, and unfortunately even well-meaning spectators can utterly screw up a slip for any number of reasons. I've seen so-called helpers make good slips go bad, and even an experienced duck hawk can get the shaft in such instances. I remember an occasion when an apprentice (not mine) completely lost his head at a duck pond. We were flushing wigeon for my peregrine x prairie hybrid and the first stoop caused most of them to splash back in, with the exception of a couple of ducks scooting out the far side of the pond. The falcon took up the chase and flew over a hill in hot pursuit. My companion's actions and demeanor resembled a bird dog that had lost his head in the midst of a covey. I yelled to him in a vain attempt to prevent him from corrupting what should have been a salvageable slip. As in the case of a berserk canine, words alone were insufficient to halt my two-legged companion. I watched helplessly as he continued to harass the ducks until he'd successfully evicted them all, at which point he looked skyward. I can still picture the bewildered expression on his face when he finally realized the falcon was gone, and he'd just cleared the entire pond in her absence. Damn!

Speaking of dogs, if you have one sufficiently trained so as to be an asset, and the falcon has been properly introduced, by all means bring him. If, however, the dog is unfamiliar with the program, you might consider leaving him home until the falcon has been entered. This will allow you to focus your attention on the falcon and the ducks only. Once the falcon has been entered, her experience will help compensate for your bobbles and other minor distractions.

Aside from the tangible aspects of entering, there are equally critical, if more subtle, factors involving the falcon's psyche—namely aggression, confidence and comprehension. In the wild, an eyas is not required to become independent overnight; they are given ample time to begin building an independent lifestyle one step at a time. Therefore, it makes little sense to attempt to enter a hand-reared eyas overnight either. By taking preparatory steps throughout the training of an eyas beginning at the second downy stage, one can cultivate a predator self-concept early on. Certainly, hawks can be entered sans preconditioning; however, to do nothing but encourage dependency in the eyas and then expect her to suddenly shift into a predator mentality at our whim, is probably short sighted and may retard the entering process.

Often, a falconer's training regimen doesn't exactly encourage aggression. Indeed, some training procedures can actually repress the naturally developing aggression in an eyas. If we fail to develop any semblance of a predatory mindset sooner, we may have to make up some lost ground later. Usually most well-fed downies won't demonstrate serious aggression unless hunger driven. Nonetheless, lower level simulations of aggression are common in both captive and wild eyases and are commonly directed at inanimate objects. Just as kittens practice swatting and biting at shoe laces in order to develop rudimentary motor skills, so, too, do raptors practice catching and killing very early in life. Psychologists have found that the first two years of a human's life are extremely formative and what transpires during this brief period will dictate much of how the individual views himself and the world around him throughout his entire life. We know that there are critical stages that occur early on in the eyas' life. The phenomenon of imprinting is one such example. Once we embrace the profound impact imprinting has on the self-concept of raptors, it's not hard to imagine there being other psychological windows opening and closing during the raptor's infancy. Most of our falconry manuals are all about the nuts and bolts pertaining to the physical aspects of raptor management, often omitting all but the scantiest reference to the raptor psyche. It's easy to get wrapped up in lures, creances and various other training aids and unwittingly pass over a critical stage during which the eyas should have been learning to be a predator, which isn't to say that she can't learn later on. But the huge irony of this lapse is that, far and away, the key element that sets a superior game-hawk apart from the others is found in the psyche. A hawk could have endless training, superior speed, bigger feet and prettier feathers, but if it doesn't have the drive, determination and aggression, it will forever be an inferior game-hawk. Therefore, I think it reasonable and wise to address the psychological development of the budding eyas.

With little effort, we can expose the youngster to a predator self-concept, thus helping ensure that we are creating the game-hawk of our desires. Anything we do that helps the eyas make that predator connection will make it easier to enter her later on. Providing the eyas with objects that she can foot and bite, such as an old lure, may encourage her to play. Add a string and you can pull her toy around the livingroom. Not only is the eyas acting out instinctive chase, catch, kill behaviors, but she is also being subtly conditioned to the lure without the use of food. Now there's cheap entertainment with a twist! Carcass recognition is another means by which the falconer can help prepare the youngster for things to come. Instead of always feeding the eyas body parts, occasionally give her an entire carcass once she's old enough to pluck and tear sufficiently. Any kind of bird carcass will help the eyas identify just what meals are made of. If it is a carcass of the quarry to which she will later be flown, all the better. Large carcasses are sometimes intimidating at first. After she finds the courage to straddle, pluck and eat a large bird carcass, you will notice the eyas gaining significant confidence. I also like to provide the occasional live bird for the youngster to kill once she is able. Small birds are ideal. Avoid negatively traumatic experiences by not giving large or highly combative birds to the youngster. It is extremely important to not allow the eyas to be severely intimidated or thrashed during this developmental stage. Since I use pigeons as part of my training regimen, I have the eyases killing pigeons before they themselves are hard penned. Once the eyas is free flying, I move directly into pigeon pursuits.

From here on, my falcon training revolves around two common themes: sharpening predatory skills and developing preferred flight style. This protocol quickly establishes the falcon's role as a predator and my role as a provider of opportunity. As the falcon's strength, stamina and flight style rapidly develop, so do her confidence and aggression. Larger bags are introduced in concert with the falcon's newfound abilities and confidence. Bagged upland game birds such as pheasants can be used, but if the falcon is to be entered directly to waterfowl, nothing is better than authentic duck bags.

When I first began hawking ducks, I mistakenly believed that duck hawks were necessarily specialists and were best not flown to upland game birds. Later, much to my pleasure, I found this notion erroneous; duck hawks in fact can be quite versatile and can be flown effectively at both game birds and waterfowl throughout the season. Therefore, the falconer with viable populations and suitable upland game bird slips certainly has the option to enter his falcon to game birds and then introduce waterfowl at a later date. In some instances this may make it possible to take advantage of young or molting game birds like our counterparts in Scotland. Falcons entered to upland game birds may require additional incentive to begin seriously chasing ducks later in the season, and this may be the reason I had been under the impression that duck hawks need be specialists. There's no doubt that many falcons accustomed to killing upland game birds only would balk at a duck slip unless given advanced conditioning. Some game-hawks may require extensive exposure to waterfowl only for a period of time to make the adjustment to killing both upland birds and waterfowl. The last falcon I entered was given both pheasant and duck bags in preparation for the season. His first legitimate kill was a pheasant; he then proceeded to take ducks on the next two consecutive flights and has continued to this day to be equally enthusiastic at either genre.

The discussion of bagged game is strewn with ethical, moral and legal questions. There are those within the falconry community who are opposed to the use of any kind of bagged quarry, and I would not be so arrogant as to condemn their philosophies. Personally, I feel that an ethical individual can use bagged game as a means to an end in good conscience. There are many predators, including raptors, that have been documented as having captured and then released quarry specifically for the benefit of their offspring in training. There is no greater impediment to entering the eyas than consistent/ consecutive failure. Bags can eliminate this potential. By preparing the hawk both mentally and physically beforehand and using bags judiciously, we can help insure that the entering process goes smoothly. Bagged quarry gives the falconer an increased measure of control; he can set the flight up without having to worry about many of the things that can go wrong when flushing wild quarry. This is a great asset for the falconer interested in establishing a particular flight style. In a perfect world, the very best bags would be freshly caught wild birds of the variety to which you are trying to enter the falcon (be advised that some countries have legal restrictions regarding bagged quarry). Properly served bags will simulate an actual hunting experience as closely as possible. Hawks that have taken a couple of bags of this caliber should have a good idea of just what they are in for. One of the nice things about a strong duck bag is that if the hawk doesn't bind or knock it down in the stoop, the duck should escape by either splashing into nearby water or by outflying the hawk altogether. This encourages the hawk to commit to a lethal attack or face the consequences of going home hungry. Unfortunately the same can't be said for most upland game bird bags. A reluctant falcon can usually "dog" one of these species until it tires and puts in and then the falcon can make her move. I don't like bagging sessions to end on this kind of note because the falcon is rewarded in spite of her lack of resolve and degenerative flight style. In so doing, the falcon learns that she need not really apply herself to the task of serious stooping; she need merely follow the easy birds to ground. To get the most from a bag session, the eyas should have to extend herself in order to succeed or she should not reap the rewards. Domestic ducks that are kept in flight pens can make good bags but probably won't have the stamina required to outdistance a semiconditioned falcon. Captive-raised ducks that have been liberated for some time would perhaps solve this dilemma. "Call" ducks resemble mallards but are smaller and a good stepping stone for smaller falcons.

When serving bags to falcons, I use the same shout that I use when serving homers. Any repetitive behavior on your part (audible and/or visual) denoting a stooping opportunity for the falcon will quickly instill a conditioned reflex. This then can be used to the falconer's advantage during (and after) the entering phase by helping induce the falcon to stoop at desired targets and bolstering her confidence. I recall an incident that occurred a few years ago that really drove this point home.

I was flying a young falcon that had been given a few duck bags but hadn't yet had any big ducks flushed under him. This day was to be his inauguration. I put the falcon up near a small pond that held approximately ten mallards. When he'd climbed to 600 or 700 feet I flushed the mallards, all of which went cleanly and flew directly under him. I held my breath and waited for the falcon to stoop. He didn't, in fact he didn't react in any noticeable way at all but he did maintain his position. Sixty yards out the mallards made a U-turn, opting to fly directly under the seemingly insignificant falcon a second time (big tactical error on their part). By then, my adrenaline was redlined and I began yelling and waving at the ducks for the falcon. Time seemed to stand still and it wasn't until the last of the ducks were passing beneath the falcon that he finally snapped into a stoop. The hit was dramatic and decisive and though it was the first legitimate duck the falcon had ever taken, it appeared as though he'd been doing it for years. There is no doubt in my mind that if I hadn't elicited the stoop from the falcon using previously established cues, the falcon would not have stooped at all. This type of conditioned response is a powerful psychological incentive and should not be overlooked or underestimated by the falconer.

When using bagged game, the falconer need always use good judgment in determining how best to challenge the hawk while building her confidence along the way. Our goal with bags is to teach the hawk that our chosen species of quarry is within her capabilities, but she must work hard in order to succeed. Falcons are constantly learning (or reaffirming) based upon their experiences in the field, therefore every flight is significant. I always try to envision a contingency plan whether I'm serving a falcon bagged game or flying a proven gamehawk to quarry. This way I know ahead of time what steps I'll take if the flight doesn't pan out as expected. The nature of falconry is that things can, and will, go wrong occasionally. When things do go wrong, it's important to minimize the damage as much as possible and make every effort to avoid consecutive set backs, which will quickly demoralize any hawk. Above all else, in the mind of a game-hawk, confidence is paramount.

Assuming that all goes to plan and that the eyas eventually manages to knock a big duck to the ground, the falconer has some options to consider involving the extent of assistance he'll give the falcon in subduing her quarry. This is a period when the eyas' confidence, aggression and determination will be tested under fire. I've found that if the falcon is given the opportunity to commit to a full on-ground confrontation and prevail, she will achieve levels of aggression and confidence beyond that which she's experienced thus far. If a falconer comes in immediately and administers the *coup de grace*, he will have denied the falcon an important facet of her life's lessons. This being said, it's important that the reader be fully aware of a big duck's ability to kick some butt. An experienced falcon can incapacitate a big duck rather quickly. However, most inexperienced falcons will have difficulty handling their first big ducks on their own. If an eyas were inadvertently beaten up by a duck that subsequently escaped, the falcon's confidence would erode and she could quickly develop a disliking for ducks altogether, in which case entering becomes all the more difficult. When my falcons are battling their first big ducks, I assist them to a point—making sure they don't get badly thrashed while simultaneously preventing an untimely escape. But, I also make certain that the falcon is completely engaged in what's happening. Once the falcon has totally dominated the duck (with or without assistance), *coup de grace* may be administered. The falcon is then given an opportunity to partially pluck and eat from the carcass before being stepped off, a sort of imprinting if you will.

It is imperative that the falconer be continually cognizant of his hawk's ever-changing state of mind. Getting into the hawk's head will add a degree of clarity that would be otherwise unattainable. At no other period in the game-hawk's career is the skill of projection more beneficial than when entering. With practice, a perceptive falconer will develop an intuitive understanding, which will ultimately prove to be an invaluable asset.

Using the hawk's natural biorhythms will assist in the entering process. Hawks are rather crepuscular creatures, exhibiting elevated levels of energy and aggression at dawn and dusk. Flying hawks during these times will greatly enhance their level of motivation. A hawk that is usually flown in the morning can be flight postponed until dusk, thus combining biorhythmic forces of appetite and heightened evening aggression. These two forces create an awesome combination if the hawk has internalized a predator self-concept, for then she'll realize that impending darkness equates with sleeping on an empty crop if a kill isn't made.

Weight manipulation is a huge ally throughout the entering process. Often, the only thing standing between a successful entry and one that is unsuccessful is appetite. Nonetheless, it would be foolish to believe that you can merely fast your way to success—it's not quite that simple. Even so, if a hawk has been trained in a state of high condition (thick), the falconer will have quite a bit of latitude and tremendous leverage. A hawk in high condition can be systematically reduced in weight at the time of entering in order to develop an intense hunger (motivation) while still maintaining an acceptable level of body mass. The falconer that has shortcut the initial training by emaciating the hawk will not be able to capitalize on this facet and is further behind in that a hawk that has been kept too low for too long will not have much energy, strength or stamina and therefore will be physically unable to compete at an upper level. Equally (perhaps more) damning is the emotional damage that an eyas in particular experiences through hard-core food deprivation. Aggressive she may be, but it's likely that her aggression will be entirely misdirected.

Still, hunger is the driving force behind heightened predatory aggression. Often, the eyas will behave like a predator in terms of chasing, sometimes giving a misleading impression of actual lethal intent. The hawk seems to be trying to make a kill, but she somehow always manages to miss her target—"Sooo close!" In reality, all to often she is merely acting out a portion of the predator role but never seriously intends to follow through. Sometimes a falcon takes bags with such aggression and enthusiasm that we are certain that it will easily catch the first wild duck flushed under her. Yet when the time comes, the quarry somehow eludes her day after day. Still, we continue serving bags in order to keep confidence up. This cycle repeats itself until at last we can no longer deny the obvious—our little darling, though capable she may be, has no intentions whatsoever of taking anything that isn't tossed from our bag. In such instances, the falconer needs to cut the proverbial apron strings and unleash the predator that lies within. The obvious tact would be to only flush wild quarry for her and feed her as little as possible until at last she sees the light.

There are additional measures that may prove useful and, indeed, may be the most viable if the falconer can't produce killer slips everyday. Serving bags via remote launcher may encourage the hesitant falcon to attack ducks that magically appear and are not visually tied to the falconer. A similar effect may be achieved with a well-hidden assistant tossing bags for the falconer or even the falconer himself tossing bags when the falcon is looking away. As long as the falcon is stooping ducks that are arising from unknown origin, progress is being made. Whatever tact is used, it's imperative to eliminate the baggy syndrome. Sometimes, in our efforts to maintain the falcon's confidence, we unintentionally foster an overdependency. Bags should be a tool, not a crutch. Bags are not a substitute for a long-term inability to produce and capture quarry. It's important that the falcon not learn to rely on bags. If, for example, the falconer conditions the falcon to expect a bag after every failure, she'll soon learn to ignore all wild game and focus on the bags only. This problem can easily be compounded if intimidation is a factor. Certainly, if the falcon balks at the big ducks you're flushing under her, intermittently serving her small bags such as pigeons, etc., is more than likely going to exacerbate the issue. Better to show the reluctant falcon nothing but big ducks and use weight management techniques until she overcomes her inhibitions.

It is important to be aware that whenever a hawk's weight is reduced below that which has been the norm, the falconer need maintain a heightened state of vigilance. The health and psyche of the hawk are in the balance. I prefer to reduce the weight of the hawk only as low as necessary and for only as long as necessary in order to accomplish that which I'm trying to do. Once the desired results have been achieved, the weight comes right back on. This kind of weight manipulation is one of the reasons why I like to get through the actual entering stage at a fairly rapid rate and this is where all the preparatory work really begins to pay off. Forward momentum is a significant factor when entering hawks. As hawks are moved through various stages of training, it's easy to see how they progress one step at a time. Raptors are creatures of habit. Consistency is the name of the game and is the path that leads to habituation.

Great game-hawks are habitual predators. Keeping the hawk in the zone, moving steadily forward, is how the eyas is transformed into a seasoned veteran. When the emerging duck hawk begins to kill her first ducks, it is good to give her a decent crop as reward for her success, however it's really easy to go overboard allowing the hawk to put on an awful lot of weight. The result is a sudden lack of motivation. Forward momentum is temporarily halted, perhaps for several days. Try to find a happy medium when feeding the hawk on her first kills. This format should provide ample incentive for the rookie to continue putting forth the necessary effort to catch, kill and eat ducks as a way of life.

Once the falcon is really in the groove and catching ducks regularly, the falconer may feel he's in the clear and no longer need concern himself with all of the details he had been so attentive to early on. In actuality, the falconer that is dedicated to flying consistent, topnotch game-hawks will find that the training never really ends entirely. In order to ensure the continued success of the game-hawk, the falconer will forever be interested in keeping the falcon's momentum moving forward, thus maintaining the groove. Even seasoned duck hawks that have killed hundreds of ducks cannot be expected to perform flawlessly if the falconer fails to preserve his end of the equation.

I have noticed that some falcons need greater incentive than others after the molt before they resume their previous season's style. An abbreviated re-entry period is called for to get these falcons back up to speed. I spend a minimum of at least two weeks reconditioning all of my falcons before attempting to fly them at wild quarry. This is ample time to get them back into reasonable aerobic condition. Throughout this conditioning process we are also reigniting the predatory fires that have lain dormant for several months. No doubt, some intermewed falcons would come around faster and require less weight reduction if a couple of baggies were utilized.

Seasoned game-hawks present a little discussed potential for aiding the yet to be entered eyas. Some of the older falconry texts refer to the use of experienced hawks as "make hawks." Make hawks were used as tutors to visually demonstrate the desired behaviors to the uninitiated pupil. Though I have barely scratched the surface in my personal exploration of this technique, I suspect there is greater potential here than has been recognized by modern falconers.

When all is said and done, entering a well-trained falcon hinges on two key elements: predator self-concept and confidence. If the falcon knows she is a predator, she will be driven to kill when hungry, so long as she believes she can.

CHAPTER 16

Slip Selection

A major facet of duck hawking revolves around competent slip selection. Perhaps more than most other falconry genres, duck hawking mandates knowing which slips to fly and which to skip in order to establish and maintain an efficient duck hawk. While it is not necessary for the falcon to kill on every flight, constantly flying a falcon over sets from which she can't possibly succeed will not only retard the development of the eyas or fresh passager, but it can also have a seriously negative impact on an accomplished duck hawk as well. When contemplating a flight, you must not only consider the set's viability, but also whether or not it is conducive to your desired mode of falconry, because a falcon's performance will be a reflection of prior slip selection and flight orchestration. In keeping with the spirit of unlimited potential, it is not my intention to dissuade anyone from exploring the outer limits of conventional duck hawking. Indeed, I feel that many a so-called barrier is only one small innovation away from possibility. This being said, there are predictable parameters involving the mechanics of duck hawking.

In determining whether or not a set is viable, several factors need to be addressed. Waterfowl habitats ordinarily include water, and it is the size, shape and depth of the water that largely dictate the level of expected difficulty. As one might imagine, the smaller the water, the less difficulty encountered when flushing ducks under falcons. As the water mass increases, so too does the difficulty in flushing increase exponentially. The number of ducks on a set will have a direct affect on the "flushability" of a pond. The larger the number present, the more inclined they are to flush cleanly. The responses elicited from ducks at the moment of flush are as varied as the ducks themselves. There are, however, recognizable consistencies among members of the same species. This makes it possible for a falconer to assess the difficulty of a set containing ducks of the sort he's familiar with. Even so, there are still elements at play that will alter the mood of any duck in question. Rest assured, ducks recognize falcons for what they are—predators. They will constantly monitor the falcon, assessing the degree of threat she appears to represent. The falcon's size, pitch, positioning and demeanor transmit a message of varying intensity. A falcon that strafes the pond before ascending is sending her message loud and clear. A falcon that is released well away from the pond and mounts to great height with seeming indifference to the pond or its occupants will be viewed as a much lesser threat than the former. The less intimidating the falcon appears, the more likely the ducks will cooperate and flush on cue. Ducks that have been hawked before will recognize the scenario the next time around and react accordingly. The more they are hawked, the less likely they are to cooperate. On the other hand, ducks that have been exposed to intense gun-hunting pressure will have an enhanced fear of man, which may well override their fear of the falcon. Probably my least favorite scenario is flying urban ducks that have all but lost their fear of man, making them extremely difficult to flush with a falcon overhead.

Putting a falcon up over a set and then being unable to flush is the epitome of absolute frustration. The more experience one has hawking ducks, the less often this should occur. Usually a duck hawker becomes intimately familiar with the favorite sets he regularly flies and sometimes even with specific groups of resident (or semiresident) ducks. Under these conditions the falconer can assess his set's potential with an enhanced degree of reliability.

Many ponds that would otherwise provide excellent slips are unfortunately laden with hazards. While even an inexperienced falcon ordinarily avoids natural obstacles, such as trees, brush, boulders, etc., man-made hazards in the form of fences, power lines and automobiles are another matter altogether. These sinister threats are so prevalent in some areas as to make it virtually impossible to hawk ducks without accepting at least some level of risk. In metropolitan areas, roads with menacing traffic often flank nearly perfect ponds. Scheduling can help alleviate some of the inherent risks involved with these types of hazards. In agricultural environments power lines are commonly stretched along at least one edge of irrigation ponds, thus providing electricity to the pumps that irrigate the fields. In ranch country, fences are regularly strewn around portions or the entire perimeter of stock ponds. If flying near fences or power lines is inevitable, doing so only during well-lighted periods will enhance obstacle visibility. But don't be fooled into believing that wire strikes are always a result of poor visibility, they are not. The sad truth is that wire strikes can occur anytime and anywhere, and inexperienced eyases are apt to hit them regardless of how blatantly obvious they are. Fences are not part of the falcon's evolutionary history, so they haven't developed an avoidance instinct. In other words, falcons are simply not programmed to automatically realize that they can't just blow through a fence.

A few years ago I was pheasant hawking in a less than ideal location. My pointer locked solid, and judging by his posture, I surmised that he was almost on top of the bird he was scenting. The falcon, still in his first season, was waiting directly overhead. Since I knew precisely where the pheasant was lying, I was confident that I could control the direction of the flush. There was a road a quarter mile to the north and not so far to the south was a seven-foot chain-link fence topped with razor wire. Since it was broad daylight, the field was relatively flat and otherwise wide open, the fence stuck out like a sore thumb. I thought there was no way the falcon wouldn't see and avoid the fence, so I opted to flush away from the road toward the fence. It makes me cringe to think of what happened next, and if it hadn't been so catastrophic the whole thing would have had a kind of bizarre comical undertone.

I circled around the pointer and approached the point head on. As expected, when I had nearly reached the dog a pheasant erupted from the depression it had formed in the grass under scanty cover. The rooster flew straight away in the direction of the fence as planned. The falcon began his stoop with a single-minded focus: hit the pheasant. As the falcon closed in on his target, I became sickeningly aware that his trajectory was all wrong. It became obvious that the stoop was going to terminate very close to the fence. To make matters worse, the rooster was still flying on the deck, he hadn't begun to climb in order to clear the fence. Then there were three impacts. The first impact was the falcon hitting the pheasant. The second was the pheasant hitting the chain link, which was immediately followed by the third impact as the falcon struck the fence. For a moment I thought, "This isn't really happening," but it was. And I felt the immediate and gut-wrenching guilt one feels when having just caused the death of a fine falcon. Ringing in my ears were those four horrible words, "What was I thinking?" After hitting the fence, the rooster bounced off and hit the ground running, looking no worse for wear. The falcon on the other hand, which I would estimate to have been traveling somewhere around 100 miles per hour, didn't exactly bounce off. In fact, he stuck. When I reached to pull him off the fence, I saw that he was still alive. The falcon's right leg was peculiarly resting on top of his tail. I straightened his leg and tried to stand him on my fist. He wobbled back and forth on my hand with dilated pupils as I put his hood on and waited for him to die. But he didn't. Maybe luck, or God, or both were on our side that day. After a couple of minutes he regained his equilibrium, and by the time I got home he was looking surprisingly good. In fact, aside from the permanent loss of one deck feather and a temporary disdain of cock pheasants, the falcon was as good as new within a couple of days.

When I look back upon this incident and analyze the falcon's line of attack and point of impact, I can only conclude that this fence strike was not a matter of miscalculation. The falcon didn't hit the fence accidentally, as in being unable to pull up in time, the falcon hit the fence because his "on-board computer" didn't register it as something that should be avoided. As far as he was concerned, the fence was a nonissue. The good news is that falcons that strike fences and survive tend to avoid them in the future. While intermewed falcons do hit fences, I would speculate that the vast majority of these strikes are entirely accidental, as opposed to a matter of indifference. This theory lends credence to the idea of fence-aversion conditioning, particularly for the eyas.

Sunday is my favorite day of the week for hawking because a lot of folks sleep late. Unfortunately, Sunday mornings are also popular with gun-toting duck hunters. It would be wise to avoid flying the areas with the heaviest concentrations of gunners.

Yet another source of concern comes in the form of check, i.e., unintended quarry. Pigeons top the list of troublemakers like none other; pigeons will suck some falcons in like a vortex—beware! While scoping the area for any possible check, it is always a good idea to take inventory of other predators, which are never too far away. Many a game-hawk has met an untimely end while encroaching on the territory of a formidable adversary.

The kinds of sets a duck hawker flies most often will obviously depend largely upon what is readily available in reasonable proximity. If a falconer has a preferred flight style it will be reflected in his choice of slips and vice versa. Thus, the orchestration of the flight will be defined in part by the set being flown. Some falconers may become interested in a particular set type or a specific species of duck and may target them only. One of the greatest things about duck hawking is the diversity of flights that are available. The monotony of a long season can easily be avoided by flying alternative sets occasionally to liven things up. Integrating a higher degree of difficulty to her routine can challenge a falcon that has mastered easier sets. Likewise, a falcon with waning confidence due to a run of bad luck can get a confidence boost from flying an easy set or two.

The last aspect of slip selection I would like to address is somewhat esoteric and has less to do with the mechanical aspects of how ducks are hawked and more to do with why. I enjoy hunting ducks virtually anywhere I can find them and am grateful for the opportunity to do so. However, I've found that some sets by sheer virtue of their surroundings can enhance or detract from the overall experience. For me, hawking is a deeply personal experience, steeped in ethereal undertones. While stepping over cow pies, dodging golfers or listening to traffic are minor distractions and a small price to pay for a decent slip, I much prefer to fly in a more natural environment whenever possible. Perhaps it is because I spend so much time in a man-altered environment that I have come to really appreciate the comparatively rare opportunities to hawk in a pristine habitat. There are few things in life that bring me more pleasure and a greater sense of totality than kicking back next to the falcon and dog after an epic flight, soaking up all that surrounds me in the natural world.

CHAPTER 17

Pond Burnout

Pond burnout may be defined as the degeneration of what was once a productive (slip-producing) pond into a consistently vacant pond as a direct result of being overhawked. Ponds located in areas saturated with waterfowl or experiencing a constant influx of migrants may produce slips daily, as can the rare piece of open water in an otherwise frozen landscape. However, I have found that the vast majority of ponds have a threshold for disturbance and once crossed the effects of pond burnout begin to surface. Burnout usually doesn't happen all at once. It is a gradual process. The observant falconer will nonetheless detect even the subtlest decreases as they occur on each consecutive visit.

Just where does the burnout threshold lie? How often can a particular pond be flown before ducks forsake the cursed waters? There is no magic answer. There are too many variables to conclude that what constitutes excessive exploitation for one location will be the rule for all others. The determining factors include such considerations as how attractive a particular pond is, quantity and intensity of harassments and how many alternative sights are available to the ducks. An area consisting of mostly frozen water with only a few thermal-heated open ponds leaves the ducks fewer options. They must tolerate the intrusions or leave the area altogether. On the other hand, in an area littered with suitable ponds, ducks have unlimited options and will select alternate, safer ponds in short order if harassed frequently. Ponds with exaggerated numbers of ducks are more resilient and somewhat slower to achieve burnout. However, I have seen ponds with large numbers of ducks flown repeatedly over the course of several days, each day there are fewer and fewer ducks on the set until one day there are none. Conversely, it is very satisfying to visit a pond only intermittently and find it holding ducks always. These sets are jewels to be cared for and cherished as sacred ground.

Making mental notes of the numbers of ducks present at a given pond each time it is visited over the course of a season and making comparisons to other ponds in the area gives one a reference for determining what constitutes an acceptable level of disturbance. The more sets a falconer has at his disposal, the less frequently he will be visiting/flushing each of them, thus reducing the likelihood of burnout. This explains, in part, why duck hawkers are notoriously possessive of "their" ponds. In areas saturated with falconers, the competition can be fierce. I find myself reluctant to divulge locations as I have had a few negative experiences. I have noticed that some falconers lack initiative and are more than happy to bombard the ponds they are shown rather than do any leg work to find their own. I group my ponds by areas and I try to avoid hitting the same area more than once a week. I suspect that in some locations this may be a bit too often, while in other locations this is a more than sufficient respite.

If, after having flown a pond, there are still ducks on the water and no other falcons to be flown, I think it wise to make a quick, quiet exit and leave the ducks on the set. The ducks that remain may feel a measure of security having survived the falcon's attack, perhaps this will encourage them to consider this pond a safe haven. At any rate, leaving them on the set provides less incentive for them to actively seek an alternative site. These remaining ducks will also act as natural decoys (the very best there is) sucking passing ducks into what is presumed a secure location. Now, that's cheap advertisement! Be kind to your ponds and, with luck, your ponds will be kind to you.

CHAPTER 18

The Psychology of Catch and Release

Game-hawking is, among other things, a form of harvest. An efficient game-hawk in the hands of a skilled falconer can readily provide for itself, the falconer and the freezer. Sometimes this bountiful harvest supercedes our ability to consume, particularly when flying multiple raptors. Wasting game is not a viable option. Fortunately, falconry offers a unique solution in the form of catch and release (referred to hereafter as C&R). Unless seriously injured or killed during capture, ducks, game birds and mammals are often quite releasable if the falconer so chooses. Aside from relieving the "excess" dilemma, there are other notable benefits to be derived from C&R. A falconer may release incidental or protected species taken unintentionally. C&R can be used as a management tool, creating zero impact on resident game population, which can be crucial to isolated habitats. C&R creates opportunities for the falconer to be gender selective, particularly useful while hunting polygamist species. Specific resident duck populations may also benefit. There is a small flock of wood ducks that permanently reside in my vicinity, maintaining a population of less than a dozen. It doesn't take a vivid imagination to appreciate the affect hard-core hunting would have on this particular flock. If the flock were hawked "mildly," the affects would be diminished. If C&R were used conjunctively, the impact would be negligible. Likewise, it is not uncommon for some of the best (or only) bunny and jack fields in developed areas to be small isolated islands surrounded by oceans of urban sprawl. These fields, with their finite game populations, are highly susceptible (if overhawked) to burn out. A wise and foresighted austringer can adopt a C&R policy to help insure a continuous, viable game population.

C&R can also be useful as a public relations tool. Most falconers hunt on private land they do not own. While some landowners may be indifferent, others seem to appreciate a C&R ethic, even if it is practiced on an occasional basis only. A friend of mine lost hunting rights to a pond after the owner witnessed his prairie falcon beat a coot to a pulp. It was simply more violence than this individual could tolerate. Clearly, some sights are better left unseen by the public at large. The immediate liberation of uninjured quarry goes a long way toward easing the anxiety of the nonhunting public eye.

Undoubtedly, the self-confidence and mental stability of a game-hawk are enhanced by consistently catching the quarry it pursues. This in no way necessitates that a death must occur at the termination of a successful pursuit. The raptor's urge is to catch, kill and eat. This, of course, is an oversimplification of the many dynamics involved in these driving forces. An understanding of the mechanics involved in this sequence of events will allow the falconer to thoughtfully manipulate the game-hawk throughout the C&R process. If handled with consideration and finesse, the game-hawk will not resent the C&R process and may in fact appreciate your intervention. Certainly the majority of game-hawks are grateful for assistance in subduing combative quarry. Anything that facilitates a quicker, smoother transition into the pleasurable eating phase will be tolerated by most raptors and enjoyed by many. Violent confrontations are inherently dangerous for raptors. They are subjected to a variety of defensive behaviors from various prey species including being kicked, bitten, scratched, drowned, dragged and hit just to name a few! Injuries range from mild feather damage to serious trauma or even death. Wild raptors that sustain any injuries that compromise their ability to hunt are not likely to survive. (Though, there has been speculation that the consummate rule-breaking Harris hawk may support incapacitated members of their colony, *NAFA Journal*, 1996, L. Morrow, "Harris Hawks in Chained Brush.")

Terrestrial conflicts present an additional hazard in the form of other predators; it is during this period that raptors are most vulnerable to predation or elimination themselves. I've witnessed a myriad of predators heading for my game-hawks that were disadvantaged and distracted, struggling with resistant quarry. Some predators are interested in pirating an easy meal while others seem intent on eliminating a competitor from their ecosystem. I suspect that some prey species use this to their advantage. The unmistakable squeal of a captured rabbit will attract the attention of any predator within earshot. Ironically, this may be the rabbit's last/best chance to survive. Once, while hawking jacks in the Mojave Desert with an eyas goshawk, I observed just such an occasion.

The gos had taken a fairly long slip and had bound to a jack. The jack began to wail and suddenly a coyote materialized, sprinting toward the sound of dinner—salivating no doubt. I was too far to offer the hawk direct assistance and felt rather helpless. The best I could do was holler, but the coyote seemed less interested in me than the commotion up ahead. I feared the worst as the coyote was nearly upon them before the gos became aware of the shaggy intruder. Her response was immediate; she released the jack and took flight. The jack's response was equally quick, making good its escape and leaving the coyote in the dust. As a young boy, I was an unwitting player in a similar scenario. I was hiking the chaparral-covered hills near my house in Southern California when I heard the distinctive squeals of a cottontail rabbit emanating from the brush just ahead, off the trail. As I approached to investigate, I startled a female Cooper's hawk causing her to relinquish her prey as she blasted out of the brush. Meanwhile the bunny she'd caught bolted in the opposite direction. Sometimes it does pay to be heard.

I could sight incidents of various predators attacking game-hawks engaged with quarry, just as I'm sure many of you have tales of your own. One need not look hard to find cases of falconry birds killed under these circumstances. The eyas, inexperienced and naïve, is particularly vulnerable, but even a seasoned wild haggard is not immune to the natural selection process. In light of these high stakes, the dynamics associated with the catch/kill/eat behaviors become more meaningful to the observant. There is somewhat of a divergence between the behaviors of a hawk and that of a falcon throughout this process. A hawk's catch/kill/eat methodology may be summarized as follows, the hawk's intent is to bind and subdue prey as quickly as possible. Large prey items are not usually killed on contact and often violent struggles ensue. The hawk uses wings and tail for stability, the legs and neck may stretch back in an effort to avoid head trauma, nictitating membrane flicks, shielding vulnerable eyes when necessary. Needle sharp talons and tremendous foot strength are the hawk's greatest killing assets. The hallux (rear toe) is equipped with a considerably longer talon and is capable of exerting far greater pressure than the three forward toes. The hallux is responsible for the greatest damage inflicted upon a prey item. Convulsive foot spasms drive the hallux talon deep into the body cavity of victims, piercing vital organs. Talons are grooved on the underside, preventing them from operating as plugs, instead allowing blood to channel and flow. Just as there are differences in flight speed and agility between buteos, parabuteos and accipiters, there are also differences in foot speed and dexterity. There are also individual idiosyncrasies that may affect foot placement upon initial contact with quarry.

Slow motion cinematography of a goshawk binding to its jack has revealed what is too fast for the naked eye to register. The gos strikes the jack in the hind quarters as she approaches from the rear and literally runs up the jack's back in a series of binds and releases until it reaches the head, whereupon the jack somersaults coming to rest with the hawk firmly in control. Most hawks end up at the head and shoulder area of large mammals but may take longer to get there.

Due perhaps to its social hunting tendencies, the Harris hawk may exhibit somewhat different intent. Some Harris hawks adopt a binding technique that is clearly nonlethal. My sonoran tiercel Harris virtually always binds to large jacks with one foot on the rump and the other on the belly or chest with his own chest pressed up against the butt and straddled by the legs of the jack. This sounds and looks awkward, but it does have its advantages and he has employed this technique quite successfully for over a decade now. Though he is in no position to dispatch the jack himself, neither is the jack capable of kicking him; in fact, jacks respond to this hold by becoming rigid and fully extended. It is likely that the jack is intent on keeping the hawk as far away from its head as possible, thus the full body extension. What the hawk realizes, which the jack does not, is that I am coming and will be there shortly to assist. Wild solitary species of hawks have no such luxury and must rely upon themselves. The longer it takes to kill or incapacitate quarry the greater the danger. The hawk focuses energy and attention to this task and the level of aggression is intense, accentuated with elevated body feathers and hackles. The hawk's relatively pliable plumage enables them to withstand a great deal of rough and tumble before feather damage occurs.

There is an interesting interaction that takes place between hawks and prey throughout these struggles. After the initial explosive attempt to escape has been thwarted by the hawk, the victim may tighten up, remain still and give the appearance of having given up. Occasionally the hawk takes the opportunity to adjust its hold. This shift often causes the victim to thrash again and the hawk responds with foot spasms, kneading the victim, attempting to penetrate deep with the saber-tipped hallux. Sometimes victims are still not mortally wounded but once again cease to struggle and may appear to be in shock. Now the hawk becomes more interested in surveying her surroundings, scanning for predators that may pose a threat. Occasionally I have seen a strange sort of mental detachment at this juncture, manifested in a trancelike state of the hawk. I suspect this condition reflects internal changes (psychological/chemical?) in conjunction with some vague or distant perceived threat. Eventually the hawk switches her attention back to her prey and may or may not attempt to drag its meal to a more concealed location. In either instance, prey sometimes reanimate for one last bid for survival, giving every impression that they were less in shock than they were biding their time, waiting for the right moment to catch the hawk off guard and escape. This effort is probably futile when used on seasoned haggards but perhaps pays off on passagers. I've seen it pay off on my eyases after they have diverted their attention and relaxed their grips.

Assuming that the hawk has successfully squelched its quarry's resistance and satisfied its desire for privacy, the hawk may begin to pluck and/or eat. It makes little difference whether or not the victim is actually dead, as long as it does not disrupt the eating process by thrashing about. If at any time the hawk perceives danger (most commonly in the form of another aerial predator) she will pause, she may flatten out over her kill and remain motionless (trancelike) visually tracking until the threat has passed at which time she will resume her meal. If she is detected by another predator and attacked, she must quickly decide whether to defend or abandon the kill—fight or flight. This choice can literally carry life or death consequences. The hawk must weigh the merits and likelihood of a successful defense against the possibilities of injury or death at the hands of a rival. Sometimes these decisions are cut and dry; other times the choice is clouded such as when the intruder is of roughly equal size. Appetite is no small factor and the hungrier she is, the more compelled she will be to stand her ground. Extreme winter conditions exacerbate the situation. A winter-stressed hawk may be just as likely to die of starvation if it surrenders its kill, as it would be to get killed in an attempt to defend. I once read of an encounter that took place between a great horned owl and a wild goshawk in Montana on January 1, 1999.

The weather had been brutal with excessive snowfall and temperatures hanging at minus forty degrees Fahrenheit. The owl had just begun to break into a Hungarian partridge it had killed when the hungry goshawk arrived (no gender description given). The gos landed next to the owl and the two began sparing, trading off jabs for an entire hour after which the owl retained possession of the partridge. The gos then "limped" off, flew into a tree and then departed in defeat. No sooner had the gos disappeared, than the owl literally fell over dead. The owl was examined and reportedly appeared not to have died from some mortal wound but rather from heart failure. Apparently the stress of extreme environmental conditions coupled with the energy expended defending its kill was more than the owl could take. Thus, we see competition is not restricted to predator and prey, instead we find that competition permeates the predator's entire existence.

The falcon's catch/kill/eat scenario deviates somewhat from that of the hawk. This divergence is reflected in the falcon's mind and body. Falcons are masters of the sky—truly aerodynamic wonders. The impetus of falcon evolution has been air to air competition. Their bodies are capable of withstanding amazing impacts as they collide with their quarry. Falcons are well equipped to quickly and lethally terminate terrestrial confrontations. Over millennia, falcons have evolved and adapted to capitalize on the vulnerable, elongated neck of their feathered quarry wherein lies the delicate spinal cord encased in the spinal column. The falcon's head and compact beak generate impressive leverage enabling a strong bite. A jagged protrusion on either side of the cutting edge of the upper bill (tomial teeth) and corresponding notches on the lower bill are killing mechanisms. By slotting the tomial tooth between their victims' neck vertebra and wrenching with a twisting motion, the falcon separates one vertebra from the next at point of contact, severing their prey's spinal cord in the process. This highly effective technique is a hard-wired (instinctive) behavior. A totally inexperienced eyas will automatically resort to this technique when killing her first victims, though she may be a bit clumsy initially. With practice, she soon becomes expert, capable of killing large birds with mechanical efficiency.

Though falcons can exert considerable foot strength, they are not on a par with hawks. The elongated toes are useful when binding to other birds, but prevent the falcon from exerting the kind of pounds per square inch pressure capable of a shorter toe. The talons are shorter, sharply curved and designed more for holding prey than for inflicting damage. Some falcons are less inclined to endure protracted struggles with extremely combative quarry. When contest between predator and prey degenerates into a dust-flying melee, hawks have an evolutionary advantage over falcons in the form of feather elasticity. The Harris, for example, is equipped with incredibly supple feathers, which are capable of extreme contortion before reaching the kink threshold. Watching a Harris being thrown around like a rag doll by large quarry and coming out of it feather perfect is impressive. Though less pliable than the Harris, all three North American species of accipiters also enjoy a great deal of feather elasticity. The peregrine is at the opposite end of the spectrum with very stiff feathers. As a matter of aerodynamics, falcons benefit from stiffer feathers. Recent investigations by falconer/skydiver Ken Franklin has shown that peregrines are indeed capable of exceeding 200 mph in the stoop. Mr. Franklin speculates that some peregrine subspecies may even be capable of 300 mph. Stiffer feathers are required for maneuverability and control when under high G-force stress. In essence, the peregrine has exchanged feather elasticity for velocity. If a peregrine were to engage in hardcore, protracted ground struggles, feather damage would likely occur. From this perspective, abandoning seriously combative quarry is simply intelligent. Wild falcons cannot afford injury or major feather damage. Besides, easier prey is probably not far off in most instances. North American desert falcons (prairies & gyrs) are constructed with longer, more pliable tails than are peregrines, both of which are more likely to crash brush, engage mammalian quarry and sustain an attack.

    Falcons employ a wide variety of hunting techniques. Some falcons specialize in binding to quarry, while others deliver bone-crunching body blows and a few perfect their marksmanship, opting for headshots. From a duck hawker's perspective, various tactics offer advantages as well as disadvantages. A falcon that habitually binds at the termination of the stoop is less likely to inflict self- injury because she bleeds off speed before impact. She is sometimes able to use her momentum to carry ducks away from water that otherwise would have been knocked back into its liquid sanctuary. Binding is sometimes more effective on upland game birds flown in dense cover. On the other hand, falcons that bind are likely to have a bit of a struggle on their hands as they touch down with coherent, intact quarry. Binding is not my favorite method for taking ducks because the bleeding of speed somehow seems less dramatic, perhaps even anticlimactic. The body-slamming duck hawk is impressive and fun to watch. The boldness and outright aggression unleashed upon anything unlucky enough to get caught in her sights is sensational. The impacts are highly audible as ducks are cartwheeled back to earth. Large ducks usually survive the hit of a peregrine-size falcon but are disoriented and often in a stupor, therefore offering less resistance when the falcon comes to terms with them on the ground. These savage impacts can take their tolls on falcons manifested by bent bells, broken transmitters, bruised feet, fractured bones and worse. A falcon that consistently orients its strike to the head of quarry is uncommon and a genuine treasure. Their ability to pass through quarry at top speed, slicing victims from the sky with imperceptible surgical precision, leaves one in awe. Quarry is often killed outright or seriously incapacitated. Occasionally, head-shooters will entirely miss their targets; we're talking about millimeters.

Whatever style the falcon adopts as her preferred takedown method, once she comes to grips with her quarry on the ground, she, like the hawk, is interested in immediate control. Sometimes falcons will procrastinate the terrestrial portion of the confrontation if their adversary seems capable of mounting a strong defense. Cock pheasants are a prime example of a bird that, once knocked to the ground, is often still very capable of an impressive defense and may openly challenge the falcon on the ground. These confident roosters are not merely bluffing; talon-like spurs on the back of their legs present a serious health risk to any falcon that doesn't subdue these fighting cocks efficiently. I have seen many falcons intimidated, refusing to engage the pheasant "hand to hand." Instead, the falcon initiates a barrage of low-level stoops, hoping to either injure the rooster with a hard strike or to encourage it to take to the air where it can be attacked from behind. It is a bit strange to watch these confrontations; often the pheasant jumps up as the falcon hurls itself at its adversary. The falcon more often than not misses its mark, sailing under the unscathed pheasant. After a few such passes the pheasant may finally take to the air, always flying in the opposite direction of the falcon and usually beating her to some form of refuge.

Sometimes the falcon's reluctance to immediately engage powerful quarry on the ground pays off handsomely. For many years I flew a hen peregrine x prairie hybrid named Omni. She was a formidable predator and an extremely hard hitter. Omni had never shown much of an interest toward ground quarry, but on this day some unknown catalyst piqued her interest. We were hawking pheasants in an open field by an airport when a large jack popped up. Omni immediately launched an attack at the fleeing hare, slamming the jack solidly in the rump, flinging it end over end. The deadly intent of the falcon was obvious from the onset and there was nothing for me to do but stand by and observe as she attacked a type of animal she'd never attacked before, using a method she'd never used before. While I watched, a law enforcement vehicle approached and a deputy sheriff stepped out with a video camera in his hand. He said nothing but began to roll tape on what is to this day one of the most violent encounters I have ever witnessed. The flight covered a relatively small area because each time the falcon smashed into the jack and sent it flipping through the air, the jack would right itself and take off in the opposite direction. As the minutes ticked by, I began to understand what the falcon knew instinctively. The jack was beginning to tire. The energy expended from having to constantly regain lost momentum was taking its toll and the jack was literally flown to a state of exhaustion at which time the falcon easily bound to its quarry who had not the strength to defend itself. I picked up the falcon and walked back to my car and into the lens of the still-rolling camera. Though I hadn't crossed any fences or seen any postings of No Trespassing, I was apprehensive about a starring role in a police video.

The deputy quizzically asked for a narration of what had just been seen. Now I was really nervous and wondered if I was being set up. I asked the officer if this would be used against me in any way. He replied, "There's nothing you can do about it either way." I detected a faint note of humor in his voice, which gave me a small sense of security. I chose to ingratiate myself and indulge his curiosity, offering a brief monologue. I explained to the camera that I was holding a hunting falcon—a predator. I described how the falcon had attacked in order that she might eat, just as wild predators do. I pointed out the strength and speed of the jack and its failed attempts to escape. The monologue concluded with a synopsis of falconry, after which he lowered the camera, smiled and said "Good bye." I breathed a sigh of relief as I watched him climb back into his squad car, leaving me with the distinct impression that he couldn't wait to show this one to the boys back at the station.

Experienced falcons control large ducks on the ground by concentrating on the head and neck, with one foot wrapped around the duck's bill and the other foot bound to the neck. The falcon tips the duck off balance, compromising the duck's ability to defend itself. Ducks chiefly defend themselves from falcons on the ground by beating them about the head with the butts of their wings (unless they happen to be near water, in which case they often attempt to drag themselves back to the pond, falcon in tow). Big ducks have very strong pectorals, thick wing structure and the ability to knock a falcon senseless with a good flogging. By controlling the head and neck of the duck, the falcon has direct access to the neck vertebra. However, as the falcon bends to deliver a bite she puts her head within the duck's clubbing range. The more experience a falcon has at killing ducks, the more efficient she becomes, reaching in with quick powerful bites, as she shields her eyes from incoming blows using her nictitating membranes. Falcons learn that the sooner they sever the spinal cord, the sooner the duck stops fighting back. Throughout this process, falcons tend to be more in touch with their surroundings than are hawks and are less likely to allow themselves to be completely consumed with the task of killing prey. They are acutely aware that their highly visible hunting sorties rarely go unnoticed. So they periodically pause in order to scan the horizons, watching and listening for signs of danger. Emotions run high during this phase, for the falcon is well aware that this is exactly when she's most vulnerable. If after having killed she detects a possible threat, she'll freeze, keeping constant watch over the potential danger, hoping to go unnoticed. If she is spotted by another raptor, she may issue a vocal threat in an attempt to ward off the intruder. Larger raptors may ignore this warning and successfully drive the falcon from her kill. Some falcons don't easily give up their kills however, and she may indeed turn the tables on her would-be pirates, venting her rage in a barrage of stoops and expletives. The pirates best not ignore these stoops, lest one catch them on the skull. If the thief tries to vacate the area with the falcon's kill, he may be in for a real beating. The falcon will strike mercilessly at the departing enemy who will find it difficult (or impossible) to roll and defend itself without first dropping the stolen kill.

Competition and opportunism are as much a part of predator's lives as is sleeping and reproducing. It is not uncommon for even well-adjusted falconry birds to occasionally view the falconer with some suspicion. They will sometimes make it difficult for the falconer (sans telemetry) to locate them when they are on kills. If, as the falconer approaches the general vicinity of where the kill has taken place, eye contact is established the raptor usually resumes plucking or eating. If, on the other hand, the falconer is unable to make visual contact, she may respond by reverting to her freeze mode. Locating the game-hawk at this point is tough because she'll not move, rendering her bells useless. This behavior should not be misinterpreted by the falconer and viewed as indicative of some sort of flaw or shortcoming in his training. It is simply an innate, survival behavior. We elicit analogous responses with children while playing hide and seek, we send children off to hide and begin the ominous countdown, then search them out, chanting malevolent phrases such as "I'm gonna get you!" Kids get into this hiding game; some will scarcely breath. When the child is discovered, he or she will almost explode in a sort of terror-riddled fun.

If a falcon does manage to eat in peace, they tend to be quite meticulous and will go to great lengths to prepare their meal. When they feel comfortable and secure, they seem to enjoy this preparation, and some will pluck virtually the entire bird before breaking in. Falcons relish eating kills and they do show taste preferences toward body parts with higher fat or nutritional content.

As noted previously, falconry birds benefit from the presence of the falconer at the kill site in terms of safety. The falconer can also be useful by helping them subdue combative quarry and assisting them in breaking in. These direct benefits give the game-hawk ample reason to tolerate, perhaps even appreciate, the falconer's participation. It is in this spirit of cooperation that we can most effectively manipulate the game-hawk to execute C&R techniques without creating an environment of distrust or hostility. In order to minimize damage inflicted upon perspective C&R candidates, we must move quickly and efficiently. Our goal is to transition the game-hawk out of her aggressive combat mode, into a relaxed eating phase as quickly and smoothly as possible. The C&R techniques I use to remove quarry from hawks are principally the same as those I use for falcons, yet mechanically, there are slight modifications. Obviously, handling various types of quarry will also effect the procedure. Regardless of what prey species we're dealing with, priority number one is to physically control the quarry. Sometimes the game-hawk has this taken care of prior to our arrival, other times the battle for control rages on as we arrive. In most cases it is wise to immediately step in and aid the raptor; this directly benefits the soon-to-be-released quarry as well. However in some instances a distraction created by the falconer's intervention may be problematic when dealing with quarry that bites, such as squirrels. Pausing and allowing the hawk to establish the upper hand may decrease the likelihood of her receiving a bite. Surprisingly, I have never taken a venomous snake with any of my hawks, but I would imagine that they would probably be best left to handle these fanged reptiles solo.

Constrictors are another matter. When I was a boy, I flew a

passage tiercel red-tail named Sundance. One afternoon while hawking a favorite bunny field (now covered in concrete, asphalt and buildings) the hawk launched off my fist, flew a short distance, winged over and crashed into the grass. Immediately I saw a portion of a large snake rise above the grass then recoil, disappearing once again into the grass. I ran to the location, arriving within moments, quite shocked at what I found. Sundance had bound to the wrong end of the serpent and was being strangled to death by coils of the five-foot snake looped tightly around his throat. Eyes bulging, beak open, tongue stuck out, the red-tail lay on his side in the dirt quite unable to breathe. I immediately reached down and unwrapped the snake from the hawk's neck, restoring its ability to breathe. Upon release, the snake slithered away, while Sundance began to regain his composure. I mused over the irony of the preceding events and how quickly the tables can turn. Had I not been there to intervene on the hawk's behalf, he surely would have died, just as do the majority of wild passage red-tails before having learned many of the skills necessary to survive.

As with hawks, there is a learning curve for austringers and a need to learn about which creatures warrant caution. I once saw a squirrel shred the welding glove of a young austringer, and as he removed the glove, we watched the blood begin to flow freely. Understandingly, most falconers probably do not C&R squirrels, though it is possible. I learned how to handle squirrels while flying a goshawk that seemed to have a knack for planting her hallux talon in the mouth of squirrels and did so on a muskrat she had bound to.

I had slipped her at a group of mallards in a ditch and, to my surprise, she flew over the ducks and slammed into the muskrat on the opposite bank. I used the same technique to release the muskrat as that I had learned on squirrels. I held the rodent's body with one hand to prevent it from squirming and scratching and then compressed the mouth between thumb and earth at the juncture of upper and lower jaw to prevent it from inflicting damage on either the hawk or myself. With the mouth forcibly held in the open position, the hawk was able to release her grip and remove her undamaged talon with impunity. Fortunately, rabbits are easier to deal with. Having taken hundreds of jacks and bunnies, I have never seen either species resort to biting in self-defense. This allows the falconer to concentrate efforts on controlling the body contortions of thrashing rabbits with no risk to himself or his hawk of being bitten.

When hunting jacks, some austringers prefer to assist the hawk as soon as she binds, while others opt to wait until the hawk is in full control before stepping in. It is well understood that a jack may intensify its efforts to escape (kicking, bucking, rolling or dragging the hawk) when the falconer approaches. I don't think one formula works best for all hawks and situations. I believe a hawk's size, individual style and hold, best dictate the austringer's response. A hen red-tail, for example, with her large size and powerful foot, may sometimes benefit from being left alone momentarily in order to shift her grip for a better position and hold before the austringer approaches. On the other hand, my tiercel Harris appreciates help as soon as possible. Usually, he has the jacks immobilized immediately, but if he has missed his preferred hold and is taking a beating (or a ride), he looks to me for aid and you can almost see the message in his eyes; "Hurry up!" If the terrain is covered with some form of vegetation, the outstretched wings of the Harris act as a drag, slowing the rabbit appreciably. If, however, the ground is devoid of such obstacles, the jack can generate quite a head of steam in spite of packing the extra baggage (hawk). In such cases, it is not uncommon for the hawk or myself to tire before the jack gives out. (You can bet the next time out after such an episode, I'll make every effort to approach from the jack's blind side in the hopes of avoiding a repeat performance.) As soon as I reach the pair, I firmly grip the jack by the back ankles (a loose grip would probably result in the jack kicking loose), and even if the hawk isn't kicked in the process, she'll think you're an idiot for letting it go! Jacks are a very muscular animal; you can't really comprehend the strength they can muster until you've held one in your hands. The back muscles are used in conjunction with front and rear legs as the jack tries to wrench itself free. If the upper body is not controlled simultaneously to the back legs, big jacks can still flip around quite violently.

The tiercel Harris that I am currently flying, Arizona, always wants to transfer to the head of jacks after I arrive. He is not happy otherwise and would not be inclined to surrender the jack until he has achieved this position of control. The additional injury inflicted upon the jack is virtually always quite minimal. I do not attempt to control the jack's upper body until this particular hawk has transferred to his desired hold. As the hawk is making the transfer, he is liable to bind to anything between the jack's rump and head including any of my body parts—so I am careful to stay out of his way! Once the hawk has transferred to the head and neck area, I place my left foot or knee gently on the jack's chest. This does not require much pressure and a lot of pressure would interfere with the jack's respiration and may cause internal injuries as well. The objective is control. As soon as the hawk is happy with his positioning, the jack must not be allowed to squirm. As long as the jack is actively resisting, the hawk will continue to remain in his combat mode, he will grip with all his might and he will not be interested in releasing his grip to transfer off the jack. By restricting all movement of the jack (except respiration), the hawk can begin to lower its level of aggression, ease its grip and be coerced off its quarry. As long as the jack remains motionless, the transfer is easily accomplished. Occasionally I use a carcass as the transfer item, laying it out over the toes of the hawk; more often I use a prepared food item such as a leg, wing, etc. By placing exposed meat in the gloved fist over the hawk's feet, the hawk's view of the jack is effectively blocked. Out of sight, out of mind is applicable. Also, the sight of flesh sharply accelerates the hawk's transition from catch/kill mode into eat mode. The hawk is allowed to tear a couple of bites from the food while I hold it firmly. This is further incentive as once he's tasted blood, felt meat slide into his crop, he'll be mentally ready to complete the transfer from the nonvisible jack in his feet to the visible food above. It is simply a matter of stepping the hawk up onto the food, to which he has already emotionally committed. As the hawk bends and pulls the meat for a third bite, the hand rises with the pull, preventing the hawk from tearing a piece. The only way for him to tear is to hold the food in his feet and the only way for him to do that is to disengage the jack and make the transfer. The hawk in essence is not being asked to relinquish anything; rather, he is being given an opportunity to eat, which he will gratefully accept. As the hawk steps off his quarry, the jack must be restrained. If it is allowed to thrash, the hawk will immediately seize the jack again, shift back into combat mode, inflict more damage to the jack and, worst of all, he may resent your interference and the seeds of distrust will have been sewn. If the transfer is smooth, the hawk engages in eating and I stand, firmly holding the jack by the back legs. The jack hangs limp and is suspended on the opposite side of my body so as to remain unseen by the hawk. I make no attempt to stuff the jack into a bag because it is awkward, delays the release and is entirely unnecessary. I walk away from the site of the capture, which helps the hawk mentally detach from the prior events and concentrates his focus on eating. Within ten or fifteen yards, the jack, having been deemed fit for release, is nonchalantly dropped behind me while the hawk is engrossed in his meal. Usually the jack runs in the opposite direction of my travel and remains unseen by the hawk. If the hawk does catch a glimpse of the departing jack it is of little concern to him now, as are any of the other jacks that may pop up on my way back to the truck, because he is thoroughly out of hunting and into eating mode. The C&R process from start to finish can be accomplished in the span of about one minute. The quicker the hawk transitions, the easier the transition will be. The less time the quarry spends under the hawk, the less mental and physical trauma it will incur.

Transferring game-hawks off waterfowl is equally simple and is detailed in relation to falcons as follows. Once waterfowl have been put to ground, it is imperative to arrive as quickly as possible. Unless killed, stunned or seriously injured by the stoop, ducks will put up quite a fight. Big ducks like mallards can really enrage the falcon with a sound thrashing of wing butts. With the falcon's level of aggression peaked, she will go after the duck's spinal cord with a vengeance. Any delay on the part of the falconer to prevent spinal cord damage can easily result in the quarry necessarily being placed on the nonreleasable list. It would be unwise to protect the duck and neglect to prevent the duck from slamming the falcon and you could hardly blame a falcon for resenting such inconsiderate intervention. The solution is a very easy procedure. The left (gloved) hand is used to cover the duck's head and neck, while the right hand simultaneously pins the duck's wings to its sides. This simple maneuver gives the falconer immediate and complete control over the situation. The duck isn't being bitten, the falcon isn't being pummeled and nobody is going anywhere. The falcon may bite the gloved hand. Instinctively, she is compelled to perform the biting/wrenching behavior, preventing her could quickly become a source of frustration. Avoid frustrating her by offering an appropriate surrogate item to bite. As with hawks, I prefer not to use a lure at this juncture. A bird carcass is very convenient though certainly not necessary. With the falcon bound to the head and neck, I assume a kneeling position with the duck's body (tail first) between my knees. This frees up my right hand, allowing me to remove the surrogate carcass from my hawking bag, while still covering the duck's head and neck with my left hand. The carcass is then presented with the head and neck in position for the falcon to bite, in order to vent her aggression. She will alternate between biting the surrogate and scanning. As long as I restrict all movement from the live duck, the falcon's aggression quickly recedes because the bird that she is looking at and biting is obviously dead. As the falcon continues to bite the limp neck of the surrogate, she may want better leverage or she may simply want to take possession of the carcass, either way she should willingly disengage the live duck and seize the surrogate. Once the falcon has made the transfer, the live duck is surreptitiously placed in the hawking bag (large ducks require large bags). Remember raptors are visual animals, if the falcon sees you with her duck and is made aware that it is still alive, she may forsake the carcass in favor of killing the live duck. Certainly if the falcon sees the duck squirm or flap around, things will get ugly. Avoid this scenario by being precise in your action and movements—out of sight, out of mind. The removal of live quarry from the falcon should be accomplished easily and smoothly with an elapsed time of less than one minute. I delay the release of the duck for an additional couple of minutes allowing the falcon ample time to make the mental transition into a relaxed plucking/eating mode. Otherwise, the sight of her duck flying off before she has become mentally prepared will cause a considerable amount of anxiety. In her mind, the duck is escaping and even if she overcomes the urge to give chase and remains on the surrogate carcass she'll feel torn. By postponing the release long enough for the falcon to switch modes, the subsequent release will be of little interest to her then. Once the falcon has relaxed and begun to eat, the sight of a duck flying off will not set her off. Just the same, it behooves one to release the duck when the falcon's head is down tearing another bite.

Ducks, along with other feathered quarry, are best released into the air as opposed to being planted in cover. I have noticed a reluctance of some birds to take to the sky after having been caught by falcons. Their nerves are fried and their confidence is shot. Putting them forcefully back on the wing seems to restore a bit of their confidence in their aerial abilities. Ducks will fly back to the security of water and game birds will fly toward some form of cover and in so doing they will benefit by being more difficult for scent oriented predators to locate. There is an awful lot of ground scent laid down around the site where the capture took place. To mammalian predators armed with a keen sense of smell, the kill site is like a beacon advertising a likely spot to scavenge a carcass. Ducks planted in such cover would be easy pickings. Even nimble-footed pheasants are at high risk while they are temporarily psychologically disadvantaged immediately after release.

The long-term survivability of released quarry is very high. There have been instances of falconers retaining quarry and having them subsequently die at home, perhaps giving the false impression that released game animals experience high mortality rates. In my opinion, stress is a significant factor. I have seen firsthand that stress alone can kill. The longer quarry is retained, the greater the impact stress will have on their bodies. This is why I promote the concept of virtual immediate release, which is common practice among fisherman. Another misconception is the underestimation of an organism's ability to heal. I've witnessed pin-holed jugulars spontaneously coagulate. I've seen birds in deep shock, near death rebound after spending a couple minutes in a darkend hawking bag where their frazzled brains could regroup. Anyone with extensive experience throwing pigeons under falcons can dispel the infection myth. Homers sustain moderate or sometimes massive injuries and survive though occasionally requiring a few stitches from the falconer. I once had a chicken survive an attack from a wild raptor but suffered nerve damage and lost entire function of one leg. Within a few weeks the hen's leg was fully functional again. Obviously, I am not advocating the release of seriously injured quarry. I'm simply documenting the abilities of organisms to heal some types of injuries sustained through encounters with aerial predators. An assessment must be made of all injuries prior to the release of any quarry. Those candidates deemed unfit for release should be euthanised quickly and humanely. The C&R techniques I have outlined in this chapter are safe, effective and will not upset or discourage the gamehawk. Rest assured, so long as she has been duly rewarded, she will expend little energy mulling over the merits of whether or not something actually died. You, the falconer, on the other hand just might enjoy watching valiant quarry taken in fair chase sail away, perhaps to be chased again some other day or maybe to procreate providing for future generations and the seasons yet to come.

CHAPTER 19

Coup de Grace and Field Dressing

The means by which falconers dispatch and otherwise "prepare" hawk food is, understandably, a little discussed subject. Taken out of context such discourse may appear morbid or overly graphic. Still there is no escaping the fact that birds of prey are just that –birds of prey. They catch, kill and consume. Falconry is not for the squeamish ... nor is the following.

The French phrase *"coup de grace,"* loosely translated as "strike with grace," has been a long-standing falconry tradition. That falconry's ancient practitioners adopted this is evidence of a deep respect for the quarries they pursued and the lives they took. Modern falconers still honor this tradition, dispatching quarry with efficiency and dignity. Over the years, I have experimented with various forms of *coup de grace*, carefully mindful of both predator and prey. I have never felt totally comfortable with knives, spikes or game shears in close proximity to hawks struggling with quarry. I once was part of a gallery of spectators accompanying an austringer and his tiercel Harris hawk out in the field. The hawk put on a wonderful show, binding to a large jackrabbit. As the crowd rushed in, I was shocked to see one of the onlookers recklessly thrust a knife blade into the melee as the hawk and jack flipped about. The austringer eventually secured the upper hand and waived off the well-intentioned

277

spectator and, fortunately, neither hawk nor man was lacerated (or worse) in the incident. I have found the use of hazardous implements entirely unnecessary for dispatching most types of quarry including waterfowl.

Probably the easiest and safest means of administering *coup de grace* to waterfowl is to break the neck with an over-rotation of the head. Quite often, however, this technique is difficult to perform due to the fact that most falcons bind to the head and are reluctant to relinquish their grip. Fortunately, there is an alternative that is equally efficient and very simple to administer, though I do suggest the reader practice the technique on a dead duck or two beforehand. As the falcon stands on the head and neck of the duck, pin the duck's wings to its sides with one hand. Use the thumb of the free hand to penetrate the duck's skin directly below the sternum by applying pressure, pushing toward the inside of the sternum. This allows direct access to the duck's heart. Insert index and middle fingers, palm facing upward, tracing the course of the sternum to the heart. The heart may be immediately detached with a curling motion of the fingers and fed to the grateful falcon. Described on paper, this sounds barbaric; nonetheless, in terms of practical application it is humane. Meanwhile, the falcon has not been endangered, nor has she been forced to release her grip on the duck's head. Whatever methods are used to dispatch waterfowl, it is imperative to restrain them for several seconds afterwards because upon death, their bodies will erupt in a series of extremely violent spasms. Even in death, a big duck is capable of giving the falcon one last thrashing and an everlasting impression.

Field dressing should occur not long after death and takes only moments, with or without the falcon still in possession of the carcass. Again, I use no sharp instruments for this procedure, so I run no risk of injuring the raptor or perforating duck intestines and contaminating the body cavity with its contents. If the duck has been dispatched via the heart removal method, the first step of this procedure has already been completed. If not, a puncture is now required as previously described. Now, placing both thumbs in the aforementioned opening and pulling lengthwise in opposing directions (head/tail), the puncture is enlarged. Reaching in, grasp the gizzard and begin removal, pulling the esophagus until it disconnects in the throat area, then roll the entire body cavity contents out. The intestines will still be connected at the vent. The index and middle fingers are placed at this juncture and the entire vent is now pulled free, completing the process. Ducks thus eviscerated may be sealed in airtight plastic bags and refrigerated temporarily or deep frozen indefinitely.

If the falconer wishes to dismember portions thereof, this may also be carried out without the use of tools; large ducks will require considerable exertion. Place one hand on each of the duck's wings, as close to its body as possible with the duck's back to your chest. Pull evenly in opposing directions and one of the wings will tear free with corresponding pectoral muscle attached. The remaining wing may be removed by holding the duck at the base of the neck with one hand and the wing in the other, once again pulling in opposing directions. This wing and accompanying pectoral muscle will detach much easier than the first wing did. Usually, this wing will also have the sternum attached when it pulls away from the carcass. The sternum can be removed from the pectoral muscle by manipulating your thumb in between the muscle and the bone starting at the top, then just sliding the thumb down, separating one from the other. At this point, the sternum will still be joined to the wing at the top by tendons. Rotating the sternum three or four times in a circular motion will weaken this connection enough to allow a good tug to complete the separation. Be careful here because parts of the sternum are quite thin and sharp enough to cut careless fingers! Duck legs may be removed by holding or standing just above the "hip" joint and pulling forcefully toward the tail. Turn the duck over and repeat to remove the other leg. This should insure that the entire leg detaches cleanly.

CHAPTER 20

Lost Hawks

I wasn't really awake, but I wasn't exactly asleep either as the alarm went off. I rolled out of bed, dressed in shorts, socks and a T-shirt. I slipped a sweatshirt over my head, pulled on my boots and went outside to check the morning air. There was an undeniable chill in the predawn, but I could tell the day would be even warmer than it had been the day before. I was a little disappointed, as I had been yearning for some really cold weather—the kind that gets a falcon all fired up. Even so, I was still excited because I had almost an hour on the sun, and I knew if I didn't mess around I would have Omen airborne by first light. Within short order I had three hawks, two pointers and a box of homers loaded into the truck and we were on our way. Forty-five minutes later, I began to ease up on the accelerator as our destination came into view. Glancing to my left, I scanned the silo for pigeons. Thankfully, there were none. Up ahead on the other side of the road, I noticed a female Cooper's hawk, which probably explained the absence of the silo flock. I offered the little hawk a silent thank you as I rounded the last bend, pulled over and parked.

Our timing was perfect and I bristled at the prospects of flying Omen at Pete's Field in the first light of day. Though far from ideal with its bordering fences, roads, power lines and pigeons, Pete's Field is still outstanding because it has good cover, is rarely shot over and has, in realtor's speak, location, location, location. In short, it's a Mecca for game. Ordinarily, I hunt this field off and on all winter long. But this year had been different. I was writing this book, so I focused almost exclusively on hawking waterfowl with my falcons, placing less emphasis on game birds. Therefore, the pheasants at Pete's hadn't seen much of me as of yet. Now that duck season had closed, things were about to change.

Here we were at the tail end of pheasant season and I still had a virgin field. I stepped out of the truck and sampled the air once more, finding it, as expected, considerably warmer than it had been at home in the foothills. Ever the optimist, I wasn't about to let a little warm air bring me down, after all Omen had been flying in spectacular fashion all season long, so I was definitely anticipating something in the phenomenal range. I paused, momentarily captivated by the sight of small bands of pintails passing overhead 700 or 800 feet up. The distinctive cackle of a nearby rooster pheasant caught my ear and refocused my attention. Hoping to pin the pheasant with the presence of the mounting falcon, I hurriedly tightened the lid on the Marshall transmitter and tuned the receiver. I tried to bewit (fasten) the transmitter to Omen's leg but fumbled the job in my haste. As is so often the case, the urgency in my desire to speed things along only slowed things down. Clearly agitated, Omen rebelled, shifting about on the cadge and making the task all the more difficult. I pleaded, "Hold still for just three seconds; three seconds and I'll get this transmitter on and you can fly." I knew all too well that the rooster would probably make the most of our little delay and vanish, the way only a pheasant can. Only after lifting the toes of Omen's other foot was I able to keep him off balance long enough to finally get the transmitter on. I slung the hawking bag over my shoulder, unsnapped Omen's swivel from the cadge and gently stepped him onto my gloved fist. I checked for oncoming traffic, but there was none to be seen. God bless Sunday mornings! Off went the leash, swivel, jesses and hood.

Omen immediately came to life, exuding an aura permeated with the very essence of predator. Suddenly, a dove fluttered among the small trees edging the road and the falcon exploded into flight, igniting the sky as dozens of terrified doves rocketed out of the trees. Their fears, though understandable, were unnecessary. Omen the Headhunter was looking for a head but not that of a dove. In a way that I can't quite define, the sight of all those flushing doves sparked the falcon further, as if there were some sort of transfer of kinetic energy. I watched briefly as the energized falcon ripped a hole through the sky in a steep ascent, seeking power. I mentally noted Omen's relative position and approximate height before taking my eyes off him long enough to grab my binos and camera, leash the pup and let both dogs out of the truck. I punched the keypad to set the truck alarm then looked up to check the falcon's progress. Thus far, things were looking good; Omen was 200 yards out, 500 feet up and climbing as if possessed.

I was feeling better than ever as the dogs and I crossed the rusted barbed wire fence. I kept the pup on the short lead and sent the old dog, Latham, directly toward the patch of cover where I hoped he would locate and point the rooster. I glanced up to recheck the falcon's progress but wasn't able to see him. Perhaps it was the trees blocking my view? It wasn't a big deal since I hadn't yet gone far from the truck. I figured I'd just swing back to the truck with the dogs, grab the receiver and reconfirm the falcon's location. Moments after deploying the receiver's elements I drew a bead on him. He was slightly to the north and about 1,000 feet up, wings rhythmically pumping as he clawed at the sky for more height. I contemplated carrying the Field Marshall receiver into the field with me, Lord knows it's compact enough, but I already felt overburdened with equipment so declined. I replaced the receiver into the back of the truck, let both dogs out again, reset the alarm and crossed the fence again.

Once into the field, I sent Latham ahead into the cover where the rooster had been, though I fully expected it was probably on the other side of the field by now. Latham worked the cover, confirming my suspicions. I turned my gaze skyward. Omen was nearly overhead some 1,500 feet up and still climbing as hard as ever. I wasn't too concerned about the absence of the rooster; I knew there'd be others. I cut the pup loose, Omen following attentively, at pitch, ready to come down at any moment like the arm of the Reaper. I can remember thinking,

"This is going to be good!" I watched the pointers devour cover for a couple of minutes, and then I looked up to check the falcon; he wasn't there. Considering Omen is a falcon with a nearly impeccable sense of positioning and never rakes, the whole thing seemed weird. I hoped that I just wasn't seeing him. After all, he'd be pushing the 2,000-foot mark by then. But this time, there were no trees to block my view. The sky was clear and fully lit. No doubt about it, Omen was gone. I knew that something had caught his attention, but I didn't know what or where. With that kind of pitch, the Headhunter would have quite the killing cone indeed. I prayed he hadn't engaged the silo flock. Regardless of what form of temptation he'd surrendered to, the bottom line was simple he had either killed, in which case he would have to be located and picked up, or he'd missed his target and would be back overhead shortly. Of course there were other less appealing possibilities. Considering Omen's history and habits, however, all else seemed unlikely.

The sensible thing to do was to back out of the field yet again and consult the "magic box." I called the dogs in and headed them toward the truck once more. By then, they probably thought I'd gone insane with all the back and forth nonsense, but they both had the good sense to comply. Back at the truck, I picked up the receiver and pulled the trigger, and the box came to life. There's a strange thing that sometimes happens when I first turn on a receiver after a falcon has disappeared. The first thing I want to hear when I turn the unit on is a solid beep, indicating a strong signal, good reception and cause for at least a little relief. What actually happens, however, is quite often something else, or at least it can feel that way. Most transmitters pulse at roughly one-second intervals. Ordinarily, one second is a relatively short period of time. That is unless you happen to be listening for that all-important first beep and you happen to turn the receiver on at the very beginning of that lag. In that case, one second can seem like eternal damnation. Sometimes when I turn the receiver on and I don't hear a beep within the first half second or so, I get nervous and after three-quarters of a second, I start convincing myself that there never will be a beep and start to imagine a variety of horrible scenarios. If I happen to have been flying a questionable slip in the first place, I'll toss in an extra heaping of guilt. Then I'll start questioning my intellect and my ability to manage a flight! When that first beep does come (and it always does) I exhale in relief and put most of the negativity behind me just as quickly as it came.

Finally, the regular cadence of the transmitter's signal broadcast loud and clearly across my receiver, soothing my delicate nerves. I determined that the falcon's position was due west. It sounded as though he was fairly close and stationary. So he did kill, I thought. As luck would have it, the falcon's direction nearly paralleled the road, veering only slightly further south. I hopped in the truck and drove a mile before reaching the first crossroad. I turned left, heading south in order to intersect with the imaginary line I'd drawn, denoting Omen's direction from my original position. One quarter of a mile down the road with the receiver out the window, I quickly determined that I'd overshot Omen's position. This was good news because now I not only knew his direction, but I also knew that he was within the mile stretch between the positions of my initial and most recent reading. I drove back along the mile stretch, taking readings out the window as I went. I stopped the truck when the signal peaked directly to the south. At that point, I had three rather precise points of reference (triangulation) and therefore knew almost exactly where the falcon would be found. I walked directly toward the intersection of the imaginary lines I'd drawn, zeroing in on the signal all the while. As I drew near to the downed falcon, my mind ran through a series of possible scenarios of what I might find. I hoped a pheasant, flushing wild, had drawn the falcon's stoop. But the demons in my head were conjuring images ranging from troublesome to horrific. The hypothesis that held the most credence involved the silo pigeons, not because it was necessarily the most likely, after all, in three seasons Omen had only checked on pigeons twice. On both occasions, Omen stooped from well over 1,000 feet, killing both as they crossed through our field, unaware of the danger far above. The silo pigeon theory, however, was more a compromise between the good and evil possibilities responsible for Omen's disappearance.

The signal began to boom. I was getting close. I turned the gain down and the demons raged. I guess it is my way of preparing myself for the worst, just in case. Fortunately, I didn't have long to torment myself. I heard the high-pitched tinkle of Omen's bell above the lower-pitched tone of the receiver. I stopped and listened intently, cocking my head slightly sideways for better directionality. Then it came again—the crisp tinkle of a bell in its prime, the melody carrying well in the still morning air. Just a stone's throw to my right stood Omen, placidly plucking his kill in the rice stubble. Cool, I thought, he's in one piece! The demons were silenced.

Finding Omen intact was a relief; the fact that he was standing over a bull sprig was icing on the cake. The site of the kill was a mere 300 yards from where I'd last seen the falcon mounting overhead. With a minimum pitch of 1,500 feet and quite possibly considerably higher, the pintail was well within the falcon's killing cone when he flew through Omen's airspace. I imagined what it must have looked like as the falcon slammed into the duck, several hundred feet up in the sky, almost certainly a headshot—pity I missed the view.

The fact that I was able to recover the falcon within a minuscule ten minutes of his disappearance is remarkable. The use of radio-telemetry technology transformed what would have taken falconers of old, on a prolonged best guess search, into a systematic speedy recovery. Losing hawks is a scourge that has plagued falconry for thousands of years. In the past, falconers relied heavily upon their wits, experience and intuition to relocate lost hawks. They were also intimately familiar with the interrelationships between raptors and other wildlife. Often, it was mobbing corvids that led them to their wayward gamehawks. Modern falconers would do well to adhere to these fundamental resources. Unlike our predecessors, however, today's falconers have access to radio-telemetry tracking aids that have completely revolutionized our ability to recover lost hawks. Using this technology, we are able to recover hawks with an efficiency that could not have been imagined just a few short decades ago. A common complaint registered by pretelemetry era falconers cited not only the untimely, permanent loss of game-hawks, but that the hawks lost were virtually always their prodigies. This, of course, isn't surprising since the most dynamic fliers would also tend to be the more accomplished hunters and were therefore less dependent upon man as a meal ticket. These types of game-hawks are predators in the purest sense of the word and will kill with or without input from the falconer. Meanwhile, the hawks that would just as soon eat from the falconer's bag as chase quarry (which it probably wouldn't catch anyway), would more than likely hang around for as many molts as the falconer would care to endure. From this perspective, it's clear that radio telemetry doesn't just help to recover lost hawks, it helps to recover our best hawks, thus enabling us to intermew our finest performers year after year. These intermewed hawks have been likened to fine wine—they keep getting better with age. There is no doubt that telemetry is largely responsible for the elevated level at which the art of falconry is currently practiced throughout North America and much of the world today. This is particularly so in the case of waiting-on flights that, in some respects, have taken on new dimensions.

With the specter of permanent loss almost a thing of the past, many contemporary longwingers are striving to fly falcons from extreme pitches, resulting in extraordinary flights. With so much to offer, flying hawks, particularly large falcons, without benefit of telemetry is practically inconceivable, and flying nonnative or hybrids sans telemetry is probably irresponsible. From a financial standpoint, purchasing telemetry equipment can best be described as money well spent. Falconers using a good telemetry system will recoup their investment several times over as they successfully recover lost hawks time and again over the course of many years. From a broader perspective, the monetary loss incurred when a cherished game-hawk is lost pales in comparison to the emotional toll exacted on the distraught falconer, who will never know the flights that might have been. In my opinion, telemetry has become as essential to serious game-hawking as the weight scale. Bare in mind, however, telemetry is no substitute for training, nor is it a valid excuse for sheer recklessness. Personally, I like to think of telemetry as an insurance policy, something I hope never to need, but I'm sure glad it's there when I do.

I make a point of tracking errant hawks as infrequently as possible; it is way too stressful. When one of my hawks causes me to search due to aberrant behavior, I try to find the catalyst or source of the malfunction. Deciphering why hawks do the things they do is paramount to positively shaping a hawk's behavior. Sometimes the reasons a hawk rakes are obvious and clearly defined, other times the hawk's departure may seem to defy all logic. Whatever the case, an immediate solution need be found because raptors can form bad habits almost instantaneously. Some of the more common issues involve improper weight management, enticing check, i.e., pigeons, etc., keeping the falcon on the wing too long (which is usually synonymous with insufficient amounts of game) and generally poorly managed flights. Unsuitable weather conditions can have an additional adverse affect on the problems listed above. Sometimes a departure signifies the hawk's lack of understanding as to just what her role is in this arena. Whatever the case, solve the riddle and find a solution.

In spite of our best efforts, the prospects of tracking a lost hawk sooner or later are rather inevitable. There are few things in life that are capable of more intensely focusing a falconer than searching for his prized game-hawk. At such times, all energies are directed toward locating the missing hawk. It is a dangerous world out there for any raptor; the competition that exists among predators can easily turn lethal. A lost and wandering game-hawk can elicit extreme aggression as she passes into the occupied territories of other raptors. Younger, inexperienced eyases naive in the ways of the wild are vulnerable indeed. The hazards that exist in a man-altered environment are plentiful, and for a hawk that has little or no fear of man the danger is ten-fold. Just within my circle of acquaintances, I've known of truant game-hawks which were shot, stomped, ran over, caged and extorted for ransom. The horror stories of atrocities committed to tame hawks abound and the evil deeds often occur within the first hour of the hawk's disappearance.

When I'm tracking a lost hawk, I can't get there fast enough.

Even if she's safely tucked out of sight plucking a kill, I'd much rather arrive before she completely crops up and spoils not only one day's hawking, but an additional day or two as well. When a game-hawk is lost, every effort is made to recover her as quickly as possible. Sometimes, however, a little restraint and patience is preferable to a hasty, ill-conceived response.

A falcon that has gone beyond visual perception isn't necessarily lost. Some falcons fly out of visual range with regularity. By and large, most people probably underestimate a falcon's ability to orientate itself. They are, in fact, quite capable of returning to the point of flight origin after having ranged considerable distances, and never more so than when they're flying in familiar territory. Were it not so, highly migrant falcons such as the tundra peregrine (*Falco peregrinus tundrius*) could hardly be expected to navigate the widths of two continents during their migration between North and South America.

The late and great falconer Ronald Stevens capitalized on the homing instincts of his falcons, intentionally nurturing this innate ability. Mr. Stevens' technique largely revolved around flying his falcons in one general locale, allowing them time to familiarize themselves with a specific perch site, such as a tree or rock. Once the falcon had established a fondness for a selected site, Ronald would begin to venture farther. In so doing, he was able to engage the homing behavior in his falcons. When his falcons were lost (figuratively), they would return to their favorite perch and there they would wait to be reunited with Ronald. In his book, *Observations on Modern Falconry*, Ronald reports of an interesting incident involving a falcon named Leila. The story is fascinating from both homing and sociological standpoints. In an experiment, Leila was intentionally left in a field nearly 100 miles from home. She was literally given the choice between liberty and resuming her life with Ronald. Leila chose the latter and flew the distance to prove it.

I do virtually all of my training in one location and I, too, have had falcons home from as far as fifteen miles, returning to the training fields where they have spent so much time. However, in my case I do a great deal of hawking far from home and depend on telemetry to bail me out when things really go awry. Nonetheless, electronics alone are not the solution. Developing a sense for interpreting the hawk's actions and intentions will assist in her recovery in a monumental sort of way. When the rapport between hawk and man is such that the falconer can accurately assess the cause of the hawk's absence and predict her subsequent reactions, he may then speed the recovery, in part by not making critical errors.

The term lost hawk can be somewhat of a misnomer. Sometimes a so-called lost hawk isn't lost at all, as in the example that began this chapter. Omen killed from his "pride of place," I just didn't happen to be watching. At the other end of the spectrum, imagine a falcon caught up in the migratory urge and headed for a new latitude on the horizon. These two extremes leave a lot of middle ground wherein a falcon might otherwise be indisposed. More often than not, a seasoned gamehawk that has gone AWOL will return to the falconer in short order, unless of course she has killed elsewhere.

When deciding whether or not a missing hawk warrants tracking, several bits of information need be considered. The signal being emitted by the transmitter will relay important clues regarding direction, distance and whether the hawk is stationary or on the move, etc. This vital information coupled with an intimate knowledge of a particular hawk's track record (no pun intended) will partly dictate the falconer's course of action. Location is also an important consideration, not just the immediate area where the loss occurred but the surrounding environment as well. Is it a game-rich habitat? What's the likelihood of the hawk killing on her own? If there is a pigeon source nearby, there's a good chance she'll be delayed, and a pigeon pursuit/kill could preclude her return altogether. Metropolitan centers with their ever-present pigeon populations attract trained falcons like magnets. There are few things more dangerous to a game-hawk than chasing pigeons through an urban jungle.

Pigeons will use any conceivable means of shaking off a pursuing falcon, trying their darnedest to kill the falcon in the process by running them into buildings, trees, vehicles, power lines, fences and anything else that presents itself. On one such occasion, my falcon chased a feral pigeon, which took to flying through backyards at breakneck speeds. This pigeon managed to escape and the falcon returned. Unfortunately, he came back without the transmitter, which was subsequently recovered in a backyard lying in the grass, deck feather and all, directly below the clothesline the pigeon attempted to kill the falcon on.

To track or not to track—that is the question. Often the answer boils down to an educated guess dosed with a heaping of intuition. If the falcon isn't coming back, the sooner tracking commences the better the odds of a successful recovery. Once the decision has been made to track, all efforts are directed toward intersecting with the falcon at the nearest possible point. Unless she's extremely close, and preferably stationary, this usually involves a vehicle. Presumably, if the falcon hasn't killed, she should be responsive to the falconer's calls, lures, etc., from a considerable distance. Therefore, if a missing falcon hasn't killed and she isn't responsive, it's likely that she's far enough out to preclude a walk-up recovery, hopefully her direction avails itself to vehicle travel. Otherwise, while you're fiddling around on foot, she may be traveling farther away at an alarming rate. The ease with which a falcon can distance herself from the falconer will be especially disconcerting to the tyro accustomed to flying shortwings.

Theoretically, tracking game-hawks is a simple matter. The directional elements of the receiving unit point the way, the falconer follows and the recovery is made. In reality, it is not always quite so simple for a variety of reasons, not the least of which is accessibility. Falcons can fly in any direction they choose, whether it be over a mountain, across a river, through a marsh, etc. Many such areas may be partially or totally inaccessible to a vehicle, making it difficult or impossible to rendezvous with the falcon in spite of knowing her whereabouts. If the obstruction can't be navigated, the falconer may have little choice but to monitor the signal and hope she eventually gravitates to a more accessible location. If, on the other hand, she stalls or moves farther into the abyss and out of telemetry range, some sort of "Hail Mary" operation may need be conceived.

As long as a signal is being broadcast and received, the prospects of recovery are excellent. When radio contact is lost, the whole affair takes on a new sense of urgency. With contact broken, the falcon's position becomes an enigma, and desperation can take a toll on the falconer's exposed nerves. Reestablishing radio contact is imperative and may not be as difficult as imagined if the falconer exercises common sense. Falcons that traverse long distances when lost are usually traveling in a very linear fashion. The direction traveled may be related to terrain, i.e., coastline, ridge line, etc. Prevailing winds are very influential and many falcons will fly directly with or against the wind. In such instances, if the falconer continues on the same bearing that the falcon had been known to be traveling, he may pick up a signal again farther down the road. Obviously, a falcon heading into a wind will make slower progress than a falcon flying with a tailwind. In the latter case it may be "pedal to the metal," just to keep pace with the falcon's progress. When the signal is lost and you have no inkling as to where to look, or if the signal being received is so weak as to make it difficult to determine direction, look for elevation. The best way to extend the reception range or get a more pristine version of the signal is to elevate the receiver. Avoid power lines, fences or any other disruptive or reflective objects if possible. Hilltops, ridge lines, freeway overpasses, bridges and buildings are all ideal vantage points, along with just about anything else that can be scaled without getting yourself killed or arrested in the process. In totally flat terrain, the top of the vehicle is very useful and readily available. Even when I'm already parked on a hill, if I'm not getting a signal I will go up on the roof of the truck. Those few extra feet may seem insignificant but in actuality they can easily mean the difference between reception and not.

Held at arm's length overhead, the antenna is methodically swept across the sky 360 degrees, scanning for a signal. Several such revolutions may be made, alternating both pitch and angle of the antenna. The best (perhaps only) chance of receiving a legitimate signal depends not only on pointing the antenna in the right direction, but also in aligning the elements of the receiver's antenna on the same axis as that of the transmitters antenna wire (polarization). A tail-mounted transmitter will be in a horizontal position when a hawk is flying and vertical when the hawk is standing erect. The transmitter may also be positioned at varying angles depending on body position. Therefore, when the falcon's location and position are unknown, all angles should be tried. When a signal is picked up, it is critical to nail down the correct direction. Quite often false signals will be picked up in the exact opposing direction. One direction denotes the falcon's actual position while the other, the back lobe, leads to disappointment. Verify the correct signal by its strength. Follow the strongest signal.

Before roaring off down the road, however, it is a good idea to make some visual references. Pick a distant landmark toward the horizon—a mountain, a building, whatever—just make certain that it is highly visible and is in the general direction of the lost hawk. While you're at it, identify the hawk's direction in terms of north, south, east or west, relative to your position. This way, no matter how the road you are driving twists and turns, you'll still know approximately where it is that you're trying to get. Additional readings can be taken en route, and by mentally combining readings taken from multiple angles (triangulation), it is possible to get a very precise fix on the hawk's location. Multiple readings will also clarify whether or not the hawk is moving and its approximate rate of progress. When following a signal, rather than using a roof-mounted omnidirectional antenna, I prefer to carefully stick the yagi antenna out the window. By periodically or continually monitoring the signal on the roads (which rarely coincide with the exact desired direction as it weaves around), triangulation occurs as a natural byproduct.

There are times when a falcon will be moving quite rapidly and continually remains one step ahead of the tracker. By the time the tracker finds a route to where she was, she's long gone. So long as the falcon travels in a specific direction, the solution may lie in plotting a course ahead of the falcon and there wait for her arrival. The rendezvous site selected should preferably be as open and elevated as possible. This will not only aid in signal reception, but it will also afford the greatest potential to make the all-important visual contact with the wayward falcon. Theoretically, if the falcon can see the tracker, she can then be called in. Whatever method the falconer normally uses to call the hawk in may be employed, but maximum visibility is crucial, as she may be quite a ways out and not necessarily looking for the falconer at this point. I, for one, am not opposed to using live lures on such occasions. Truth be known, I always carry a box of homers in the truck when I'm hawking, in part for these rare occasions. If lures (live or otherwise), whistles and yells fail to attract the attention of the lost falcon, the tracker may consider lofting a fit homer. Upon release in unfamiliar territory, strong homers will take to the air, rising in circles, perhaps several hundred feet overhead before striking out for home. If the falcon in question has been conditioned to the balloon, by all means, send it up. If these attempts fail to bring the falcon around, chances are she's still out of visual range. The tracker may have miscalculated the falcon's trajectory or she may have altered her course. At any rate, he may have to re-evaluate the signal and move accordingly.

There's no doubt that tracking can be a grueling, arduous affair that requires a great deal of perseverance. Nevertheless, so long as a signal is being received, the prospects for recovery remain excellent. Throughout an abnormally difficult tracking ordeal, the tracker may also find solace in knowing that with nightfall the tracking should get easier. On a couple of occasions, I have tracked falcons that were still on the wing well after dark, but on both occasions the falcons had somewhere specific they were headed—they were homing to the training field. Ordinarily, a falcon will take up a roost around sunset and once she's finally stationary, she should be a whole lot easier to find. Dusk also brings a couple of bonuses in terms of signal reception. Most raptors will select a reasonably high perch for a roost; my lost falcons have chosen hillsides, trees and, on one occasion, a high-tension metallic power pole. As the sun sets, atmospheric changes take place. Just as the sound of a falcon's bell is amplified after sunset so, too, is the transmitter's signal received from greater distances. The combination of a stationary, elevated transmitter and enhanced reception make for better tracking. One afternoon, while tracking a falcon, I lost the signal and had no idea where he'd gone or even which direction to look. After dark when he'd taken up roost on a large power pole, I began to receive the signal again. As it turned out, he was nearly thirty miles away, but with a clear signal he was easily located.

Unfortunately, with darkness new threats come to life as nocturnal predators start to make their rounds. The great horned owl (*Bubo virginianus*), which is common throughout North America, has killed many a game-hawk left out overnight. These formidable predators, hunting under cloak of darkness, provide a healthy incentive to retrieve falcons in the dark if at all possible, as opposed to calling off the effort until daybreak. Those who choose to wait may well be collecting their transmitters in the morning and little else. Aside from the threat of predation, leaving a hawk out overnight is risky because they often leave their roost well before sun up. By the time the bleary-eyed falconer arrives in the morning at the place where his falcon had spent the night, she may well be on the wing and out of telemetry range—especially if she's in foreign territory. For that matter, she may get spooked during the night and take off, panicked in the dark. Let your imagination run wild with the possible calamities this scenario inspires. Additionally a bird on the hand means a good night's sleep, a bird on the lam…well, you get the idea.

Once the falcon has been located in the dark, it becomes a question of how to get her down from her roost. If she can be easily reached, she may be approached slowly while speaking to her in a soothing voice to help steady her nerves. A flashlight illuminating a lavishly garnished glove doesn't hurt either. Whereas some hawks may get flighty after being on their own for some time, imprint falcons are usually fairly placid. Nonetheless, they all should be treated with the utmost consideration and deliberance of movement in the dark. If the falcon has chosen to roost in a more precarious location, making an ascent dangerous or impossible, we hope she had the courtesy to roost in a vehicle-accessible location. In that case, she may be called down by headlight. The tracker, standing in front of the vehicle in clear view of the hawk, is lit up by the high beams. He then entices the hawk down by any means possible, and by this time I'd imagine there would be few who would be entirely opposed to using a live lure! Nonetheless, if she's really hungry, she'll probably come down to just about anything. Regardless of what is used, it helps if it has got white on it for visibility reasons; a pigeon with white or light brown feathers will work nicely. In a pinch, a white sock, hankie, napkin, etc., can be tied to a lure to enhance its illumination.

When coercing a falcon to fly in the dark, the falconer is obligated to ensure that the hawk has a safe landing zone. This space encompasses not only where she'll come down, but the surrounding area as well, namely avoiding power lines and fences, which she will not see as she butterflies in. If auto headlights can't be used due to inaccessibility or hazardous surroundings, calling the hawk in by flashlight is a viable alternative. Last season I had one such episode when I was duck hawking in the Sierra Nevada Mountain Range at about the 8,000-foot level. The area I had originally planned to fly was currently being used as a landing zone for a helicopter logging operation. I pressed on, looking for slips for two falcons as the sun dipped below the mountain peaks to the west. I was quickly running out of daylight. As dusk approached, I came to a clearing in the forest with a fairly large pond containing five mallards. It wasn't an ideal set, due in part to the trees. But it was a "now or not today" proposition and the older falcon, Shaman, was sharper (hungrier) than he had been all season.

I put Shaman up and kept tabs on his progress as best as I could. His wingbeat looked good in the cold mountain air. At 400 feet I could still hear his bell and catch occasional glimpses of him through the tops of the pine trees as he climbed. For no readily apparent reason, Shaman went wide, his bell fell silent and I could no longer confirm his position. I fully expected to see him reappear in a minute or two because I knew he had seen the mallards to which he had an addiction. Maybe, I thought, he's just keeping his distance to lull the ducks into a sense of complacency? At any rate, I wasn't too concerned because it was getting dark and this duck killer was hungry!

The dog, Latham, and I went in to flush. Two of the mallards got up and left while the remaining ducks settled in at the opposite end of the pond. I watched and listened for Shaman, but there was sign of him whatsoever. Now I was concerned and hurried back to the truck to consult the receiver. I was comforted by a strong signal coming from the north, the direction the pair of mallards had chosen to leave, which was coincidentally the direction I had last seen Shaman headed. I began to suspect that the ducks had unwittingly flown under him as they traversed their way through the forest in an effort to reach the massive lake that lay at the base of the mountain I was on. Driving wasn't an option, but judging by the signal strength, I didn't expect to have to go far.

I struck out on foot, and a few hundred yards into the forest, the signal really started booming. I knew I was getting close, so I pressed on in spite of the impending darkness. The forest was heavily treed and strewn with boulders, ravines and drop-offs, all of which made for treacherous walking and wreaked havoc on the transmitter's signal. What should have been a simple retrieval became increasingly difficult as the signal was diffused through the trees and reflected off everything the terrain had to offer including the lake down below. I stumbled around in the fading light, chasing illusions here and there. I found myself torn because I really wanted to pick up the falcon, and I knew I was close. But I was also acutely aware of how dark it was becoming and the all-too-real prospects of stepping off some unseen ledge. Better to head back and get the flashlight, I thought, kicking myself for not having brought it in the first place.

Darkness fell and gave way to a pitch of black that enveloped everything. If it was tough to see the hand in front of my face, it was impossible to see my boots. The hike back to the truck was painstakingly slow. I knew the pointer could fare much better in the darkness than I, so I followed his lead through the woods, back toward the road. With Latham right in front of me, I concentrated on the white patches of fur that occasionally became visible. I turned off the receiver in order to better hear the metallic nametag jangling on his collar as he strode ahead. Having the dog out in front provided a sense of security. I figured he probably wouldn't lead us over a cliff. In fact, with him in front, I was almost certain he wouldn't lead *me* off a cliff, if you know what I mean. The fact that this neck of the woods sported a healthy bear and mountain lion population crossed my mind more than once. Nothing like a walk in total darkness in strange territory to heighten one's sense of vulnerability. I wanted to believe that Latham wouldn't stumble into anything large and hairy, but Latham is no spring chicken. And while I knew his sense of smell was up to snuff, I hadn't yet decided whether his sense of hearing was really getting worse or if he'd just finally gotten tired of listening to me after all these years.

Eventually, Latham and I landed on the road safe and sound, where visibility was only slightly better, and we made our way back to the truck. When we arrived, I turned on another transmitter and placed it on top of the truck, grabbed the flashlight, and followed the falcon's signal back into the forest. This time I could at least see where the flashlight's beam shone on the trail directly ahead. Within half a mile, the receiver was booming again; as before, the signal seemed to be coming from just about everywhere. I turned down the gain and moved through the black, calling to the falcon by name. The receiver I was using then was considerably older than my geriatric dog and though I'd used it to locate many a falcon over the years, I was having a hell of a time with it that night. Apparently, Shaman became a little impatient; he was definitely hungry. Instead of waiting for me to find him, he launched himself into utter darkness. I heard his bell, crisp and clear and I can tell you I've heard no finer sound. Though I couldn't see him, the cadence of the ringing prompted visions of a moth fluttering to light. In the next moment, Shaman crashed through small limbs, then came to rest on the receiver held in my hand. Man, what a relief. I pulled a glove over my hand and stood Shaman on my fist, giving him a once over with the flashlight. His crop was empty; there was no blood on his talons or feathers stuck to his toes. By all appearances, he hadn't killed one of the mallards or anything else for that matter. The mystery as to what he'd been up to would remain unsolved. I was just glad to be getting the hell out of there with my falcon intact.

    I removed Shaman's transmitter and shut it off, then tuned the receiver to pick up the signal from the transmitter I had left on top of the truck. The hike back was no picnic, but neither was it anything like before when I'd had no light to see with. Now it was just a matter of following the signal back to the truck with the transmitter, like a beacon, guiding us in. After replacing the falcon to the cadge, I stowed the telemetry gear and it was only then that I realized that somewhere along the way I'd dropped Shaman's transmitter. Ordinarily, it wouldn't have been such a big deal because I know better than to turn off a transmitter out in the field. But, of course, this night had been atypical in a number of ways; it seems Murphy had been working overtime. I knew the odds of backtracking and visually locating the transmitter in the dark were slim to none. I thought maybe the next day I'd get lucky and find it, but not tonight. Tonight I was content just to have Shaman back on the cadge.

    Sometimes falcons are reluctant to come off their roosts in the dark, especially if they are cropped up. If the falconer can't manually retrieve the falcon, he'll have little choice but to pick her up in the morning. I've heard of falconers spending the night near their roosting falcons. Others have left portable radios turned on at the base of the roost to ward off predators. Since I began using telemetry nearly two decades ago, I've only had two instances in which my game-hawk spent the night out. Both incidents occurred before I had switched to Marshall equipment. On one occasion, I had been hawking sage grouse near dusk. My falcon knocked a grouse down, but it jumped up again and the tailchase was on. The grouse only flew about half a mile before it bailed and was killed by the falcon. As I made my way to the general area where the two had gone down, the falcon plucked and fed on the grouse in the snow. Before I could pinpoint the falcon's exact location, the signal stopped abruptly. I flipped on another transmitter to verify that the receiver was working properly, and indeed it was. With no signal to follow, I knew the pointer was my best hope of finding the falcon before dark. I gave the command "go falcon" and the dog diligently coursed the sage, but neither he nor I could find the kill site before nightfall.

I spent the night there in the truck, which, fortunately, I had planned on doing anyway. As I woke up periodically throughout the evening, I'd flip the receiver on, just in case, always with the same result—dead air. At 4:30 a.m. I woke again and dutifully turned on the receiver. This time, the signal was there, clear as a bell. Within a few minutes, I'd located the falcon, not more than 400 yards from where I'd slept. I found Shaman ten feet up, roosting in a juniper. He was covered in grouse blood, still had a crop and, by all appearances, was one happy camper. I could only surmise that the leg-mounted transmitter ceased functioning in the snow due to the extreme temperature. Then, sometime, during the night or the wee hours of the morning, the falcon pulled that foot up and warmed the transmitter with his body heat, whereupon it began to function once again. Go figure.

Transmitters can and do fail, which is why many people advocate flying with two transmitters at all times. Now that I'm using Marshall transmitters, with their reduced antenna length, I'd be more inclined to fly with two transmitters when the potential for tracking is greater, such as when sage grouse hawking. Whereas falcons commonly kill sage grouse after a protracted tailchase, this is rarely the case with waterfowl. Under normal circumstances, the risk of losing an entered duck hawk (especially an eyas) is not very high. Most duck flights terminate one way or another, in close proximity to the pond/falconer. Out of approximately 1,000 duck kills, I have experienced very few episodes where any of my falcons flew down and killed a healthy, mature duck in a long, drawn-out tailchase. Duck hawks learn to do their killing at the pond and ordinarily don't bother engaging themselves in distant futile tailchases. Gyrs may be an exception, and I have read accounts from various sources of the relentless gyr flying waterfowl out of the sky. Though I've experienced no such difficulties with my half/half gyr hybrids, the three-quarters jerkin I recently began working has demonstrated the capacity to fly ducks down. In any case, one should never become too complacent about the possibilities of losing a game-hawk in the field.

Long-range transmitters are highly recommended whenever flying large falcons. Transmitters can be attached to hawks via leg, tail or neck mounts. While I have never felt comfortable (or compelled) to try neck mounts, I have extensive experience with both leg and tail mounts. Theoretically, the tail mount has much to offer both functionally and aesthetically. With the transmitter tucked neatly over the top of the tail, it is well out of the way and can't interfere with the hawks footing ability. It's also less likely to get fried if the hawk lands on a power pole, and it won't attract the attention of other raptors bent on pirating a free meal the way the other mounts can. From an aerodynamic perspective, it would seem that the tail mount would generally create less friction (drag) in flight. Basically out of sight, the tail mount aesthetically reigns supreme hands down. As strong as the case is for tail mounts, they have historically had one huge drawback in that they were very prone to being ripped out of an active, aggressive game-hawk. When a tail mount is ripped out, the problem is two fold in that not only is the transmitter no longer attached to the hawk, but neither is the deck feather. A pulled deck feather in the middle of the hawking season isn't the end of the world, but it is a real letdown. In some cases the raptor will generate a new feather, but even under the best of circumstances, it will be months before the tail has been fully restored. In the meantime, the hawk will fly with no noticeable lack of maneuverability, but the developing feather will be susceptible to damage whilst it is still "in the blood." If a developing feather is damaged, either nutritionally (underfeeding) or traumatically (impact, etc.), it will be pinched out at the base, in which case the regeneration process must start all over again—if you're lucky! Sometimes feather pulls result in follicle damage. The incidence and severity of follicle damage varies from case to case, and the likelihood of follicle damage will depend to some extent on the species of raptor involved. Harris hawks for example are loosely feathered, meaning their feathers are comparatively easily pulled. This in turn, causes less or, hopefully, no follicle damage. Thus, while the Harris is relatively susceptible to pulls when an antenna wire is snagged, they are also more likely to regenerate a well-developed replacement. My tiercel sonoran Harris has had several tail mounts ripped out, all occurring while tackling large Black-tail hares. My impression is that the jacks are kicking them out with their hind toes. I'm in no way inferring that Harris hawks shouldn't be tail mounted. In fact, I'm certain that many (perhaps most?) would fare well with a tail mount, depending on what and how they hunt. But I'm equally confident that my Harris will never go the season with his tail intact if he's tail mounted for precisely the same reasons.

Falcons, which are generally more tightly feathered, present a bigger dilemma. Though tightly feathered, falcons are susceptible to feather pulls when their antenna wires are snagged during high-speed pursuits, speed being the operative word. While I have had some falcons replace pulled decks, two falcons received follicle damage that was severe enough to permanently preclude regeneration. In another instance, a falcon received partial follicle damage and subsequently developed a replacement deck that was a little short and slightly twisted at the bottom. From then on, after each molt, the deck in question was similarly afflicted.

Once a falcon's tail has been permanently reduced to eleven feathers, tail mounting is no longer a viable option. Were she to lose another, the aerodynamic performance of the tail as a rudder mechanism would be substantially compromised. Furthermore, without the support of the two central deck feathers, the likelihood of additional train (tail feather) damage would be significantly higher.

In light of the possible side effects related to tail mounts, one might think the leg mount an obviously better choice. But the argument is far from over. It has been contended, better to have a tail feather ripped out than a leg dislocated, or worse, in the case of an antenna snag. Personally, I've had no such injuries. On one occasion a hawk was pulled up short when an antenna wrapped around a fence he was flying over. On another, a falcon pursuing a mallard between power lines was visibly jerked when his antenna wrapped the power line, but in neither case were there injuries to the raptor. It's likely that a leg-mounted transmitter will occasionally exacerbate the inevitable foot bruising experienced by a hard-hitting falcon, but a small bruise on rare occasion is an acceptable price and less problematic than the complications I've suffered in dealing with tail mounts, which is why I had opted for leg mounts only. Recently however, innovations in transmitter circuitry and design have prompted me to reconsider my position.

Transmitter antenna wire lengths have always been a source of concern regardless of mounting method. The longer wires were a necessary evil in order to achieve the desired range. Marshall Telemetry has pioneered the next-generation transmitter that has cut the wire length in half, while retaining superior signal strength. Additionally, Marshall has constructed a new transmitter specifically designed to meet the needs of tail mount enthusiasts. The Powermax transmitter is extremely low profile and cut the overall length by a whopping eight and one-quarter inches from the transmitter I had previously used. That's a whole lot less wire dangling from a game-hawk. I experimented with this transmitter the last three seasons on some of my falcons and love it. Just as the days of flying large falcons without telemetry are long gone, the days of flying with lengthy dangling transmitter wires are likewise coming to an end, as these relics become obsolete.

Regardless of which transmitter or means of attachment is used, unless certain precautionary measures are taken, the telemetry system may let you down at the worst possible moment. When it comes to telemetry (or falconry in general for that matter) it pays to be meticulous and prepared. Every time a game-hawk is loosed, the falconer should be operating under the premise that tracking may become necessary. All components of the telemetry system should be maintained in good working order. Transmitter batteries should be replaced well before they lose their potency. Battery contact points should be checked periodically and cleaned as necessary. Before each use, transmitters should be visually inspected to ensure that batteries are properly installed and that antenna wires are securely attached. Always verify the signal before the hawk is released. Tuning in the receiver to the transmitter's signal just prior to flight enables tracking to begin immediately without having to scan the frequency for the proper setting. For precision tuning, the transmitter should be the same temperature as the outside air. Always check that the transmitter is correctly secured to the hawk. An incorrectly positioned tail clip can easily slip out. In the case of leg mounts, a traditional bewit works very well. Alternatively, some falconers attach transmitters to the almeri cuff, usually by means of a cable tie (zip tie). I used to use this method myself, but have long since abandoned it for a couple of reasons. A transmitter hanged from an almeri will dangle considerably farther down than one bewitted directly to the tarsus above the almeri. Not only will this create an encumbrance when the hawk is footing quarry, but the antenna snag liability is also increased. Furthermore, large falcons can remove cable ties with their powerful beaks. Habituating a falcon early on in her training to wearing a dummy transmitter can alleviate the biting/picking at transmitters that may otherwise occur after the falcon has been lost long enough to get bored. Nonetheless, cable ties are not recommended.

The receiver is the falconer's lifeline to a lost hawk and, as such, should be handled with care. The Marshall receiver I use is designed to facilitate a quick battery change out, so I keep fresh batteries in the truck at all times. The last thing anyone wants to be doing in the midst of tracking is to have to stop and look for a place to buy fresh batteries.

Not surprisingly, the most critical element of any telemetry system is the operator. While I've touched upon many of the skills and techniques used to track falcons with telemetry, I have by no means exhausted the subject in either technical or practical terms. Tracking falcons is an art in itself. Essential skills will only be perfected through practice. Don't wait until a hawk is actually lost to figure out how to use the system you have purchased. Place transmitters in various locations and take readings from multiple positions in order to learn how your system responds in a variety of terrain and atmospheric conditions. Have somebody else hide transmitters for you. When you get efficient at finding them, you can raise the bar by tracking moving targets, such as vehicle. The skill you gain will not only increase your odds of quickly recovering a lost hawk, it will also give you confidence and thus help reduce your stress level while tracking her.

Take comfort in knowing that as long as a signal is being received, recovery is virtually inevitable. Remember, if a transmitter moves out of range and the signal is no longer received, look for elevation. If the available elevation isn't cutting it and you are truly stumped, aerial surveillance should be considered. If you can't pick up a signal from an aircraft, there's probably a malfunction in the telemetry system. If all else fails and the hawk remains at large, get the word out. Contact the agencies, groups and organizations that are most likely to receive the call when John Doe discovers a tame hawk in his backyard. Spread the word by any means possible, but be prepared to ask pertinent questions about any possible sightings in order to eliminate false leads and save time.

As with so many other aspects of game-hawk management, an ounce of prevention is worth several pounds of cure. Use good judgment, fly smart and listen to your intuition. Undoubtedly, some slips are better left unflown. Raptors are highly visual animals, meaning they are usually thinking about things they're looking at; maintaining visual contact, especially with an inexperienced eyas or a fresh passage is important. Out of sight, out of mind. If during a flight a falcon starts to range, whether through boredom or distraction, do something to draw its attention back to you before it flies over a hill and disappears.

In order to experience the finest that falconry has to offer, a game-hawk needs longevity. She needs to mature. Her potential is as boundless as your imagination and skill. Don't let her slip away through some momentary lapse of reason for the rewards are coming up around the bend.

CHAPTER 21

The Future of Falconry

Recently, I headed out to one of my favorite jack fields. It was the first time I've flown it since the moult. It was surprisingly difficult to find, due to the enormity of the construction that had taken place during the break in the hunting seasons. While the core of the field remained, the outlying area had been bulldozed and much of it built upon. The few remaining acres of vegetated landscape still held jacks; in fact, it was practically writhing with "blacktails." While I was grateful for the temporary abundance of quarry, I couldn't help but feel guilty about taking advantage of the jacks' plight; my heart weighed heavily as I acknowledged the passing of yet another field already in the throes of a painful, lingering death.

Unfortunately, this scenario isn't exactly unusual. Too many of us are all too familiar with the loss of a favorite field or pond to the ever-pervasive tumor of urban sprawl. We drive past subdivisions, shopping malls, and gas stations where once stood rich wildlife habitat. Memories of fine days spent hawking still linger, but the habitat and its inhabitants are long gone. The United States is currently losing wildlife habitat at a rate of 1.5 million acres per year, with no end in sight. This reduction has in turn resulted in fewer hunting opportunities and, thus, fewer hunters. Hunters are among the strongest supporters of conservation, both ethically and financially. In 2001, American hunters contributed $1.8 billion in license fees and special taxes on hunting paraphernalia; they also donated $200 million to conservation organizations, not to mention the $4 billion spent on leasing, managing, or buying land for hunting. In short, hunters are the primary funding source for government conservation agencies across the U.S. and have funded the conservation of tens of millions of acres of wildlife habitat, at least helping to slow the bleeding of a wounded world. How unfortunate that these facts are lost on the general public, many of who view hunters as ignorant Neanderthals. While loss of habitat may be the most visible threat to wildlife and falconry, there are myriad environmental and political issues that could prove equally or more devastating.

As human populations continue to swell, so do the demands placed on our natural resources, and many ecosystems are being exploited beyond all hopes of sustainability. We are fortunate in North America, that there are still millions of acres of public land where even an average guy can still hunt grouse like a king. Unfortunately, much of these high desert lands have been degraded through overgrazing of domestic livestock. When ranchers supplemented their herds' meager diets with foreign hay, they unknowingly introduced non-native vegetation that competes with the native plants upon which many animals depend. These factors have contributed to the decline in sage grouse populations that, once so abundant, are now precariously close to the endangered species list. I suspect that were it not for the socio-economic and political realities, sage grouse would have been listed long ago. The recent boom in oil and gas extraction in the heart of sage grouse territory is not encouraging. The Bureau of Land Management, which oversees these public lands, has streamlined its permit process to facilitate the massive increase in drilling in New Mexico, Colorado, Wyoming, and Montana (they're talking about 71,000 wells in the Powder River Basin alone). Additional roads, vehicles, drills, pumps, pipes, spilled crude oil, and lower water tables can do no good for sage grouse. To a grouse hawker, sage grouse habitat is hallowed ground; to a corporation, nothing is sacred—look for a drilling rig on your favorite grouse lek/moor soon. Things haven't been a whole lot easier for the prairie grouse either, more than 75 percent of the original North

American prairies are gone, having been converted to agricultural lands.

Duck hawking fanatics will, of course, be keenly interested in waterfowl habitat, i.e., wetlands. The Prairie Pothole Region on the northern prairies (lovingly referred to as 'the duck factory') is the single-most important breeding ground for water birds in all of North America. Aside from providing ideal habitat for a diverse group of organisms, wetlands are a vital part of our water cycle. A single acre of wetlands can store up to 1.6 million gallons of water, making them extremely effective at retaining flood waters, thus reducing erosion. In the meantime, wetlands constantly recharge underground aquifers with purified water. Today, more than half of the original wetlands across the United States have been obliterated, and the U.S. is still losing more than 100,000 acres of wetlands every year. Agricultural operations were once the primary cause of wetland loss, but today rural and urban development have become the leading forces behind the draining of these critical habitats. Were it not for people who love ducks, namely duck hunters, there would be far fewer wetlands across North America and correspondingly lower duck populations. Ducks and duck hunters alike have an invaluable ally in Ducks Unlimited Inc., which has taken on a leadership role in waterfowl and wetlands conservation. Quite literally, what happens to wetlands is what happens to ducks.

The coming years will undoubtedly be challenging for North American wildlife and falconers. Of particular concern will be global warming. Complex physical forces including the chemical composition of the atmosphere dictate the earth's temperature. Several compounds including carbon dioxide and methane are known to be greenhouse gasses, which trap heat in the atmosphere and prevent it from radiating back into space. As the atmospheric concentration of these gasses increases, so too does the temperature of our planet. It's my impression that most of us haven't really come to grips with just how disruptive climate change will be. In fact, a lot of people, including the current administration (Bush Jr.), don't even want to acknowledge global warming, going so far as to delete all such references from the latest environmental protection agencies' annual report. Rather than taking on a leadership role in reducing greenhouse gas emissions, the U.S. has stuck its head in the sand and chosen not to accept reality. According to Michael Dettinger, a U.S. geological survey research biologist and researcher with the climate research division at Scripps Institution of Oceanography, "Climate change is upon us. In 20 to 25 years, we really will be working with a different climate." While a 2.5 to 10.4 degree increase over the next 100 years may seem mild, the fallout promises to be substantial and potentially catastrophic. Oceans, which have risen 4 to 8 inches over the last century, may rise 3 feet over the course of this century, flooding coastal estuaries and eliminating critical waterfowl habitat. Warmer temperatures will continue to affect weather patterns and alter when, where, and how precipitation occurs. Some regions are expected to become wetter, others drier, but it's still to early to get a clear picture of just how it will all unfold. This uncertainty however, must not preclude us from taking actions now. By investing in alternative energy technologies the U.S. government can reduce dependency on fossil fuels, thereby cutting greenhouse gas emissions and once again taking on a global leadership role. Since politics will obviously play a major role in plotting the environmental course the nation will follow, the crux of a truly visionary approach will be in overcoming the greedy cooperate mentality, which currently has a stranglehold on many governing bodies. Government will also play a role in the future of falconry by way of regulations—some of which are politically driven and reflect the attitude held within the courts of public opinion. In order for American falconry to survive well into the twenty-first century and beyond, it is crucial that the public perceive falconry as a biologically sound and morally acceptable hunting art. Likewise it's imperative that falconers be recognized as the most dedicated raptor conservators on the planet. In this day of instant information, or misinformation as the case may be, falconers can no longer afford to rely upon a low-profile protocol. If falconry is to benefit from a positive public image, it is up to falconers to deliver that message. Likewise, it falls upon those of us who make the outdoors our temple to actively promote conservation, preservation, and restoration ethics among those who don't.

Raising environmental concerns in this modern era is made somewhat more difficult because the average citizen is woefully out of sync with the earth's natural rhythms. Somewhere along the path to modernization, people fell out of step with nature, as industrialization drove a wedge between them and the ecosystems upon which they unknowingly depend. Still, somewhere deep inside, people are listening to a faint call of the wild, and they are filling this perceptible void by fishing, biking, hiking, kayaking, hunting, and a host of other interactive pursuits. I believe that part of the allure of falconry today is its capacity to cut through the artificial haze enveloping modern man. Falconers experience an unsurpassed ecological intimacy, reconnecting man with the natural order, thus instilling a sense of personal balance. To be sure, falconry isn't for everybody, yet the insights revealed through falconry's unique perspective do have universal implications. Falconers see life from an elementary viewpoint while standing on the front lines of ecological battlefields. If falconry is to persist at the level of excellence and grandeur that it's being practiced today, we need to change the way we do business. All too often, we turn quick profits at the expense of our environment, and, in so doing, we deny ourselves and future generations access to future resources. If we continue to write environmental IOUs on the backs of our children's generation, then our legacy will be that of gluttony, greed, and arrogance. We will be the generation that "paved paradise and put up a parking lot." If, on the other hand, we rise to the occasion, seize the moment, and save the day, our legacy will live on in the ecosystems we preserve, thereby enabling future generations the opportunity to practice the beautiful and ancient art of falconry.

May there always be places where wild things flourish and the hearts of uncivilized men can still soar.

Glossary

Accipiter: Genus of shortwinged hawks known for rapid acceleration and extreme maneuverability.
Aspergillosis: An often fatal respiratory disease to which goshawks and gyrfalcons are particularly susceptible.
Austringer: One who hunts with hawks, especially accipiters.
Bagged game: Game artificially released by the falconer for training purposes.
Bate: Restrained hawk attempting to fly.
Bail out: As in ducks piling back into a pond.
Bewit: Thin leather strap by which bells and transmitters may be attracted.
Bind: To seize quarry and remain fastened.
Block: Tapered cylindrical outdoor perch for weathering falcons.
Braces: Straps used to open/close the hood.
Break into: The act of beginning to eat, as in piercing flesh.

Cadge: Perch designed to transport multiple falcons.
Cast off: Launching a raptor for free flight.
Casting: The indigestible portions of a raptors meal including bone fragments, feathers, fur, etc., compacted into pellet form and regurgitated.
Check: Gamehawks pursuing unintended quarry.
Cope: To trim overgrown beaks and/or talons.
Creance: A safety line used to secure hawks in initial training flights.
Crepuscular: Being active at dawn and dusk.
Crop: A storage area for food within the esophagus, above the sternum.

Deck(s): Central tail feathers.
Downey: Developmental stage before a young raptor has grown body feathers.
Duck hawk: A falcon that hunts ducks.

Enseam: To purge excess fat accumulated by a game-hawk after the moult.

Enter: The transition during which a hawk in training begins, or resumes, catching wild quarry.
Eyas: A young raptor; a nestling.
Feak: The means by which a raptor cleans its beak in a stropping fashion.
Foot: Attempt to bind to quarry.
Frounce: (pigeon canker) A protozoan infection (trichomoniasis) somewhat common in doves and pigeons and transmittable to raptors.
Game-hawk: A trained hunting hawk or falcon.
Hack: Temporary liberation of young falcons while they are still dependant on food provided by the falconer.
Haggard: Any raptor in adult plumage.
Hallux: Rear toe, strongest of the four.
Hard-penned: The completion of feather development in a young raptor, or completion of moult in older raptor.
High: Generally refers to an overweight game-hawk.
Hybrid falcon: The offspring of an interspecies cross.
Imp: Method of repairing broken feathers.
Imprint: A raptor raised by humans, thus psychologically bonded to its handler.
Intermewed: A raptor having experienced one or more moults in captivity.
Jerkin: A male gyrfalcon (*Falco rusticolus*).
Keel: Breastbone.
Keen: A state of eager readiness related to appetite.
Killing cone: The circumference within which a waiting on falcon may stoop game effectively.
Low: Underweight.
Longwing: Falcon.
Make hawk: An older, experienced hawk used to help teach an eyas.
Mantle: Raptors standing over food in a defensive posture with tail fanned and wings out.
Moult: The annual shedding and replacement of feathers.
Mount: A falcon is said to "mount" as she ascends above the falconer.
Pitch: The height which a falcon waits-on overhead.
Prairie pothole: Glacier-formed depressions becoming seasonal ponds comprising North Americas most productive waterfowl nesting habitat.
Preen: Feather maintenance performed by raptors with beak and preen gland.

Put in: To drive or intimidate quarry into cover.

Quarry: The game being pursued.

Rake away: When a game-hawk leaves the area.

Rangle: Smooth, round stones historically administered to falcons in an effort to purge excess fat.

Rat hunt: A hunt generally lacking style wherein multiple flushes are required to "rat" the quarry from its refuge.

Ring up to: Spiral ascent.

Rouse: The occasional lifting and shaking of feathers very commonly just before flight.

Serve to: Flushing for, or otherwise providing, quarry for falcons to stoop.

Set: As in set up, i.e., ducks on a pond, etc.

Sharp: As in thin keel, i.e., low weight.

Slip: An opportunity at game.

Spec flight: As in speculation, flying a falcon in an area where game is presumed or hoped to be.

Speck out: To fly beyond visible range—preferably straight up.

Stoop: Vertical free fall; as in dive.

Thermal (air): Rising column of solar heated air.

Thick: Reference as to body mass, as in not slender.

Tiercel: The male of any type of hawk, these are about one-third smaller than the females.

Tiring: Usually tough bony portions of quarry fed to hawks not for nutritional value, but to keep them active and exercised, and as preventative measure for overgrown beaks.

Train: Any raptor's tail.

Wait-on: Falcons are said to wait-on as they circle above the falconer in expectation of a serve.

Washed meat: Meat soaked and/or rinsed in cold water to eliminate nutritional value.

Wetlands: Precisely, wet lands that are ideal waterfowl habitat.

Wing-over: An abrupt maneuver, most often seen after a falcon has struck quarry to ground. Winging over, she drives herself toward the earth to seize her quarry before it can recover from the initial hit.

Weather: Hawks perched outdoors exposed to the elements.

Yarak: A Turkish work denoting a hawk that is intensely hungry and ready to hunt.

Bibliography

Adamson, Jim. "Notes on a Goshawk." *N.A.F.A. Journal*; Vol. 18&19, 1979-1980.

Anderson, Michael, Ph.D. "Scaup Update." *Ducks Unlimited,* Sept/Oct 2001.

Anderson, Michael, Ph.D. "Wetlands in a Warmer World." *Ducks Unlimited,* Mar/Apr 2002.

"The Associated Press Study: Global Warming to Substantially Effect State". *The Union Newspaper*; November 8, 2000.

Batt, Bruce; Ph.D. "A Goose of a Different Color." *Ducks Unlimited,* March/April 2000.

Beebe, Frank L. *The Compleat Falconer*. Hancock House Publishers; Blaine WA. 1992.

Bergren, Erik. "The Remarkable Redhead." *California Waterfowl,* June/July 2000.

Cade, Tom. *The Falcons of the World*. Comstock/Cornell University Press; NY, 1987.

Carty, Dave. "Is There a Chessie in You're Future?" *Ducks Unlimited*; Jan/Feb 2001.

Connolly, Michael. *Game Hawking at it's Very Best.* "Duck Hawking with Peregrine Falcons." Windsong Press, Denver, Co. 1988.

Eagle Optics – "Choosing Binoculars." *California Hawking Club Newsletter*; Vol. 28, no. 3, Dec., 1998.

Franklin, Ken. "Vertical Flight." *N.A.F.A. Journal,* Vol. 38, 1999.

Furtman, Michael. *Duck Country.* Willow Creek Press;

Minocqua WI. 2001.

Haak, Bruce. *The Hunting Falcon*. Hancock House Publishers; Blaine, WA. 1992.

Latham, Simon. *Falconry*. Jackson, 1615

Marshall Owners Manual, 2000.

McGinn, Anne Platt. "State of the World." *Phasing out Persistent Organic Pollutants*.

McLandress, Bob. The Three R's of Bad Duck Hunting. *California Waterfowl*, April/May 2001.

Moran, David T. "Magnum Hawking." *International Falconer*, May 2001.

Morrow, Lance. "Harris Hawks in Chained Brush." *N.A.F.A. Journal*, Vol. 35, 1996.

Robinson, Gordon. "Hybrids – An Opinion." *The Falconer British Journal*, 1998, p. 73.

Roy, Joe. "Catch & Release." *American Falconry*, Vol. 9, Dec. 1997.

Roy, Joe. "Pigeons; A Training Tool for Longwings." *American Falconry*, Vol. 16, Sept. 1999.

Sibley, David Allen. The Sibley Field Guide To Birds of Western North America. Alfred A. Knopf, New York, 2003

Spomer, Ron. "Strategies for Spring Snows." *Ducks Unlimited*, Jan/Feb 2001.

Sternberg, Dick & Simpson, Jeff. *Complete Hunter/Duck Hunting*. Cowles Creative Publishing, Inc.; Minnetonka MN., 1997.

Stevens, Ronald. "Excerpt." *The Falconers Journal*; Western Sporting Publications 1996.

Stevens, Ronald. *Observations on Modern Falconry*. Pilot Publishing; UK, 1987.

Wolf, Ken. "Goshawk and An Owl do Battle." *Raptor Room News*, Vol. IV #1, Spring, 1991.

Woodford, Michael. *Falconry*. A&C Black; London, 1971.

Yerkes, Tina; Ph.D. "Spring Wetlands and Pintails." *Ducks Unlimited*, May/June 2001.

Young, Matt. "Canada Goose Roundup." *Ducks Unlimited*, May/June 2001.

Young, Matt. "Mixed Bag." *Ducks Unlimited,* May/June 2001.

Young, Matt. "Plight of the Pintail." *Ducks Unlimited,* Sept/Oct 1998.

Young, Matt. "Redhead Central." *Ducks Unlimited,* Nov/Dec 2000.

Young, Matt. "The Wonder Duck." *Ducks Unlimited,* March/April 2000.

Index

accipiter, 6, 30, 33-35, 61, 97, 109, 260, 264
aggression, 16, 87, 91, 94, 106, 114, 165, 185, 198, 236, 238-240, 243-245, 261, 265, 272-274, 287
anatum, *129*
Austringer, 33-38, 89, 109, *133*, 233, 258, 270-271, 277
Barrow's Goldeneyes, *145*
buteo, 35, 126, 260
back lobe, 292
bells, 37, 217, 265, 268
binoculars, 55, 59, 216, 222
bind, 38, 54, 112, 123, 192, 204, 229, 241, 260-261, 263-265, 271-272, 277-278
bullheads, *145*
check, 101, 105, 120, 128, 161, 201, 253, 284, 287
coot, *130-131, 135*
crop, 31, 33, 71, 85, 87, 89, 98, 244, 246, 272, 288, 297-299
creance, 114, 122, 239
duck factory, 307
DDT, 22, 27
evolution, 9, 18, 40, 42, 51, 92, 100, 171, 210-211, 251, 263-264
enseam, 90
frounce, 24, 120
goshawk, 6, 29-30, 32-35, 61, 120, *138*, 229, 259-260, 262, 270
great horned owl, 262, 294
grouse, 11, 26, 59, 60, 91, 208, 211, 234, 298-299, 306
harris hawk, 9, 21, 35, *154,* 259, 260, 277, 300-301
hybrid, 10, 22-28, 51, 53, 65, 69, 74, 91, 97, 104, 111, 116, 120, 122, 124, *137, 142, 155,* 163, 169, 194, 203, 208, 219, 221, 237, 266, 286, 300
imprint, 20, 23, 27, 90, 94, 109, 207, 239, 244, 294
jerkin, *153*
killing cone, 34, 99, 102, 179-180, 283, 285,
longwing, 6-7, 33-36, 52, 67, 70, 207
mallard, *136, 144-145*
marked game, 196, 200
merganser, *138, 142*
metabolic, 88, 91-92
moult, 47-48, *136*, 305
peregrine, 10-11, 20-27, 34, 41, 49-50, 69, 74-75, 89, 97, 99-100, 110, 116, 127, *160,* 169, 186, 203, 206, 221, 223, 230, 237, 264-265, 266, 288
pheasants, 97, 161, 208, 240, 252, 265-266, 275, 281
pin tail, 30, 43, 46, 48, 50-52, 54, 99, *157*, 186, 219, 281, 285
pitch, 17, 22, 25-26, 28, 34, 36, 49, 51, 53-54, 57, 59, 62, 64, 78, 99-108, 111-112, 115-117, 119-120, 123, 125-126, 166-167, 170, 177-178,

180-182, 186, 188, 194, 196-198, 200, 204-207, 210-212, 234-235, 250, 282-283, 285-286, 291, 296
predator, 9-11, 14, 22, 28, 33-34, 39-40, 46-47, 69, 72, 94, 96, 98, 100, 113, 115, 127, *132*, 164, 169, 196, 211, 233-234, 236, 238-240, 244-248, 250, 253, 259, 261-264, 266-268, 275-276, 281, 286-287, 294, 298
projection, 17, 244
pursuing quarry, *129, 132, 133, 138*
rangle, 90
rat hunt, 60, 82, 167-168
receiver, 82, 224, 281-285, 291-292, 296-299, 303
remount, 41, 53, 78, 111-112, 118, 167, 170, 181, 189
ring neck, *146*
Ronald Stevens, 11, 15, 288
serve, 17, 75, 108, 110-114, 116-120, 126, 176, 190, 198
scale, 86-87, 90-92, 286
shortwing, 29-39, 101, 212, 233, 290
sky trials, 24-25
Spoonbill, *132*
teal, *139, 147-149, 156*
transmitter, 43, 97, 123, 207, 281, 284, 289, 290, 292, 294, 296-300, 302-304
thermals, 22, 102, 112, 115, 118, 122-128, *129, 151,* 161, 186
triangulation, 284, 292
wait-on, 9, 34, 84, 125, 166, 200
wetlands, 44, 52, 168, 197, 307
wigeon, 49-51, *144, 157,* 186, 218, 237
wingload, 61, 113, 124

bold/italics=illustration

More titles available from Hancock House Publishers

Arab Falconry
History of a Way of Life
Roger Upton
ISBN 0-88839-492-6
8½ x 11, HC, 224pages

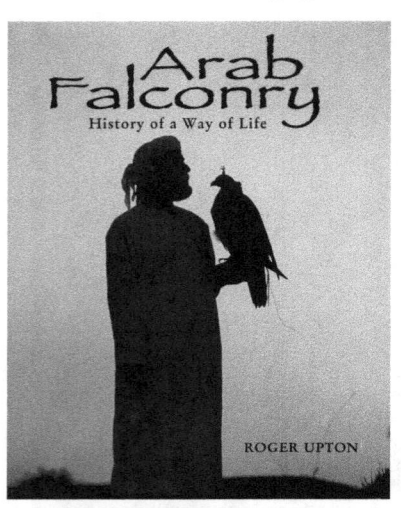

The Loo Falconry:
The Royal Loo Hawking Club 1839-1855
J. W. M. van de Wall
ISBN 0-88839-576-0
8½ x 11, HC, 144 pages

Falconry Uncommon
George Kotsiopoulos
ISBN 0-88839-450-0
5½ x 8½, HC, 120 pages

The world leader in birds of prey publishing

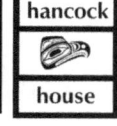

Understanding the Bird of Prey
Nick Fox
ISBN 0-88839-317-2
8½ x 11, HC, 375 pages

Classical Falconry
A Treatise on Rook and Crow Hawking
Nick Fox
ISBN 0-88839-548-5
8½ x 11, HC, 248 pages

All books available from
http://www.hancockhouse.com

Falconry in Literature
David Horobin
ISBN 0-88839-547-7
5½ x 8½, HC,
240 pages

Bolt from the Blue
Dick Decker
ISBN: 0-88839-434-9
5½ x 8½, SC, 192 pages

City Peregrines
Saul Frank
ISBN: 0-88839-415-2
5½ x 8½, HC, 320 pages

A Fascination with Falcons
Dr. Bill Burnham
ISBN: 0-88839-415-2
5½ x 8½, HC, 240 pages

Hawking with Golden Eagles
Martin Hollinshead
ISBN: 0-88839-330-X
5½ x 8½, SC, 176 pages

Hawking Ground Quarry
Martin Hollinshead
ISBN: 0-88839-306-7
5½ x 8½, HC, 168 pages

A Falconry Manual
Frank L. Beebe
ISBN: 0-88839-978-2
5½ x 8½, SC, 198 pages

The Hunting Falcon
Bruce Haak
ISBN: 0-88839-292-3
5½ x 8½, HC, 240 pages

Pirate of the Planes
Bruce Haak
ISBN: 0-88839-320-2
5½ x 8½, SC, 208 pages

The Compleat Falconer
Frank L. Beebe
ISBN: 0-88839-978-2
5½ x 8½, HC, 336 pages

www.ingramcontent.com/pod-product-compliance
Lightning Source LLC
Chambersburg PA
CBHW052229230426
43666CB00034B/2457